LOCAL RITES

PAUL DAFFEY

A Year in Grass Roots Football in
Victoria and Beyond

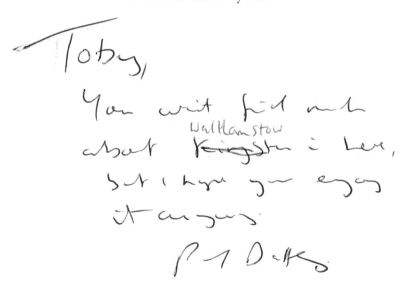

Toby,

You won't find much
about Walthamstow Kingston in here,
but I hope you enjoy
it anyway.

P J Daffey.

Black Duck Publications

Paul Daffey grew up in Melbourne,
moved away for a year here and there,
and lives in Melbourne again.
This is his first book.

LOCAL RITES.

© Copyright 2001 by Paul Daffey.

ISBN 0 646 41248 5

Black Duck Publications
PO Box 363, Flemington, Victoria 3031

Photography by Mark Daffey

Cover art by Martin Tighe

Cover photography by Sharp Edge

Cover design by Liz Vagg

Legal advice from Minter Ellison

Typesetting by Abbtype

Printing by Brown Prior Anderson

Distribution by Dennis Jones Distributors

For my family

CONTENTS

HARD YARDS

The launch was sponsored by:

Tooheys Victoria
(03) 9277 5800

De Bortoli Wines
(03) 9761 4100

Customised Catering
(03) 9333 4977

ACKNOWLEDGEMENTS

My deepest appreciation goes to the editors, Mike Shuttleworth, Brad Newsome, Vin Maskell and Paula Hurley, who all worked with skill and patience.

I thank the following for their help with production: Greg Barron, Phil Barrett, Andrew Brasier, Ashley Browne, Luke Daffey, Mark Daffey, Marie Daffey, Phil Daffey, Terry Daffey, Chris Dennis, Ken Ellis, John Farrell, Martin Flanagan, Warwick Green, Matt Harrington, Damian Hogan, Frank Hurley, Ricky Johnstone, Hayden Kennedy, Tony Leonard, Barry Levinson, Garry Linnell, Steve Linnell, Dennis Jones, Andy McElroy, Meghan McGann, Bernie McIntosh, Cathy McNamara, Adam McNicol, Andrew Muir, Andrew Nathan, Bruce Pascoe, Steve Russell, Andy Ryan, Pat Ryan, Martin Tighe, Joanne Toscano, Liz Vagg.

Dozens of people from football clubs, leagues or associations provided feedback on chapters and I thank them all. I also thank everyone who gave the time for interviews, or general football chats, during the 2000 season.

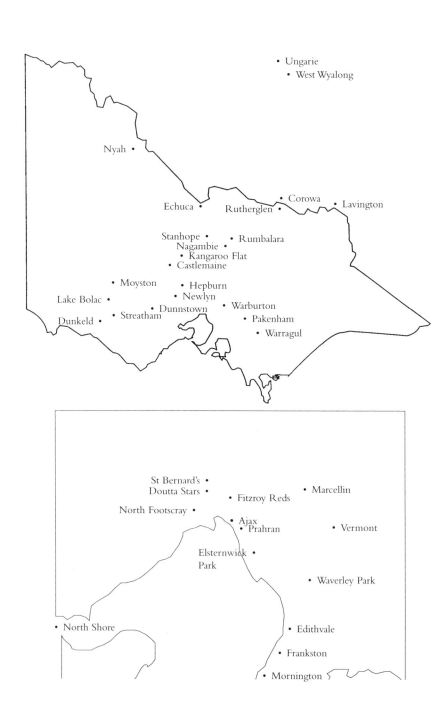

- Ungarie
  - West Wyalong

Nyah •

• Corowa
Echuca •   Rutherglen •   • Lavington

Stanhope •   • Rumbalara
Nagambie •
• Kangaroo Flat
• Castlemaine

• Moyston   • Hepburn
Lake Bolac •   • Newlyn
• Dunnstown   • Warburton
Dunkeld •   • Streatham   • Pakenham
• Warragul

St Bernard's •
Doutta Stars •   • Marcellin
• Fitzroy Reds
North Footscray •
• Ajax
• Prahran   • Vermont
Elsternwick •
Park
• Waverley Park

• North Shore   • Edithvale
• Frankston
• Mornington

INTRODUCTION

I grew up on football stories. My family drip-fed me over several years. Most of the stories were about country football. My father talked about one of his first games for Sandhurst, when a Castlemaine veteran persisted in elbowing him in the ribs or digging him in the kidneys when he was trying to work out whether to fold his arms or rest his hands on his hips. My grandmother talked about arriving at the footy in Bendigo during her courtship with my grandfather. She walked through the gates only to see a massive brawl and hear the cry: "Daffey started it." My other grandfather, who lived in the Mallee, remembered a week when sewing the crops prevented my uncle from going to training. My uncle turned up on the Saturday and was best afield. "See," my grandfather said, "a bit of hard work is better than any blasted footy training."

The stories aroused my interest in country footy. Then I left school and began to create my own stories. My stories were based in the city. I played with St Bernard's Old Collegians in the Victorian Amateur Football Association. Years later I played with another Amateurs club, Preston Marist Brothers Old Boys. I also played country footy with Golden Square in Bendigo and Rowlands in the Northern Territory. Rowlands, based in Katherine, was the only football club in the world to be sponsored by an airconditioned dairy. We trained on a rugby pitch and played in heat that scorched our throats. It's a story I never imagined while growing up in Melbourne.

This book is a collection of footy stories. For the six months of the 2000 season, I went to matches all around Victoria, as well as one match on King Island and another in the Northern Riverina. I saw a handful of great games and several duds. I saw three or four inspiring players and many modest ones. Some coaches and administrators had clear visions; others muddled along. But whether they shone like diamonds or struggled against the overwhelming forces of mediocrity, they all had stories to tell. Those embroiled in controversy were reluctant to talk, but most football people were happy to chew my ear off. At the end of the season, I was enriched by anecdotes and exhausted by travel. I was also assured of the place of Australian football in the heartland of the game. It's no longer the only show in town, but with rare exceptions it's bigger than any other. It's in deep trouble in areas, for example, where families are leaving the farms for the cities. But more often than not, football is one of the few things keeping these communities together at all. I have tried to build a picture of a season in the suburbs and the bush in my corner of Australia. The flow of the narrative required some chapters to be placed out of chronological order.

After the season, Echuca midfielder Glenn Fitzpatrick helped me with chapter 14. Fitzy is a wanderer. He played footy in northern and central Victoria and in the Amateurs competition in Perth. By the time I contacted him, he'd taken a teaching job in the Ukraine. Reading about footy produced in him a reaction that many expatriate Australians might recognise. He wanted to hop on the next flight from Kiev and return home to play footy. Once it's in your marrow, it stays. The lure of the game is strong.

Paul Daffey

FIRST BOUNCE

1

THE BOYS FROM OLD FITZROY

Fitzroy Reds v University Blacks
the Reds and the Blacks

"From the airport, I purposefully got a taxi into the city
so I could get a Brunswick Street tram to the ground."

Brisbane Lions committeeman Mac Tolliday

The old Royboys gathered in the poky rooms beneath the grandstand at
the Brunswick Street oval. The Fitzroy Reds, a club of engineering
students, finance industry workers and inner-city eccentrics, were about
to run on to the old ground in the maroon and blue. The jumper looked
a bit funny on top of the red socks and the red shorts of the Victorian
Amateur Football Association club but, then, Fitzroy was a hotch-potch
club itself. The Roys were jumbled from the moment they left Brunswick
Street after the 1966 season. For 30 years, they wandered and battled,
always fighting to stave off the creditors, and always looking for a place to
call home. The club eventually receded behind a veil of tears after losing
to Fremantle at Subiaco Oval, a few blocks from the Indian Ocean. Then
it jumped into a lopsided merger with Brisbane, to play on balmy nights
at the Gabba. At least now players in Fitzroy guernseys would be fighting
for the ball in Merri Creek mud, with the No.12 tram rattling along
behind the goals. It might be D2-section in the Amateurs but, for the first

time since the departure from Brunswick Street all those long years ago, the Fitzroy guernsey was coming home.

Big Norm Brown was among the Royboys who reminisced in the belly of the Brunswick Street grandstand. Former wingman Ray Slocum rolled up his sleeves to show his muscles for the photo. Bernie Drury was smiling from ear to ear. Drury played six games in the maroon and blue in 1966. His son Stephen grew up watching the Roys at the Junction Oval, when Garry Wilson scooted around packs and Bernie Quinlan kicked goals from the wing. At 18 years of age, Stephen joined the Reds because he wanted to play at Brunswick Street. Now he was standing in the rooms listening to the stories from the days when his father played at Brunswick Street. The old Royboys talked about the flimsy screen that separated the teams in the rooms. Each team was clearly able to hear the opposition's secrets and lies. After the match, the screen would be folded back and players and officials would mingle over beers. Stephen Drury had to stretch his imagination to picture current league players discussing the match over beers. "Now they'd get fined $10,000 if they did that," he said.

A century ago, the Brunswick Street oval was a suburban colosseum. Ironworkers and bootmakers converged from the factories and lanes to cheer Fitzroy against their hated neighbors from Collingwood and Carlton. A group of larrikins known as the Fitzroy Forties required extra police to be stationed behind the Brunswick Street goals. In 1922, the Roys won their seventh premiership and were considered the most glamorous club in the land. The next year, they defeated Essendon before a record home crowd of 35,000. The club slowly declined in the following decades, but it took until the '50s before football was threatened in Melbourne's first suburb.

By 1954, the British and Irish no longer comprised the largest group of foreign-born residents in Fitzroy. Italians outnumbered them. Greeks, Yugoslavs and Poles were also concentrated in enclaves around the suburb. The football club began to feature Italians and Greeks in the senior side, but the Roys' fortunes dwindled as the population of immigrants grew.

Doctor June Senyard, a Melbourne University historian and former president of the Fitzroy History Society, said that by 1966 the proportion of Australian-born residents in Fitzroy was less than 50 per cent. The suburbs of Collingwood and Richmond were also absorbing large numbers of immigrants, but they were a decade behind Fitzroy. The first suburb was known for its progressiveness. Senyard described Fitzroy in the '60s as "the laboratory of Australia". It had advanced welfare programs and the first legal-aid service. Residents cherished the urban streetscapes and the parklands in the Edinburgh Gardens. In 1966, the Fitzroy Football Club applied for a $400,000 loan for improvements to Brunswick Street. A clergyman campaigned against the improvements because he figured that sport led to gambling. "I think he represented the old view of Fitzroy as the working class who couldn't control themselves," Senyard said. The Fitzroy council was unimpressed when the football club revealed that it planned to build a carpark in the Edinburgh Gardens. The car was the transport of the future, the club argued. The loan was rejected and the club decided to play home games at Princes Park.

The Roys continued to train at Brunswick Street during the late '60s, while pushing for plans to refurbish the ground. Its aim was to improve the facilities and return to playing home matches at Brunswick Street, but a strong Fitzroy residents' group opposed the plans. The residents didn't want football fans traipsing through their suburb and they didn't want money spent on sport. They wanted the ground to be a park. Before the 1970 season, talks between the Fitzroy council and the Fitzroy footy club broke down and the footy club set up a new home across the Yarra River. The Roys began training and playing at the Junction Oval.

During the '70s, distaste for football at Brunswick Street received symbolic support when the grandstand that was next to the main grandstand burned down. In 1982, the walls surrounding the ground were knocked down and, for the first time in Melbourne, a park was created from a former league football ground. Four years later, the Fitzroy Cricket Club departed for Doncaster. The football club tried to develop the oval into a training base but the plan was resisted. In 1992, the Brunswick Street oval was renamed the WT Peterson Community Oval. Peterson had pushed for development of sporting facilities in the suburb, but he was not a close friend of the football club. June Senyard said the decision to name the ground after the former Fitzroy council mayor was the final insult for the Roys. She said the council turned its back on history of national significance when it named the ground after a local councillor. She suggested the ground should be renamed after Haydn Bunton, who danced across

Brunswick Street on his way to three Brownlow Medals in the 1930s, or Neil Harvey, the Test batsman who was one of six brothers to play cricket for Fitzroy.

While the oval was off-limits to the Roys, its availability for local sport was fortuitous for the Reds. During the 1980s, the Reds were known as the University Reds and played home matches on Sundays at the Melbourne University oval. In 1991, opposition clubs made it known that they didn't fancy playing on Sundays. The Reds wanted to play at the university oval on Saturdays but the ground was fully booked. Their brother clubs, the Blues and the Blacks, shared the ground on Saturdays. As the Reds were a distant third in the pecking order of the Melbourne University Football Club, they were forced to move on. Reds president Peter Hille proposed a move to Brunswick Street.

Hille first went to Brunswick Street in 1954, when he was six years of age. His uncle took him to see the Roys. Hille continued barracking for the Roys in the '70s when they were at the Junction Oval. In 1978, at 30 years of age, he rediscovered the urge to play football. He ended his retirement by going to University Reds' training with three mates. "We doubled the numbers," he said. Hille kicked hundreds of goals for the Reds until retiring at the age of 44. In his final years of playing, Hille was also president. When opponents revealed their displeasure at playing on Sundays at the university oval, he negotiated the move to Brunswick Street. "Taking the Reds there was a bit like taking friends home," he said.

The club came to regard Brunswick Street as home, but so did four soccer clubs and an American football club. The busy schedule forced the Reds to host the occasional home game away from Fitzroy. Some games were held in East Brunswick, or Clifton Hill, or by the train tracks in Parkville. Sometimes the university oval was available. But the soul of the club came to settle in Fitzroy. The drift from the university took the club away from its base of students and graduates. The Reds now attracted comedians, techno disc jockeys and a sculptor. Justin Doyle, a competition best-and-fairest winner, was a skateboard entrepreneur. AFL commentator Anthony Hudson played for the Reds around this time. The change in personnel earned the attention of the Melbourne University Sports Union, the umbrella organisation for sports that receive university funding. The sports union wanted to know the percentage of students and graduates at the Reds. In late 1997, the Reds tired of overstating their proportion of university people and shed their links with the Parkville campus. The decision cost them $10,000 in funding but it attracted more recruits with no university links. Many players were artists or professionals or country exiles looking for a club in the inner city. After shedding the university link, the first step in the new direction was a new name. Fitzroy Reds was the obvious choice.

The Fitzroy identity was strengthened by adopting the Royboys' guernsey, but soon after this decision the club was forced to move from Brunswick Street because of renovations to the oval. The Reds wore the Fitzroy guernsey but they played at Ramsden Street in Clifton Hill, on the western bank of the Merri Creek. Before the 2000 season, the Brunswick Street renovations were completed and the club returned to the oval. The first match would be at home to University Blacks, the former brother club. It would be the first match in which the Roys' guernsey would be worn on its rightful patch since 1966. A ceremony was surely in order.

Reds president Chris Tehan and Fitzroy Football Club members set to work. Fitzroy had ended their AFL days with a small kitty from gaming machines in the club hotel in Northcote. The football club continues to operate, with a membership of 1200, and the money is put towards promoting football in the northern suburbs. For the 2000 season, the Roys sponsored Coburg in the VFL, the Reds in the Amateurs, and Fitzroy Juniors in the Yarra league. Representatives of the three clubs would be invited to the ceremony. A Brisbane Lions representative would also be invited, while the special guests would be the players from 1966, the last Royboys to wear the old guernsey at Brunswick Street.

In the lead-up to the match, Fitzroy Football Club secretary Bill Atherton approached the Yarra City Council, which had replaced the Fitzroy council in the early '90s. He asked for funding for new goalposts. Atherton and Chris Tehan erected the goalposts on a Saturday morning in March before stepping back to admire their handiwork. "This football ground is coming back to life," Atherton said. Two days before the match, the Fitzroy Football Club held its 115th annual general meeting in the bowling club behind the Brunswick Street grandstand. All members were encouraged to get along to the Reds' match.

Chris Tehan welcomed the guests into the pavilion by the grandstand. The president had made the ultimate sacrifice to ensure a smooth ceremony: he'd pulled out of the first match of the season. "Duty calls," said the dogged defender. His reserves side chugged away under a murky April sky. Behind the pavilion, tennis players traded forehands and backhands on the red courts that spread beneath the canopy of trees in the Edinburgh Gardens. Vice-chairperson Elaine Findlay was the guest of honor for Fitzroy. Coburg president Robert Evans represented the VFL Lions; Mac Tolliday was from the Brisbane Lions. Tolliday was a lifelong Fitzroy supporter and a member of the Amateurs executive before he left Melbourne for Brisbane in the late '60s. Now he was back at Brunswick Street as a Brisbane committeeman. "From the airport, I purposefully got a taxi into the city so I could get a Brunswick Street tram to the ground," he said. "I haven't caught one for 30 years. It was wonderful."

Chris Tehan also welcomed leading Reds such as Ben Pickett, who was captain of the 1995 premiership side before taking an agriculture job in Yarrawonga. The heartiest welcome was reserved for the nine former Fitzroy players. Most of them were wearing the maroon and blue at the last game at Brunswick Street in 1966. The Roys lost the match to St Kilda by 84 points. The ceremony was suitably humble.

Over a buffet lunch of meat and vegies, Fitzroy board member Colin Hobbs established the truth about the most memorable incident from the match against St Kilda. Hobbs was a teenage wingman and *provocateur* when, according to a newspaper story before this ceremony, imposing St Kilda ruckman Carl Ditterich took a swing at him, missed, and hit centreman Daryl Peoples. Hobbs said he backed into Ditterich and trod on his toe. Ditterich grunted threats and shoved Hobbs out of his way. The wingman replied by elbowing the blond Saint in the stomach and commenting on his German heritage. "One was impetuous at 19," he said.

When play resumed, Ditterich cursed and steamed and took out the first player in his path, who happened to be Daryl Peoples. Ditterich was reported and suspended for four matches, denying him a place in St Kilda's only premiership side. "I had a capacity to aggravate," Hobbs said.

Ditterich said during a phone interview from his home in Swan Hill that he remembered little about the incident. "It was a long time ago." But he did recall that Daryl Peoples was the Fitzroy player in his path, and he believed he shouldn't have been reported. "It was a fair bump," he said.

The old Royboys finished their lunch and filed into the dressing-rooms in the belly of the grandstand for the unveiling of the plaques. About 50 guests squeezed into a space that was barely bigger than a Toorak en suite. Light filtered through the thin windows that separate the roof and the brick walls. Chris Tehan invited Bill Stephen to step forward. Stephen was born in Freeman Street, which runs along the southern wing of the Brunswick Street oval. His Fitzroy career began in 1947, when league clubs still had a handful of players who grew up within roaring distance of their ground. He played 162 games for Fitzroy, always in a back pocket. He coached the club in three stints for a tally of 11 years. He also coached Yarrawonga and Essendon. On his 72nd birthday, Stephen spoke of dedicating his life to Fitzroy, the club of his heart. "It was a tragedy – and a travesty of justice – that Fitzroy was eliminated from the league," he said. He made sure that everyone knew he believed the club was eliminated.

The small man with the neat crop of silvery hair peeled off the sheet to reveal an elegant plaque listing the first Fitzroy side and the last Fitzroy side to play at Brunswick Street. The first game was in April 1884, just before trams began rattling past the ground. The Roys kicked no goals and 14 behinds to defeat Richmond Union. The last match was in August 1966, when St Kilda kicked 17 goals and the Roys kicked five. The Fitzroy side for the last game featured Stephen as coach and Norm Brown in the ruck, but few other household names. Only four players topped 100 games. Stephen nodded his head and accepted the applause. The mood in the small, dark room was respectful, even wistful. There was none of the back-slapping that accompanies most football ceremonies.

Chris Tehan then revealed the Reds' honor board, which listed the officials and the award-winners in the two years since the club had entered the Fitzroy family. The golden names floated at the top of the board, leaving plenty of room for additions in the decades to come. The boards of the Roys and the Reds hung side by side, one representing a storied past, the other a link with the future. D2-section in the Amateurs is a far cry from league football, but not a galaxy away. All football clubs are underpinned by the desire to have a kick and to belong. It's just that some clubs are more intense than others. Tehan received warm applause as he stepped down from the bench that stretched along the brick wall.

Stephen Drury listened to tales of the partition and the dark years of decline. He looked on as his father joined the old Royboys for the photos. Bill Stephen was in the middle and big Norm Brown held up one end. Ray Slocum laughed and tried to push out his modest biceps while folding his arms. After the photos, the Royboys headed into the light. Maroon and blue streamers swished from the iron lace at the front of the grandstand.

The Reds captain led his side on to the cherished turf under moody skies. A Fitzroy guernsey with a yellow No.33 was draped from his angular frame. After barracking for Fitzroy all his life, Stephen Drury was now entwined in the club's history, in a modest kind of way. "It means everything to me," he said. The Reds took their positions feeling 10 feet tall. Several were playing with the Reds because they liked the ground. Now, in their Fitzroy guernseys, they were guardians of the ground. The visitors wore the traditional guernsey of Melbourne University: black with a blue "V".

The Reds opened the match strongly. Patrick Jackson, the midfielder with frightening sideburns, bullocked his way from pack to pack and Todd Clarke, who had his sideburns shaved off for the big day, was yappy in defence. Up forward, Paddy Haephy provided a target after returning from two years in Warrnambool, his home town, and two years in Queensland, where he mustered cattle. His helicopter kicks suggested he mustered from the air. Haephy's kicking drew good-natured derision from the Reds crowd. Former captain Greg Cook was among the leading culprits. I knew Cook from university. His morning had been spent sitting yet another exam in medical research. Going to the footy proved a worthy way to relieve his stress and the former full-back had plenty of advice for his old teammates.

Most Reds spectators were more interested in the full-forward at the other end. Tony Wilson was playing his first game for a few years. As a teenager, Wilson was drafted by Hawthorn but after four years at the Glenferrie Oval, plus a few more at Prahran and Preston, he became distracted by fame. He won *Race Around the World*, the ABC travel competition for film-making novices that was almost too groovy for words. He then went on to host public radio shows, write lively features for *The Age* and settle into the life of a media man about town. But after a couple of years of wine and song, he disliked his flabby tummy. At 27 years of age, he put distractions aside and his goggles on and lined up for the Blacks. He wore goggles because he has a wrinkled cornea. He played with the Blacks to maintain family links. His brother Ned was his fellow key forward. Their father Ray, a Blacks premiership captain, watched from the sidelines. The Wilson brothers, with Tony conspicuous in his chunky eyewear, helped turn the match the Blacks' way in the second quarter. Ruckman Michael Laffy, the former Richmond player, and coach Kane Bowden, the brother of Richmond midfielder Joel, drove the ball forward and the Wilson brothers plucked it from the air.

Ray Wilson was smiling proudly. Not only were his sons thriving in their first game together, but he was able to relive his glory days. Ray Wilson was captain of the Blacks' A-section premiership side in 1965. The next year he joined Hawthorn and, in his only match on the Brunswick Street oval, scored three Brownlow Medal votes. At the end of the year, he won the Hawthorn best-and-fairest. His opponents during the match at Brunswick Street included fellow former Northcote High students. A particular memory of the match was the punishing treatment from John Benison. Wilson smiled and said Benison was the toughest player he came up against. He turned around to see Benison laughing in front of the grandstand.

Benison was telling yarns with the former Royboys. John Hayes, the Fitzroy captain in 1966, said rivals turned up their noses at the Merri Creek mud. "They said it stank, but we couldn't smell it." The former defender pointed across the ground to the terrace houses in Freeman Street. He recalled spectators watching from the balconies.

Elaine Findlay was watching the match just along from the old Royboys. In 1985, Findlay capped a lifetime of devotion to Fitzroy when she became the first woman to be elected on to a league board of directors. Back at Brunswick Street, she recalled jostling through the turnstile behind the grandstand in the '50s. It was a lively era for the Roys. In 1958, they lost the first semi-final to North Melbourne by four points. In 1960, they lost the preliminary final to Collingwood by five points. Butch Gale was throwing his weight around in the ruck and Tony Ongarello was taking the ball from the sky. Ongarello's problem was kicking for goal. In his exasperation, he became the last league forward to resort to place kicks. Findlay recalled the color and verve of Brunswick Street. Her friend Pauline Morant, who in the '80s became the first woman to join the Gold Lions coterie group, recalled standing behind the Brunswick Street goals when a menacing drunk tottered forward. Morant hit him with her umbrella, which drew the attention of the drunk's wife. The Brunswick Street end had never been a place for faint hearts. Morant feared retribution, but she needn't have worried. "The wife came along and said, 'Don't hit him with your umbrella, hit him with your fists'." Morant's boyfriend was so impressed with her gallantry that he proposed that evening.

The stories continued to flow as the match struggled on. In windy conditions, the margin was never more than three goals. Stephen Drury, the key defender and stockbroking assistant, rose to the challenge of matching Tony Wilson, the revived forward and media star. Drury and midfielders Patrick Jackson and Simon Greenwood dragged the Reds into the game, providing a chance of victory over the former brother club.

Some supporters would never have believed that the two clubs were playing each other. By the time the Reds began their humble existence as University Reds in 1955, the Blacks had won nine A-section premierships. The Blacks were renowned for producing the Cordner brothers, who represented all that was good and noble about Amateur football before taking those values to Melbourne. In 1946, Don Cordner became the only footballer to win the Brownlow Medal as an amateur. Two years later, Denis Cordner was rushed into Melbourne's grand final side a fortnight after being captain in the Blacks' premiership side. He played at centre half-back in the tie against Essendon and in the replay, which Melbourne won. The Cordners remain the first family of Amateur football. The Blacks, with 11 A-section premierships, remain the most successful club in Amateur football. They won their last A-section flag in 1974, when the Costello brothers were at their peak. Six Costello brothers played for the Blacks. In the '80s, they watched their club become a B-section club. In the '90s, the Blacks plummeted through the grades until they faced the ignominy of shaping up against the Reds.

The university fraternity always considered the Reds a bunch of ratbags. The club made the E-section finals in its first four years. The lifeblood of this side was Mark Marsden, who in 1956 kicked 100 goals and organised the Olympic torch relay. But the club was known for eccentric parties more than sporting prowess. "The Reds have always had an equal commitment to off-field enjoyment and on-field success," said Peter Hille. In 1981, the Reds lost the E-section grand final to North Brunswick. They lasted one season in the giddy heights of D-section before being relegated. In 1995, the Reds won the E-section premiership but, again, were relegated after one season. A few years later, the grading system was up-dated. D-section became D1, while E-section became D2, and so on. The change was made because footballers prefer to say they play in D4-section rather than G-grade. Whatever the Reds thought about the grading system, it surprised them as much as anyone when they became foes of the mighty Blacks.

In 1998, the Rouge et Noir Cup was struck to commemorate matches between the clubs. The cup was named after the flamboyant 1836 novel *Le Rouge et Le Noir*, by French writer Stendhal. Only in the Amateurs could football and French literature be mentioned in the same sentence. The Reds threw themselves into every contest in this match against the Blacks in an effort to keep the treasured cup. With minutes to go, Steve Drury smothered a kick and the ball was whisked away to give the Reds the lead. The Blacks then replied. The final minute was a desperate scramble, befitting a contest between warring brothers, before the siren went with the visitors five points ahead. The thoroughbreds with the Cordner pedigree had defeated the brumbies from Brunswick Street. Players and supporters gathered in front of the grandstand for the presentation.

As the Blacks received the cup, Reds defender Ricky Johnstone was in Sicily preparing to give a talk at a conference on cancer research. His engagement by the Mediterranean Sea put him in two minds. He was proud to be contributing to the international community of medical research, but he was distraught that he was unable to play at Brunswick Street in the match that celebrated the return of the Fitzroy guernsey. Ricky and I studied science together at university. We had opposing views on the merits of test tubes and petri dishes, but we bonded instantly over footy. I once joined him for a season in the Amateurs at Preston Marist

Brothers Old Boys, where the dressing-room offered a parade of tattoos. Going to the showers was like stepping into a cartoon show. The club folded the next year and Ricky joined the Reds while I returned to St Bernard's. I lived around the corner from the Brunswick Street oval and sometimes trained with the Reds because it was convenient. If I were more honest, I would admit it was because I loved the ground.

The Brunswick Street oval is among my favorite stretches of turf in Melbourne. I often enjoyed a kick with mates on its lush surface. When going for a run, I always included a lap around its perimeter. The ground offered respite from the tight rows of terrace houses. It also offered a sense of history that I was only beginning to associate with my own city. I grew up in East Keilor, a suburb where nothing was old and the only constructions of note were the parish church and the local pool. At Brunswick Street, there was iron lace on a grandstand that watched over the turf on which Haydn Bunton, Chicken Smallhorn and Dinny Ryan earned five Brownlow Medals in six years. There was the familiarity of football, the only aspect of life I knew in any depth, and the grandeur of iron lace and Brownlow Medals. It was a heady combination for a boy from the suburbs.

My regret is that I never played a game on Brunswick Street. The ground has an allure than can be known only to footballers who spend childhood with stars in their eyes and adulthood trying to get a kick as best they can. Playing at Brunswick Street offers a small link with the big time; it offers a small link with childhood dreams. The Reds felt like keepers of the flame in their Fitzroy guernseys. Stephen Drury felt like he was receiving the premiership cup during the first round of the season. Ricky Johnstone was crying into his lecture notes in faraway Sicily. Those who renamed the Brunswick Street oval after a former mayor never knew such feelings. The ground should be called the Haydn Bunton Oval or the Chicken Smallhorn Recreation Reserve. Maybe it should be the Tony Ongarello Place Kick Park. Whatever the name, it should reflect the familiar and the grand. I doubt that any footballer would argue with that.

The presentation concluded as streamers and balloons swished and bobbed from the iron lace on the grandstand. The University Blacks clutched the Rouge et Noir Cup as the crowd drifted across the turf towards another fine Fitzroy landmark, the Lord Newry Hotel. The No.12 tram clanked along behind the Brunswick Street goals.

The Blacks won the D2 premiership but the Reds finished a distant last and were relegated. Midfielder Peter Caccaviello won the Blacks' best-and-fairest. Tony Wilson discarded his goggles mid-season after an opponent stepped on them. He went on to kick 63 goals and lead the Blacks' goalkicking. Stephen Drury and rover Steve Addicott shared the Reds' best-and-fairest. Ricky Johnstone returned from Sicily and became a rock in defence. During the season, the Reds established a Hall of Fame to provide a link between the club's university years and its reinvention in Fitzroy. Financial problems forced Coburg to drop the link with the Fitzroy Football Club and align with Richmond.

2

FROM WILD CARDS TO
SHORE THINGS

North Shore v Leopold
the Seagulls and the Lions

"I don't know how many times I told him,
'No, the last club I'll ever coach is North Shore'."

Seagulls legend Gordon Hynes

From the first instant, Max Evans gave the impression of a man who gets the job done. The 66-year-old had just unfurled the flag for North Shore's fifth consecutive premiership, a task that would bring a wide grin from most football people but, from Evans, earned a wry smile and a quip about another day at the office. I'd been told that the retired toolmaker would be the best man to explain the club's dominance. "Follow me," he said, spinning on his heel and leading me into the social club. His eyes brightened as he outlined the Seagulls' rise from a home for rough-heads in the industrial north of Geelong to one of the most respected clubs in country Victoria. There would be no more quips about offices.

Evans stopped at a wall that was plastered with memorabilia and pointed to the photo of the 1937 premiership side, the club's first. He was the mascot in the middle of the front row. His father was a member of the side, which was just reward for his role in the club's history. Bill Evans founded the North Shore Football Club in 1927 and won the best-and-fairest in its first year. His wife, Margaret Evans, achieved life membership and unfurled premiership flags. Their son would later make a habit of unfurling premiership flags. North Shore has always been an enormous part of life for the Evans family. And while Bill Evans founded the club, Max Evans prepared the way for its burgeoning success.

In the post-war years, Max Evans was a teenager who organised football matches of six a side around Norlane and North Shore. Before long he wanted to raise the stakes, so he cycled up the road towards the oil refineries, to Geelong Grammar, where a student named Graeme Richmond agreed to rustle up a side. Graeme Richmond would go on to become the power behind the Richmond Football Club's premiership years from 1967 to '80. For Evans, the success of the match against the Geelong Grammar side prompted him to organise games against more sides from nearby schools and suburbs. And so junior football was founded in Geelong.

Evans continued organising junior matches after beginning his senior football career with North Shore in the 1950s. In this decade, the population of Norlane and North Shore began to grow. No longer were there occasional houses separated by paddocks in the shadows of the smokestacks. Young families moved into the area to take up jobs in the steelworks and the meatworks, and at companies such as Ford and International Harvester. With the rising population, Evans recognised a recruiting bonanza. Whenever he saw young fellas kicking a football in the park, or jumping off the swings, or hanging out at the shops, he would invite them along to play at North Shore. "I'd drag them off the streets from everywhere," he said.

The difficult part was persuading them to stay at North Shore. Evans said opposition clubs called the young Seagulls slum kids, then tried to recruit the most talented ones. The raiders' favored tactic was to tell the best players that they were too good for the scum at North Shore; they said the boys should join a club that gave them a chance in life. Evans said that all he could do was tell his players not to listen. To this day, he shudders at the practice of preying on the insecurity of the boys and parents from the housing-commission areas.

In 1961, Evans was club president when North Shore won their first under-15 premiership. The breakthrough remains a highlight in a lifetime of service to the club. Evans said it showed the calibre of the teenagers coming through the junior program. Four decades later, he was able to recite the stations in life of the four main players: two are school principals; one is a senior naval officer; and Leigh Crawford, who played senior football for Geelong, manages a meat company. These teenagers were talented and responsible, traits that provided the base for success.

Evans had begun recounting the tale of the club's rise to success when former umpire Ray Gurrie strolled through the social rooms. Gurrie was the man in white in several grand finals that North Shore won. "They were a magnificent club in the '70s," he said.

Evans corrected him. "We were a good club before the '70s."

"Well, you were probably a bit rough."

"We had the image of being a bit rough."

Gurrie hesitated and looked at me. "They had an image."

Evans recognised a non-believer when he heard one, prompting him to launch into an animated defence of North Shore's conduct over the decades. But the fact remains that opponents in the Geelong league considered North Shore a bunch of brawlers for many years.

The club began to change under the presidency of Bill Nicholls. As a player, Nicholls was one of the first full-forwards to be known as the Coleman of the Bush. In 1967, he broke his ankle while playing with North Shore and retired after a long a distinguished career at clubs throughout Victoria. He became a trainer, renowned for swirling his towel above his head when he needed to attract attention to an injured player, before becoming president in 1969. One of his first moves as president was to entice John Bligh to join the club as under-18 coach. Bligh set about instilling discipline into the teenagers.

The masterstroke of Nicholls, however, was hounding Gordon Hynes to become senior coach. It was through the legend of Gordon Hynes that I first became curious about North Shore's dominance. I was on a trip to the coast with a few journalists when we came to Norlane, at the un-lovely entrance to Geelong. One of the journalists, Ondrej Foltin, who would go on to become the sports editor of the *Herald Sun*, explained that behind the grit and traffic was a strong community. Foltin had grown up in the area and played all his footy at North Shore. He explained that the

Seagulls were an underachieving club until Hynes imposed the discipline that earned success.

Hynes had begun his senior career at Geelong in 1963. Within a few weeks he was suspended for eight matches for kicking, a penalty that earned him a black mark in the eyes of many, but failed to stop him playing in the premiership in his debut season. He was only 18 years of age. Six years later, his league career ended and he transferred to North Geelong.

When Nicholls approached him about coaching North Shore, Hynes was uninterested. He believed the Seagulls' main interests were drinking on Friday nights and brawling on Saturday afternoons. He hated playing against them and wanted nothing to do with them, but Nicholls began dropping in to see him on a regular basis. "I don't know how many times I told him, 'No, the last club I'll ever coach is North Shore'," Hynes said. "But he kept at me and at me and at the finish he broke me down."

Hynes's friends said he was mad. His decision even cost him one or two of those friends. But he believed he could turn the club around if two conditions were upheld: if a player didn't train, he wouldn't play; and there would be no grog late in the week. On Friday nights, he and Nicholls trawled the pubs in the northern suburbs looking for sly drinkers. So many were dumped from the team that Nicholls feared the club would be left without a senior squad, but Hynes held his ground. He could see the long-term gain.

To fulfil his training requirement, Hynes accommodated shift workers in the meatworks and the refineries by holding sessions at dawn and at lunchtime. Everybody was expected to attend Sunday morning training, but those who arrived late were punished when the session was over. They had to go on a run; the length of the run depended on how many minutes late they were. Sometimes players would bolt from their cars to the dressing-rooms only to be told they'd failed – they were a minute over time. Their teammates would form a guard of dishonor and jeer them on to the ground. Counting down the minutes until the start of training became a regular feature of Sunday mornings. Latecomers would feel they'd let the club down. Discipline and strong bonds resulted. Eager teenagers replaced the sacked drinkers and the Seagulls reached the preliminary final. Hynes continues to believe that a couple of injuries cost his side the distinction of rising from wooden spooners to premiers in a single season.

The next year several teenagers made big contributions as North Shore won their first premiership in 26 years. The friends who'd doubted Hynes's sanity for taking on North Shore were forced to think again. In the club history, *The Seagull Soars*, Bill Nicholls recalled his pride at accepting the premiership cup at the Palais in Geelong: "After giving a couple of two-finger signs to a couple of clubs, we sat down to savor the enormous pleasure of this night."

Hynes went on to coach six premiership sides. The centreman also won seven consecutive best-and-fairests, as well as a league best-and-fairest, and later served the club as president. In recent years, he's been the president of the North Shore Sports Club, which is the umbrella organisation for the football, cricket and bowls clubs. The social rooms at North Shore have been named in his honor.

In front of the Gordon Hynes Pavilion, John Bligh sat on a table with a radio to his ear. His Bombers T-shirt suggested he was intent on the Essendon match. His left foot kept his dog's leash pinned to the ground while his right foot swung freely. Spectators strayed into groups all around him but Bligh, the legendary under-18 coach, remained alone with his head cocked towards his radio and his eyes on the play. I felt guilty interrupting his reverie.

Bligh revealed how Bill Nicholls had lured him from St Peter's to North Shore. "He said come out here and see how you go. And I'm still here." North Shore greats from the past 30 years list Bligh among their biggest influences, but he admitted his iron rule was not always appreciated. "I thought they were going to hang me in the early days."

He offered loyalty and doing everything together as reasons behind the club's success. Then he paused. He said he'd been with the Seagulls so long that it was not up to him to suggest why they dominate. He ran his finger along the volume knob and returned to the Bombers. "We sort of don't know everything," he said. "You'd be better asking someone from outside."

Mick Atkins is an outsider. The centreman joined Footscray as a teenager before enjoying success with Wodonga and Old Xaverians. He arrived in Geelong after giving up journalism to buy a fish-and-chip shop and, with a view to choosing a club, spent a season watching Geelong league games. His study concluded in favor of North Shore; his study proved sound. Before this match against Leopold, Atkins hadn't played in a losing side in his five years with the club.

I chanced across him in front of the North Shore rooms. He was watching the reserves in shorts and sandals, with his ankles taped. Atkins is proud that he does his own strapping. He said it was a habit he learned in the Amateurs, a competition he enjoyed because there was no money to fuel jealousies. In this sense, he said, the modest pay scale of North Shore appeals to him. Players pull on the blue jumper with the yellow sash for the right reasons. He scraped his sandals on the concrete and said honesty is also a trait behind the club's success. "You just know everyone you run out with is going to have a go. That puts pressure on everybody else."

Atkins ducked into the dressing-rooms to warm up for the match. I worked with him in 1997 at *The Sunday Age*, where he was an astute football reporter before resigning because he wanted to return to the midfield at North Shore. He said he prefers playing football to writing about it. Before this match against Leopold, I was impressed that, at 33 years of age, he was still passionate enough to play in a major country league, but it should have been no surprise. In the mid-'90s, Atkins returned from a European holiday, jumped straight into his car and drove four hours to Wodonga to play in the reserves. He overcame jetlag to finish best afield and was back in the senior side the next week.

Atkins kicked the first goal of North Shore's premiership defence. After receiving the ball in the forward pocket, he was forced towards the boundary line. The temptation would have been to swing his left boot across his body and hope the ball ended up near the goals. Atkins, however, took a couple of steps to straighten. There was barely time to squeeze out a handball, let alone steady himself to kick, but he dropped the ball perfectly on his right boot and squeezed the ball through the goalposts from an improbable angle. It was a goal of rare class. Leopold defenders looked on with horror.

While Atkins is an outsider, and there were outsiders on every line, most supporters were unwilling to concede that outsiders had played a part in the club's success. The supporters all held fond memories of the 1990 premiership team because it was almost entirely local, but they ignored the rising number of outsiders that had helped the club towards six premierships over the next decade. Most guessed that the side playing Leopold had two or three outsiders, but Ken Ivermee, the Seagulls president, revealed that half the side had not come up through the juniors. Ivermee said the Seagulls' record was increasingly a magnet for those seeking success. "It's not money," he said. "They come here because they want to play in a successful team, and better their football."

He said all players received the same money. My request to reveal how much brought a smile, but no enlightenment. "I can't tell you that."

I walked with Ivermee from the huddle. The skinny former half-back had played in 120 games for three premierships before becoming a selector and committeeman. He looked relaxed and in control in his first year as president and said that strong support made his job easy. Then he cast his eye over the sea of former players traipsing from the huddle, not all looking as fit as him. "You won't find too many here who haven't played in a premiership," he said.

The lure of premierships entices North Shore products to return after seeking their fortune elsewhere. Against Leopold, Mark Hildebrandt was playing his first game after stints in Queensland, Perth and Griffith in the Riverina, and Matt Kershaw was back in the blue and gold after leaving as a disgruntled teenager. Kershaw fell out with a Seagulls coach because he wanted to train with the Geelong under-19s. He went on to play at Lara, Port Melbourne and St Kilda, but his return to Windsor Park was considered unremarkable.

North Shore supporter Jack Deppeler thought it was the most natural event in the world. "They all come home," he said. Deppeler shouted at Kershaw as if the midfielder had been missing for a few weeks, rather than almost 10 years. "Oh, Matty, you've done it again. You've hooked it." Minutes later, Kershaw held out one opponent while another flew over the top of him. He stood his ground to take a clever mark on his chest before splitting the posts from an angle. It was a goal of strength and subtlety. "That's what you needed, Matty," Deppeler said.

Deppeler, a former Corio shire mayor, began following North Shore during the '60s, in the rough-and-tumble days when the club had few supporters and many enemies. For the Leopold match he was dressed as a bayside cowboy. He wore an Akubra hat and Wrangler jeans, and the sleeves of his checked shirt were rolled up to his elbows. He believed that North

Shore's ability to deal with anything was behind their success. "If they're not versatile, they don't click," he said.

The make-up of the side supported his view. Ruckman Wade Bowyer was the only player of imposing height or strength. Frank Fopiani, Nathan Lewis and the coach, Glenn Keast, were in the rover mould, but the rest could have been rotated through all positions. It was a team of ruck-rovers, superbly fit and disciplined, like the West Coast sides of the early '90s, and a team that confirmed the history of the club. North Shore sides have never been rangy. In the mid-'70s, Bob Benson was the ruckman. His successor in the late '70s was Leo King. In the tradition of the Seagulls, King had been pulled off the street to join the club. He went on to play four games at Geelong, but his achievement failed to have a flow-on effect in producing ruckmen at Windsor Park. The Seagulls continue to be more athletic than tall. Versatility remains the key.

Tom Hall epitomises this versatility. In 1999, Hall played at centre half-forward for the Geelong league and full-back for the Victorian Country side. At the end of the season he won the Geelong league goalkicking award, with 88 goals, and the competition best-and-fairest. He also broke the strangehold of Frank Fopiani on the North Shore best-and-fairest but, in this first game of the 2000 season, he found himself in defence. After half-time, he was moved to the forward line, where he confirmed North Shore's dominance. He was pale and, at 185 centimetres, hardly a giant, but he had a simplicity that stripped the match to its core. He was the sort of player no one seemed to touch. He marked in front and kicked straight. Even his name is old-fashioned. The lack of fuss and clamor normally linked with key forwards is a large part of his appeal. Hall grew up two blocks from Windsor Park, on the flat grid of weatherboard houses that spreads across the northern suburbs. The Seagulls supporters revere him.

In the social club, Hall was in the photo of the 11 Seagulls who represented the Geelong league in 1997. The picture paints a thousand words: North Shore comprised half the side that made the grand final of the country championships. Ovens and Murray defeated the Geelong league but the North Shore representation indicates the strength of the club in the '90s. A rundown of the 11 players at the back of this book shows the calibre of the sides that dominated the Geelong league in this period.

The heart and soul of these sides was Ron Watt. His performances in the midfield were crucial, but it was his nature that most impressed. He had the ability to create harmony and generate affection. After every match, he was in the habit of asking supporters at random for their view of the game. The supporters loved him for it and he became entrenched as a favorite of the football club and the suburb. His pupils cried when he left his teaching post at North Shore Primary School, which backs on to Windsor Park, to join the coaching staff at Geelong.

Watt continues to drop into North Shore when commitments allow, a practice that is common among former premiership Seagulls. The most decorated premiership player of all, John Albon, has never left the club. Albon was one of the teenagers who lifted the Seagulls to the flag under Gordon Hynes in 1974. His career ended when he was captain-coach of the 1990 premiership side after 309 senior games, the club record, including 12 grand finals and seven premierships. He continues to serve the club by working on the committee. I found him selling cold cans behind a makeshift bar, where he looked like rugged former Richmond defender Robbie McGhie. He had dark skin, cropped hair and tattoos stretching down his sinewy arms. It was no surprise to learn that he played almost every game at centre half-back. Albon said he continued to work for the club because he believed in the people.

The people saw a match that was pedestrian. North Shore moved the ball with skill and discipline but, apart from a Leopold flurry in the second quarter, the atmosphere was as flat as the suburban terrain. Sam Graham, the 195-centimetre brother of Geelong captain Ben Graham, fancied his chances of influencing a game against a team of almost uniformly medium height, but his efforts were in vain. The Seagulls swept to victory by 42 points, with Mick Atkins and Wayne McElroy kicking five goals each. Nathan Lewis, who played on a wing, ranked with Atkins for my choice as best afield. Forward Corey Chapman, a grandson of Bill Nicholls, was also among the best. His brother Wade, meanwhile, was struggling in vain to return from injury and get his AFL career back on track at Port Adelaide.

The Chapman brothers grew up around the club at North Shore, tearing around in Seagulls jumpers in a sight that must have pleased their grandfather. Early in his presidency, Bill Nicholls regretted that young boys cycled around the northern suburbs wearing St Peter's, St Mary's and

Newtown jumpers. His goals included building a club that would inspire the young boys to wear Seagulls guernseys. From all reports, he achieved his aim. The gritty streets of North Shore and Norlane are dotted with blue and gold. The football club is a source of great pride.

North Shore won their sixth consecutive premiership. Mick Atkins was best afield in the grand final. Frank Fopiani won his fifth best-and-fairest. Injuries forced Wade Chapman to retire from AFL football. Half-back Andrew Merriman won the Leopold best-and-fairest. Sam Graham injured his shoulder playing with Carlton reserves and headed overseas.

3

NO PLACE LIKE HOME

Castlemaine v Kangaroo Flat
the Magpies and the Roos

"As a sportsman, he ranks with Geoff Southby and Craig Bradley for all-round talent – except that he chose not to leave Castlemaine."

Former Carlton coach David Parkin on Steven Oliver

On Easter Saturday in 1990, I emerged from the rooms following an inglorious game with the Golden Square reserves and stumbled on a phenomenon. I'd grown up in the city hearing tales from my father and uncles about legends of the bush. At 24 years of age, I was looking forward to investigating the land of those tales when I moved out of Melbourne to begin a journalism cadetship at the *Bendigo Advertiser*. And here, in my second week in Bendigo footy, was a baby-faced forward kicking four goals in a quarter, all from impossible distances. The tales had come to life.

Steven Oliver blew away the mighty Golden Square, the premiers of the previous two seasons, with an early blitz in the senior match at Wade Street in Bendigo. The 19-year-old lined up for his first goal after taking a mark near the wing that runs alongside the Golden Square pool. I couldn't believe he was going to have a shot, but a drop punt sailed through at post height. Minutes later, he soared over his opponent, the feared and respected Phil McEvoy, to take another mark. This time he was closer to the flank near the pool. Another drop punt sailed through, again at post height. Soon, he soared to take another effortless mark and kick a long torpedo. By the fourth goal, the match was over. McEvoy looked embarrassed.

The Golden Square supporters were at a loss. Some blushed for McEvoy, who was becoming more human by the minute, while the wise ones fixed their eyes on something in the distance. I was staggered. Every story that I'd heard about bush champions at family celebrations, over drinks at birthday get-togethers or bowls of plum pudding at Christmas, was embodied in Oliver. With his lack of muscle tone, he looked like he'd been training on plum pudding, but it was apparent that, if he hopped the fence and lined up from inside the enclosure of the Golden Square pool, the ball would have still sailed through the goals at post height. A few years later, when it was revealed that Geelong superboot Billy Brownless had won a bet by booting a ball over a silo in the Riverina, I came up with the idea of Brownless and Oliver embarking on a national tour kicking footballs over country icons. Maybe my imagination was taking one bounce too many.

Oliver slowed down after quarter-time, kicking two more goals to finish with six. Golden Square coach Brian Walsh, who once topped the goalkicking at Carlton, later confirmed to the *Bendigo Advertiser* that the teenager's early blitz was the difference between the sides. "He should be playing full-forward for Carlton, not down here," Walsh said. But at the house of the O'Farrells, our family friends who admittedly are Sandhurst people, the tales of the Castlemaine prodigy struck no interest. The O'Farrells said he'd been taking marks and kicking goals with Castlemaine since he was 16, when Carlton drafted him. His talent was far from being a secret, but this failed to deter me from believing I'd made a big discovery.

Two years later, Oliver began the season with two games in the Carlton seniors before returning to Castlemaine. Soon after his return, he kicked 17.7 at Northern United before succumbing to exhaustion and falling over in the goalsquare as he struggled in for his eighteenth. I rang *The Sunday Age* and, in something of a career breakthrough, four paragraphs duly appeared in which I described Oliver as a reluctant Carlton forward. Before long, the newspaper followed up with a feature on country stars who turned their backs on the city. It reeled out old favorites such as Ron Best and Tony Southcombe, who preferred the Bendigo league to the big league in the '70s, and Wayne Beddison, the Dimboola flyer who returned to the Wimmera after a handful of games with Essendon. I once heard Kevin Sheedy chide Beddison because he had the world at his feet and kicked it out of bounds on the full. To Sheedy, the back-pocket plumber who scrapped his way to 251 games and three premierships with Richmond, this amounted to criminal neglect. But Beddison reportedly didn't care for Melbourne, or the expectations of others. Steven Oliver was the same.

As a teenager, Oliver gave the city a shot. He went down to spend a pre-season with Carlton but injured his back while playing for the Victorian under-17 cricket team, which he captained. The stress fractures forced him to spend his pre-season with Carlton in the pool. He became frustrated and returned home, where he resumed kicking goals for Castlemaine and playing golf off single figures. The next summer, he roused himself to play a few games of district cricket for Essendon as an all-rounder but, the next autumn, he showed no inclination to return to Princes Park to play football.

He was having too much fun at Castlemaine. The team had half a dozen of his mates from Castlemaine Tech and it was winning enough games to keep the young Magpies interested. After failing to win a premiership since 1952, Castlemaine had modest expectations, upgraded maybe once a decade by a talented side with ambitions of a flag, but mostly there was no pressure on the young Magpies to do much more than enjoy themselves. The week after I saw Oliver perform party tricks against Golden Square, Castlemaine lost to a middling club at home. At the end of the season they finished fifth and nobody thought twice about it.

In 1991, the Magpies moved up the ladder when weight of talent finally shone through. About halfway through the season, they clicked. Oliver and his mates took over the Bendigo league and spectators from throughout central Victoria began turning up to see what the fuss was about. Oliver alone was worth travelling to see – opponents went into every match conceding he would kick eight goals – but he was far from the only star. To see Derrick Filo, the son of a Samoan father and Castlemaine mother, bulldoze through pack after pack was to see one of the most exhilarating sights in football. Tom Kavanagh, Brent Crosswell's son, streamed from the half-back line and Simon Jorgensen was ever artful on the ball. After every brilliant cameo, the young Magpies treated the moment like they were still having a kick after school. It was the most charismatic side I've seen in football. More than 10,000 crowded into the Queen Elizabeth Oval in Bendigo for the grand final, only to see the experienced South Bendigo hold off the challenge.

The next year, Castlemaine met Golden Square in the grand final and an even bigger crowd turned up. Golden Square defenders hit Oliver with a house but he continued to lead and fire at goal and the Magpies got up by five points. The celebrations were long and loud after the club's first premiership in 40 years, but then the exodus of talent began. Oliver sensed it might be time to move on himself.

Carlton eventually won him over by accepting his wish to live in Castlemaine. Three times a week Oliver left work in the office at Castle Bacon at 3pm and arrived at Princes Park 10 minutes before training. The Blues played him mainly off the bench. His moment in the sun came at Subiaco Oval when he took several gliding marks at centre half-forward and turned a game against West Coast. It was the performance that finally confirmed his talent on the biggest stage but, after eight goals in 13 games, Oliver quit the Blues for good. When I spoke to him at his Castlemaine sports shop after the 2000 season, he said the journeys to Melbourne for training had sapped his desire. "Towards the end I finished up on the side of the road after falling asleep. I thought, 'Ah well, that'll do me'."

Oliver has played with his beloved Castlemaine ever since. He coached for three years before handing the reins to Shane Robertson, the 1987 Carlton premiership defender, who brought several handy recruits with him from Daylesford. I went to Castlemaine's first game of the season to see if Oliver still had the magic. The fact that the Magpies were playing Kangaroo Flat would provide a double act.

The Kangaroo Flat coach was Derrick Filo, the human train. Like Oliver, who is his cousin, Filo had short stints in the city but failed to find his feet. Several Castlemaine supporters hinted that Carlton and Collingwood were unable to rein in a teenager who was wild at heart. "He played pretty hard, Derrick," said one supporter. Filo himself told me it was a matter of preference: "I was more comfortable in the country than in Melbourne."

Either way, he returned to Castlemaine and won four best-and-fairests before moving on to Balranald with Simon Jorgensen. This pair had shared Castlemaine best-and-fairests during the Magpies' surge in the early '90s, so it was unsurprising when Balranald won the Central Murray league premiership. Filo then took the coaching job at Kyneton, where, in his first season, he pulled the Tigers through the finals like a team of horses dragging a stump. Kyneton won their first Bendigo league premiership for three decades. The next year, Jorgensen coached Kangaroo Flat to victory over Kyneton in the Roos' first Bendigo league grand final. Then he went to Robinvale and led them to a premiership.

Before the 2000 season, Kangaroo Flat pulled off one of the biggest coups in country football when they reunited Jorgensen and Filo. Although longer in the tooth, the pair were still held in awe along the length of the Calder Highway, from Kyneton to Mildura. Filo was appointed coach, with Jorgensen, who was in a cleaning partnership in Melbourne, his assistant. Their signatures dominated summer footy talk and sparked a recruiting bonanza, with Bendigo Diggers centre half-forward Simon Elsum rejoining his old Kyneton teammate Filo and several 1996 premiership players returning to Kangaroo Flat. Most significantly, David Lancaster returned after stamping himself as the standout player at the Diggers.

Castlemaine had also picked up their share of recruits, and many regarded Oliver as a recruit after breaking his arm and having a knee operation the previous season. Still, the Magpies had finished runners-up to Maryborough and, on the morning of the new season, the *Bendigo Advertiser* tipped them to go one better and win the flag, with Kangaroo Flat to finish runners-up.

Camp Reserve in Castlemaine is one of my favorite country footy grounds. It has a tree-lined perimeter and an eccentric shape, with a straight wing under the towering trees and a forward pocket that banks steeply. My first sight upon parking the car was Derrick Filo having a kick and a smoke with his teammates at half-time in the reserves. He was still fit and solid, but less imposing in his jeans and woollen jumper, and he wore glasses. In the other forward pocket, Oliver wandered around in front of the orange-bricked clubrooms, stooped as always, as tall as his cousin was solid.

In my mission to establish their place in the pantheon of Magpie greats, I was pointed towards Jack Jefferies, the 72-year-old treasurer who was on canteen duty. Jefferies untied his apron strings and looked me over with the beginnings of a frown. "What's wrong, son?"

I told him nothing was wrong and said that I wanted to know whether Steven Oliver and Derrick Filo are the greatest Castlemaine players of all time. There was no better man to ask. Jefferies made his senior debut with the Magpies at 16 years of age and played in the 1952 premiership. His place in the side is celebrated in the social rooms, where his jumper is encased in glass alongside the jumper that his son John wore in the '92 premiership side. Jack's jumper is black with a white V; John's guernsey has the Collingwood stripes. Both men played more than 200 games for Castlemaine before continuing to work for the club off the field. Jack Jefferies said Wally Culpitt, the former Hawthorn forward, was the best player of his generation but he was unwilling to compare players from different eras. "It's like comparing Phar Lap and Tulloch," he said. His conclusion was that Oliver and Filo are among the best.

He was more specific, however, about Oliver's decision to leave Carlton and return to Castlemaine. "It was disappointing, really, because we wanted a hero," he said. He rejected my suggestion that the town would have appreciated the return of its most prodigious talent. "We would have all loved to see the boy kick on."

As a young man, Jefferies was quietly pleased when he received an invitation to play a practice match with Melbourne. His regret is that it was at Olympic Park, not the MCG, the ground that young footballers continue to hold sacred. "It was disappointing for a country boy," he said. It was not hard to sense that Jefferies would have cherished another chance to play at league level. He believed that Oliver had every chance to establish himself in a key forward post at Carlton, even in the Stephen Kernahan era, but he chose not to. "Of course he should have made it. He's the best talent that I've ever seen to never make league footy. He didn't want to make it."

Jefferies believed Filo was also a phenomenal talent. When pressed for a feat that sticks in his mind, Jefferies recalled the 1995 grand final, in which Filo forced the ball from the wing to centre half-forward, cleaved a pack and kicked a goal while running towards the boundary. He said Kyneton were never going to lose after that performance. "Next to Oliver, he's the best footballer in this league over the last 20 years."

Oliver had the first impact on the new season when he launched himself at a pack in the opening minutes, taking a strong mark and earning a satisfied roar from the Castlemaine crowd. The 30-year-old barely pushed his foot through the ball but it sailed though the goals from 40 metres. Magpie supporters nodded and murmured about his follow-through. Oliver's foot normally swings through a mighty arc, but it was obvious he was still carrying the hamstring injury that had limited his pre-season.

The Magpies went on to kick four goals in 15 minutes. Kangaroo Flat then woke up and rebounded through rovers Ash Wilson and Wayne Landry, who split the game open with darting runs. It was their first game together and already they were revealing a close bond. They both had choppy running actions and dyed blond hair, and seemed to revel in their pairing. The senior partners in Filo and Jorgensen were slower to ignite. Filo was far from the possession magnet that he was in earlier years and Jorgensen was bulkier, and balder. He spent the first quarter trying to keep up.

Simon Elsum was in better shape; with his bulging arms he looked ready for a body-building contest. Towards the end of the quarter, he killed the notion that it was all for show when he summoned breathtaking nerve to launch himself towards a pack with the flight of the ball. A crisp thud sounded as the ball hit his chest and opponents sprawled beneath him. In lining up for goal, his sharply defined arms contrasted with the shapeless strength of his opponents. Several Roos looked chiselled and buffed, whereas the Magpies looked gym-shy. Elsum kicked a behind, earning advice from the crowd that big muscles won't help him kick straight.

The Roos gained momentum in the second quarter as the Magpies' limited pre-season began to tell. The seeming shortage of gyms in Castlemaine had been compounded by the unavailability of the ground. Shane Robertson forced himself to keep following the ball but, at 36 years of age, he was laboring. My first memory of Robertson is reading about him winning the 110 metres hurdles at the Catholic schools' sports in Melbourne in the early '80s. Against Kangaroo Flat, he looked unable to hurdle the boundary line. His team trailed by five goals at half-time.

I spent much of the next quarter asking supporters whether Oliver should have stayed at Carlton. Many had vivid memories of the game at Subiaco and said it showed that he could have created havoc. Others believed the Subiaco match had shown what he could do, so there was nothing more to prove. Steven McCoomb, who taught Oliver and his talented friends at Castlemaine Tech, recalled his precocious talent. "When he was 16 or 17, he'd take three steps and stand on blokes' shoulders." Almost every interview ended with a shrug and a version of the line: "He's a country boy." This catch-all explanation was sometimes expanded to: "He's like his father." In the end, the consensus was that it was Oliver's life and it was up to him how he lived. Nobody gushed about the fact that he preferred Castlemaine to Carlton, or that the Magpies boasted the best forward to pull on a boot since The Great McCarthy. It was accepted that he wanted to live in central Victoria rather than central Melbourne and there was nothing more to it.

The next step was to seek out Charlie Oliver, Steven's father, who, in his youth, had the chance to go to St Kilda but stayed in Castlemaine. Jack Jefferies remembered him as an elusive centreman; others claimed he was a brilliant forward. All agreed he was an easy-going footballer with an aversion to fuss, and all seemed keen to protect him from the prying visitor. "He might be up the back somewhere," one supporter said. "You wouldn't find him."

He was right. But it was with interest after the season that I read of Charlie Oliver's words to his son Ben before the teenager made his debut in the Victorian cricket team. Charlie Oliver had advised Ben as he left to try his hand in district cricket at Geelong that, if he was going to have a crack at the big time, he should do it properly or not at all. Ben Oliver opened his first-class career with the wicket of Brian Lara.

One method employed to divert my attention from the whereabouts of Charlie Oliver was telling me about the brown paper bag. In the early '90s, Carlton coach David Parkin reportedly stuffed the bag with money and drove up the Calder Highway to sign Steven Oliver. The big forward refused. Not to be dissuaded, Parkin got a bigger bag and stuffed it with more money and headed up the Calder Highway. The big forward refused. Parkin tried again and again, taking fistfuls of cash and stuffing them in brown paper bags and driving up to Castlemaine until his car was worn out. Still, Oliver refused. The tale of the brown paper bag conjured images of SP bookies taking bets in narrow lanes rather than football in the corporate age, but I was happily surprised when Parkin confirmed the legend himself.

I asked him at a government awards function, where he was effusive in his praise of Oliver and recalled his trips up the Calder Highway. In a formal interview, Parkin said he made Oliver lucrative offers. He admitted Oliver's refusal to fulfil his potential annoyed him, and even dented his ego, because few footballers have resisted his recruiting efforts. But in the end he respected that Oliver wanted to fulfil his potential in walks of life other than football. The young forward rejected the bright lights and the brown paper bag because he wanted to bring up his family in his home town. "As a sportsman, he ranks with Geoff Southby and Craig Bradley for all-round talent – except that he chose not to leave Castlemaine," Parkin said.

Oliver remembered Parkin making a dozen trips to Castlemaine accompanied by officials such as Ian Collins or Col Kinnear. Oliver laughed, as he did freely during the short interview, at the suggestion that they were persistent. "Persistent's a good word," he said.

Persistent, as unlikely as it might sound for one so brilliant, was also a good word to describe his performance against Kangaroo Flat. He took a series of marks by planting his 196-centimetre frame in front of his opponent, then sprayed a series of behinds. With his reluctance to follow through, it looked like he was giving the ball a delicate tap, but it sailed further from his boot than any other. He finished with four goals through sheer volume of shots.

At the other end, David Lancaster was on fire. Before he went to the Diggers, Lancaster won a Kangaroo Flat best-and-fairest after kicking 100 goals from full-forward. At the Diggers, I once saw him take 20 marks on a half-back flank. He was like a one-man wall in long sleeves. Now he was back at Kangaroo Flat and back at full-forward, despite his modest dimensions of 183 centimetres and 80 kilograms. Against Castlemaine, he constantly outmarked taller opponents and kicked eight goals. It seemed the bottom line with him was talent.

Towards the end of the game, Derrick Filo took himself off. The 32-year-old had swapped between half-forward and the midfield and gained his share of kicks without being the dynamic player of his youth. He smiled as the Roos' bench applauded his debut in the green guernsey with the white kangaroo, then slipped on his glasses. He folded his arms and watched the nimble Roos run out winners by 59 points.

The match served as a reminder that even the brilliant ones fade with age. Oliver, despite kicking four goals on one leg, was no longer the player to make spectators gasp. It seemed he'd passed that baton on to Lancaster. Filo, despite his inclusion among the best players, was far from the dominant figure of a decade before. He'd passed that baton to the rovers with the dyed hair and sculpted muscles. The performance of neither player compared with the performances of a decade before, but the brilliance of their youth remains fresh in my mind.

In the social rooms, Oliver slumped in his plastic chair in the same manner that he stoops when he walks. I explained that my visit had its origins at Golden Square on Easter Saturday in 1990, and he laughed. To him, the match was a vague memory. I said my survey of Castlemaine supporters had shown that, even if they were disappointed in his decision to quit Carlton, they supported it. He said he had no regrets and mentioned former Geelong defender Ken Hinkley as another country footballer who shied away from the city. "I probably had the skill but I didn't have the work ethic," he said. "My story's not so special. There's probably a lot of guys out there just like me."

His daughter, one of his three children, sat on his knee and showed him every chip from the packet before putting it in her mouth. Her father smiled and lifted a light beer from the trestle table to his mouth. In the Castlemaine clubrooms, with his daughter on his knee, amid the ricketty tables and photos of Magpie sides from down the years, Steven Oliver struck me as a happy man.

Castlemaine won every remaining match, culminating in a 12-point defeat of Kangaroo Flat in the grand final. Steven Oliver kicked 135 goals for the season; David Lancaster kicked 112. Derrick Filo kicked seven goals in a quarter against Gisborne. In the grand final, held on a windy day at the QEO, Lancaster kicked two goals and Oliver, playing at centre half-forward, kicked none. His opponent was Brett Gloury, who, in 1986, played his first of four games for Collingwood at full-back on Paul Salmon. Centreman Shannon Milward won Kangaroo Flat's best-and-fairest. Oliver won his third best-and-fairest for Castlemaine. Shane Robertson retired after playing in the premiership side.

4

TO THEIR CREDIT

Lavington v Corowa-Rutherglen
the Blues and the Roos

"We don't need pokies for today's jackpot."
Albury banner before 1982 grand final against Lavington

When I was a teenager visiting relatives on their farm near Wangaratta, my
uncle clicked his tongue, cut the twine of the hay bales and muttered about
this mob from Lavington. He said their money was ruining football in the
region. The poker machines in the Lavington sports club were enabling the
Blues to buy the best players and it didn't seem fair. His words must have
made an impression. Almost two decades later, I still believed that
Lavington splashed out the money for the best players. Like the "foreign
legion" at South Melbourne in the 1930s, it all sounded quite glamorous.
While visiting the farm outside Wangaratta over the Easter break, I
decided it was time to go to Lavington and check out the claims. My
father offered to drive and we headed up the Hume Highway.

   The Lavington footy ground revealed itself beyond the brow of a hill
on the western outskirts of Albury. Huge light towers craned over the concrete grandstand that backs on to the road. Next to the ground, the sports
club was a boxy, brown building. Large gums edged on to the car park and

the Murray River was just over the range. Until the late 1960s, the land at the base of the Black Range was a turkey farm. The Lavington football and cricket clubs bought the farm from the Divine Word Seminary, built the sports club and filled it with pokies. Victorians poured over the border by the busload and poured their money into the machines. The football club signed recruits with the pokies money and prepared the way for entry into the powerful Ovens and Murray league.

But the Ovens and Murray league clubs feared a monster. All that money was bound to leave the rest of the competition floundering. Lavington were forced to bide their time in smaller competitions on either side of the border for almost a decade before, finally, in 1979 the merger of Corowa and Rutherglen left a vacancy. The Ovens and Murray clubs gritted their teeth. Lavington were invited into the competition.

The Blues stepped up their recruiting. Players were signed throughout north-east Victoria and the Riverina. A handful of key players turned up from Tasmania while Warren Stanlake, a glamorous centre half-forward from Bairnsdale, crossed the mountains in his friend's Tiger Moth aeroplane. The grand entrance of Stanlake stoked the gossip that surrounded the Blues. If a recruit was on $200 a match, rumors raised his payments to $500. If a player from a rival club wanted more money, he made up stories that Lavington were interested in him. The rival club would raise their star player's earnings to keep him away from the Blues. Lavington officials shrugged and learned to make jokes at their own expense. They put out the word that the pokies were rigged. If a star recruit wore No.3, you must steer clear of the third poker machine. If a recruit wore No.9, the ninth pokie should be avoided. And so on.

In the first few years, Lavington sorted out the players who were prepared to work. Enthusiastic coach Ken Roberts, the former Essendon defender, trained the Blues for hours. One night, a committeeman walked on to the ground and asked what time training would finish.

"Why?" Roberts asked.

"Because it's 20 to nine."

"Is it? I didn't realise."

Many recruits proved more than willing to work; some stayed for a decade or more. Warren Stanlake played 200 games. Local products such as Ralph Aalbers, Peter Copely and Ray Mack also notched 200 games. At the junior level, the Lavington Sports Club oversaw what was reputed to be the biggest little league competition in Australia, with 600 boys racing around ovals in the west of Albury on Saturday mornings. Ken Roberts combined his role as senior coach with his role as junior development officer. The juniors progressed to the seniors and Lavington climbed the ladder.

In their fourth year in the Ovens and Murray league, the Blues made their first grand final. Their reward was resentment. Albury ran through a banner that read: "We don't need pokies for today's jackpot." The Tigers won the flag but Lavington were undeterred. The club developed more juniors and signed more recruits, most notably the former Geelong defender Jeff Cassidy, who coached the Blues during their golden era. In the eight years from 1982, Lavington played in seven grand finals. The 1990 grand final proved a portent for rough times ahead.

Lavington lost the match to Wodonga after a massive brawl. Television stations continue to wheel out footage of the brawl when seeking to make a point about violence in football. Off the field, telling blows were landed when legislation to introduce pokies in Victoria was passed under the state Labor Government in 1991. Victorians could now remain in their home towns and gamble their days away; there was no need to head over the river to Lavington or Barooga or Murray Downs. Tourist buses stopped pulling up outside the boxy building on the outskirts of Albury, and the sports club fell into a debt of $6 million.

A stable committee enabled the football club to raise its own money and remain competitive. Since the mid-'70s, the club has had only three presidents, and one of them served for only one year. Brian Chalmers became president in 1975 and did the job for 16 years. He continues to serve the club. His offsider, Tom Gittings, joined the club as the senior runner in 1980, went on to the committee and also continues to serve the club. I joined the pair in the press box at the top of the Hartley Stand, which backs on to the road that rises over the Black Range. They were like the two old hecklers in the stalls on *The Muppet Show*, keeping score and watching over their domain. They took me through the club's history, from the days when it was based in a tin shed on Urana Road to the glory days, when their riches of talent were envied throughout country football. They didn't deny that money from the pokies enabled them to gather talent, but they made the point that every New South Wales sports club had the right to apply for a gaming licence. In the early years, Lavington was the only club with the foresight to do it. The Blues also knew how to work. It was a trait that got them through the '90s, when the sports club proved unable to make a dint in the debt of $6 million.

For this game against Corowa-Rutherglen, the hecklers expected a struggle. Lavington lost the 1998 grand final to Wodonga Raiders. In 1999, Lavington lost the elimination final to Corowa-Rutherglen by a point. A year later, Corowa-Rutherglen were tipped to move up the ladder. Lavington had lost a few players, prompting them to bring on a few teenagers. Matthew Murray, the 15-year-old brother of Port Adelaide forward Derek, led the Blues out on to the ground for his first game. His jumper hung in folds over his skinny frame as Tim Sanson, the coach, hovered at his shoulder. Murray gained some promising touches in the early part of the match before being swept away like a cork on the tide.

On the sidelines, policeman Darren Holmes did some stretching exercises after missing the opening of the match because of his duties at the station. Lavington recruited Holmes from Walla Walla, a small town just down the road, before the Swans lured him to Sydney. At Sydney, he achieved a measure of fame when he caught the piglet that raced around the SCG with the word "Plugger" in big red letters on its hide. After taking the field against Corowa-Rutherglen, Holmes ran hard on to a pack to take a strong mark.

Corowa-Rutherglen established an early break through midfielders David Teague and Luke Henderson. The pair had joined the Roos from their home town of Katandra because they had to be aligned with a major-league club if they were to play in the VFL. Corowa-Rutherglen had five players who moved between their Ovens and Murray league club and the Murray Kangaroos. President Rod Campbell believed his club's riches of talent were due reward after the steady flow of players seeking higher ground. Over the previous decade, a dozen players had left Corowa-Rutherglen and made it on to AFL lists. Campbell, leaning on the fence on the wing, said it was about time his club had some luck. The Roos had been unable to win a premiership since the merger in 1979, battling away against larger rivals from Wodonga and Albury, but the form of his midfield recruits suggested they might be ready to break through.

Teague, especially, was having a picnic against Lavington, his floppy hair shining in the sun as he took the ball from the centre with coolness and precision. Up forward, curly-haired David Willetts, another Murray Kangaroo, forgot his crumbing role and leapt on to his opponent's shoulders. In the ruck, Brendan Eyers was presenting the midfield with the ball on a plate, with a choice of salad or vegies on the side. He'd come a long way from his student days in Bendigo, where I played with him at Golden Square. In those days, Eyers was a young giant, yet to grow into his body. By his mid-20s, an age when many gangly sportsmen begin to find their feet, he was among the leading ruckmen in country football. At least one of us had kicked on.

Late in the third quarter, Eyers imposed his authority when he held out a crowded goalsquare to take a towering mark. He kicked the goal and lumbered jauntily back to the centre circle as his teammates took their cue to ease off in the dreamy autumn sunshine. The Roos coasted early in the last quarter, prepared to rest on their four-goal lead, before Lavington mid-fielder Kerry Bahr led the charge for the home side. Bahr won his first best-and-fairest in 1989. More than a decade later, he was still throwing himself into packs like a teenager. Small and unrelenting, he gave the impression that he would walk tenaciously to the corner shop.

In attack, Tim Sanson was wearing a bandage that stoppered his nose before looping around his head. The rangy centre half-forward made a series of fierce leads before hanging on the back of his opponent, parallel to the ground, and taking an inspiring mark. His goal from 40 metres, on an awkward angle for a left-footer, showed his mettle as a leader under pressure. The Blues were only two or three goals behind – it was hard to tell because Tom Gittings, the old heckler, kept turning on his microphone at the back of the Hartley Stand and correcting the scoreboard. The spec-tators, who for most of the afternoon had lounged on the concrete ter-races looking pleasantly bored, stirred to life. With Sanson firing, victory was possible.

Then Damien Houlihan shifted up a gear. The 24-year-old is the old-est of four brothers, three of whom have played league football. Damien made his debut in the forward line at Collingwood as a teenager but he was unable to fulfil his considerable potential, drifting back to the country before returning to the AFL at North Melbourne. Corowa-Rutherglen were quietly ecstatic when he was lured home and in the last quarter against Lavington he justified their faith. It was the most casually brilliant quarter you could wish to see. Houlihan drifted into every passage of play like he was taking a stroll by the stream, pulling down marks and loping forward from the half-back line to lead his side to a 29-point win. The Roos named him as their best player but I thought David Teague had shown industry throughout the match and deserved to be best afield.

The performance of Houlihan was enough to give the spectators a measure of satisfaction as they shuffled across the concrete towards the turnstiles. My father tucked his radio under his ear and picked up the league scores in Melbourne as we made our way across the carpark. Just as Lavington had toiled in vain, the sports club was looking solid but dated. The boxy, brown design was obsolete in an age when even Corowa-Rutherglen were threatening for a premiership. My uncle would have to be informed that the pot of gold was no longer to be found at Lavington. We headed back down the Hume Highway for a family dinner.

Corowa-Rutherglen defeated North Albury by 108 points in the grand final, with Damien Houlihan kicking 10 goals in a best-afield performance. Lavington missed the finals and amalgamated with Sydney rugby league club Penrith Panthers as a means of solving the sports club's debt. The Lavington Blues have since been renamed the Lavington Panthers. Midfielder Carl Dickins won the Corowa-Rutherglen best-and-fairest. David Teague graduated to the Kangaroos' rookie list. Midfielder Darryn McKimmie won the Lavington best-and-fairest.

5

FIGHTING WORDS

Bungaree v Dunnstown
the Demons and the Towners

"You can't change a lot of things that happen in football.
Individuals can only be guided as much as they choose to be."

Hepburn co-coach Jamie Grant

This an edited version of the story which appeared in *The Sunday Age* on
April 30, 2000, entitled "The fight that grew":

The Paul Kelly song *From Little Things Big Things Grow* might
well be adapted to the saga over the brawl between Hepburn and
Dunnstown before their match on April 15. It is a saga that shows no
signs of dying.

Before the seniors match, a Dunnstown player broke from his
team's warm-up routine to separate two boys who were fighting. One
of the boys, an eight-year-old, complained to his father, a Hepburn
player, as the Burras were leaving the rooms to run on to the ground.
The father let the Dunnstown player know that he shouldn't touch his
son and an ugly brawl erupted that led to spectators joining in, officials
trying to intervene and the arrival of police cars and an ambulance to
ferry three Dunnstown players to hospital.

Both clubs agree that the fight was over in 90 seconds but the exuberance of witnesses and the magic workings of pub talk have extended the brawl to 10 minutes. Whatever the duration, it was long enough for the umpires to walk off the ground and declare the match abandoned. Police and league investigations ensued and interest in the incident culminated in reports on the Channel Seven football show The Game, which is hosted by Dermott Brereton and broadcast around Australia. In the weeks since, Ballarat's *Courier* has run five front-page lead stories on the brawl, rivalling the Queen on her recent visit to the former gold mining town.

Yesterday, Hepburn broke its silence and agreed to an interview with *The Sunday Age* that, fittingly, began small and then mushroomed. President Gordon Torrance and vice-president Eddy Comelli sat down to outline the club's view at a small table in the Burras' social rooms on the edge of the spa town outside Daylesford. An hour later, players and committeemen had expanded the forum to more than a dozen. The atmosphere was solemn rather than chaotic as the club tried to rectify what it believes is an unfair media portrayal.

They were able to talk on a Saturday because their match at home to Clunes had been cancelled. Clunes secretary Dennis Coon said his club was happy to play but the Ballarat Football Umpires Association had announced during the week that its members, concerned for their safety, would not officiate in any Hepburn matches until the Central Highlands league investigations officer, Ray Harris, had completed his findings. Harris has another week of his allotted 21 days to finish the investigation and is able to apply for an extension.

The umpires continue to officiate in Dunnstown matches but all Hepburn sides are off limits. "The thing that we really can't understand is that the umpires can't come and umpire a game between the kids," Torrance said.

All netball matches involving Hepburn have been cancelled as well. The under-14 footballers were training during the interview and some reserves and seniors turned up expecting a game because the club had not informed them of the cancellation. Torrance said there had been no time to tell the players of the cancellation – he was ringing the league until late Friday night in the hope of resurrecting the game.

In their statement of events, Hepburn acknowledged that the club had a reputation for toughness and it regretted its behavior on April 15. "We knew there'd be repercussions and we imagined there'd be an investigation because the game didn't proceed," Torrance said.

The statement also said that the boy reported to his father that he had been assaulted and that his father, Darren Elderfield, remonstrated with the Dunnstown player. "He was then set upon by Dunnstown players and all hell broke loose," Torrance said.

It was estimated that six to eight players from either side were in the brawl. Feelings were high partly because a Hepburn player had been taken from the ground with a broken nose in the dying seconds of the reserves and because Hepburn had won with the last kick of the match. It was denied that players had been attacked while lying on the ground and the report of a Dunnstown player having his head belted against a goal post could hardly be true when the goal post is padded.

Half a dozen Hepburn players had received black eyes and cut lips and one had received concussion. They had obviously been punched but it looked worse for Dunnstown because the reigning premiers' Jarrod Bickley had been taken to hospital with a broken jaw. The umpires left the ground immediately and returned to Ballarat without filing their reports to the ground manager, as is required under league rules. The Central Highlands tribunal this week dismissed reports against three Hepburn players because the umpires had filed their reports back in Ballarat.

Torrance said the umpires were not under threat and he did not know that reports had been made until the Monday. "We think they might have made their minds up later."

The fact that the umpires had not named the Dunnstown players who were the alleged victims can't have helped the umpires' case. Elderfield, who in 297 senior games had never had his number taken, was reported for interfering with an unknown player. Darren Harris was reported for assault and joint coach Michael Brown was reported, in full, for assaulting an unknown Dunnstown player by multiple blows to the head and assaulting an unknown Dunnstown player with fists to the head.

Brown's fellow coach Jamie Grant, who played five senior games for the Western Bulldogs, where his brother Chris is a favorite son, was horrified about rumors that Hepburn had planned to start a fight before the match. "I will dispute that till the day I die," he said.

To order a fight against Dunnstown would be stupid, not that he would make such an order. Grant said he almost played with Dunnstown after leaving North Ballarat before the 1999 season, and that he had married into a Dunnstown family. He called the players together after the brawl and told them to focus on the match, not realising it had been cancelled. He said he did not berate any players at the centre of the brawl. "You can't change a lot of things that happen in football," he said. "Individuals can only be guided as much as they choose to be."

Grant also lamented that some reports had mentioned his brother for the sake of introducing a high-profile name. Clubs throughout the Central Highlands league share his distaste for association. Opposition clubs believe the media has besmirched the name of the league, with the result that the shutters have been put up. League officials have not returned phone calls and opposition clubs have acceded to the league's advice against talking to the media.

The Sunday Age has occasionally struck anger, and even legal threats, for trying to unravel the events of the brawl. Officials and a policeman have claimed that fights are common in country football. This response is subdued when it is pointed out that few brawls break out before a match and require the attention of police and an ambulance.

The main regrets are that the cancellation of matches is unfair on those drawn against Hepburn and that the good name of the league is under question. The league's good name is not under question, but this reaction is understandable when volunteers contribute many hours to making their league work.

The Sunday Age yesterday followed its Hepburn interview by going to the match between Bungaree and Dunnstown to further piece together events. But officials would make little comment until the investigation is completed.

Bungaree president Shane Frawley said: "Dunnstown is a good football club on and off the field." Dunnstown committeeman Gary Bridges said: "Our players are slowly recovering and we'll make further comment when the investigation is finished."

The match between the neighboring towns proceeded without a hitch, as they usually do, although the players taken to hospital a fortnight ago – Jarrod Bickley, Craig Jenkins and Paddy Leonard – did not take the field. Dunnstown, the premiers for the past two seasons, won by 55 points to retain the Mount Shield, which was struck in 1982 by the publicans of the two towns.

The shield is named after Mount Warrenheip, which separates Dunnstown and Bungaree. Now, an isolated incident separates the league from the football world. Hepburn and Dunnstown could be fined or suspended. Recommendations will be made after Ray Harris finishes his investigation. In the meantime, the Central Highlands league would like to be left alone to play football.

The Sunday Age

The story had begun for me the day after the abandoned match. I rang the Daylesford police to check that three police cars had attended the ground. The policeman on duty confirmed the number of cars but added that he failed to see what the fuss was about. He said there were brawls in country football every weekend. I replied that few brawls require the attention of three police cars and an ambulance and end with three players in hospital. The policeman's defensiveness was the first sign that emotions were raw.

The following Friday, I rang Hepburn president Gordon Torrance in the outside hope of piecing together a version of events. Torrance falteringly invited me to Hepburn because the club was unhappy with its treatment by the *Herald Sun* and *The Courier* in Ballarat; I was invited purely because I was from *The Sunday Age*.

I was nervous when I arrived at the Hepburn ground at 10am on Saturday. My only resolve was to try to give both sides of the story. The Burras were drained. They felt the league, the police, the media and the football public were against them. They just wanted to be heard.

I wrote the first third of the story in a back room at the Daylesford tourism office before proceeding on to Bungaree. Dunnstown officials were firm but polite in refusing to comment. I was less interested in the Bungaree views, but president Shane Frawley was determined to support his neighbors by refusing to comment. Relations were strained. The clubs agreed to give me a single statement and I repaired to my car to complete the story. On the final siren, I drove into town, knocked on the door of strangers, asked whether I could plug my laptop into their phone line, and filed 1500 words. It had been a tense day.

History shows that it didn't stop there. The story of the Hepburn brawl would lurch on for a while yet.

Centre half-back Tony Trigg won the Bungaree best-and-fairest. The seasons of Dunnstown and Hepburn continue in the next two chapters.

6

RUB OF THE GREEN

Dunnstown v Newlyn
the Towners and the Cats

"It knocks you around, so it does."

Dunnstown supporter Paddy Leonard

Almost three weeks after my tense afternoon reporting on the brawl, Hepburn became the first country club to have their seniors and juniors banned. The decision sparked pandemonium, with news convoys and helicopters racing to the spa country in central Victoria to report on the suspension of almost three years for all grades, from seniors down to under-14s. Television stations led their news bulletins with the ban and newspapers weighed in with reports and columns. *The Age* ran a picture on the front page and Channel 7 host Naomi Robson piled indignation on a Central Highlands league official. The story featured violence and justice taken too far. For the metropolitan media, it was also a chance of redemption.

After failing to feel the pulse of the bush in the lead-up to the 1999 state election, in which city champion Jeff Kennett was sent to the bottom paddock, the Melbourne media were sensitive about their disregard for rural issues. The Hepburn story offered the chance to please everyone. The idea of wild men from the bush sorting things out with their fists connected with a view of Australia that many continue to uphold, whether in the country or the city. Others recoiled at the punishment of 13-year-olds for the actions of senior footballers, especially after seeing pictures of boys with skinny arms and baggy jumpers and nowhere to play.

The shot at redemption lay in the issue of rural decline. Hepburn was portrayed as a beautiful town in a flawed world. High unemployment was corroding the youth but the football club offered a binding force when so many strands of life were coming apart. The ban until the 2003 season put the club in jeopardy, especially when there would be no juniors coming through. The media pursued the line that, if the club died, the town would surely follow. The footballers had been violent, but it was over-zealous officials who had committed the greater offence.

An independent tribunal – that is, independent of the Central Highlands league – had imposed the harsh penalties, but much of the reporting pointed the blame at Central Highlands officials. The officials had worried in silence since the brawl erupted on a nondescript Saturday in April. All were volunteers: farmers or plumbers or accountants trying to make sure their league kept going in the region around Ballarat as it had done for decades. None had any experience of dealing with a crisis that attracted media attention in the next town, let alone across the state or around the nation. The advice from leading country football administrators to maintain their silence until Ray Harris, a policeman of 30 years, had completed his investigation for the league was accepted with a measure of relief.

Headlines piled up after the Ballarat umpires announced they would refuse to officiate in Hepburn matches. The headlines continued when rival clubs refused to play the Burras. Further headlines erupted when the tribunal threw out reports against three Hepburn players because the umpires had failed to follow the correct reports procedure. Hepburn broke the media silence in the interview with me, but opposition clubs remained silent and league officials held on to the rails in the hope that the storm would pass. Harris completed his investigation in the allotted three weeks and made his recommendations. By the time of the hearing, it was just over a month since the brawl.

The decision of Burras ruckman Matthew Brown to heed legal advice against giving evidence failed to stop the hearing continuing from early on a weekday evening until 3.40am. The tribunal found the club guilty of bringing the game into disrepute and handed down the bans. Central Highlands league officials had no input into the severity of the penalties but were forced to deal with the backlash. The storm, rather than passing, gathered strength. The saving grace was that rival clubs knew where they stood and could get on with the season. I decided to see what Dunnstown thought about all this.

Dunnstown no doubt thought plenty but they saw little sense in saying much. The club from the potato fields on the southern fringe of Ballarat had arrived at Hepburn for a game of football and left in shock with three of their players in hospital. Five days later, on Holy Thursday, the day before the Easter break, emotions continued to simmer as 140 supporters jammed the clubrooms for a crisis meeting. The supporters were angry and bitter but they agreed there was no purpose in talking to the media. The club-rooms and the Shamrock Hotel would be their only platforms for dissent. Everything would be kept in-house.

After the penalties had been awarded, they saw little reason to crow. They believed the Burras should have been punished, but the extent of the ban shocked them. A few journalists flew in or dropped by, but Dunnstown gave little away before sending the show-offs back to the maelstrom at Hepburn. I thought the public sympathy for Hepburn might have sur-prised Dunnstown, or left a sour taste, but they appeared too drained to worry about what went on beyond Mount Warrenheip.

Hosting a game at their ground at the base of Mount Warrenheip offered the chance to return to the comforting routine of kicks and hand-balls and raffle tickets in the bar. The atmosphere in the first quarter against Newlyn was decidedly flat, but this was a result of rain and mud and inept opposition as much as weeks of worry and the marathon hearing. I watched the home side draw to a five-goal lead, with rover Damian Wood in a class of his own, before wandering over to the huddle, where coach Gerard Cahir saw little reason in getting worked up. In 1983, Cahir played the last of his 11 games for St Kilda when it became apparent that the for-ward line wasn't big enough for both him and North Ballarat recruit Tony Lockett. After this dominant opening against Newlyn, Cahir more or less shrugged his shoulders and advised his side to keep the pressure up.

In the opening minutes of the second quarter, Wood took front position and reached up to outpoint a defender who was inches taller than him. "He's a strong little prick," one spectator said. The mark defied physics and confirmed that Newlyn had no hope. Attention switched to Jarrod Bickley and Paddy Leonard, who were playing their first games since the ambulance had ferried them from Hepburn to the Daylesford hospital. Bickley's depressed cheekbone had mended and Leonard had recovered from the concussion that had given him headaches for two weeks. Craig Jenkins, the other Dunnstown player who'd been poured into the ambulance, would later return, but in his second game back on the field he received a knock in the spot where his jaw had been broken. The bone was split again and Jenkins spent the rest of the season considering retirement.

I put off my interviews by soaking up the flavor. This means standing around and listening to everyone else talk, a regular practice among procrastinating journalists. In front of the Dunnstown dressing-rooms, the reserves players had finished their showers and were busy ribbing each other. They made no mention of the brawl or the Hepburn ban, preferring to limit their comments to the senior player who'd hobbled from the ground with a strained hamstring. The most entertaining conversation was between a seconds player and a boy in tracksuit pants and mud-caked boots who presented himself with his footy before his grown-up friend.

Grown-up: "You want to have a kick with that footy?

Boy: "Yes."

"With me?"

"Yes."

"But we can't."

"Why not?"

"It's a North Melbourne footy. Haven't you got a Collingwood one?"

"No."

"Ah, well."

The grown-up pointed at the boy.

"That's a good haircut. But why didn't you get one like your father – shave it all off? That might have looked all right."

"I wanted to be like Dad."

"Why didn't you?"

"Mum wouldn't let me."

Tommy Owens accepted that he would have to find someone else to kick the footy and wandered off. The back of his Dunnstown guernsey had the No.18 of his brother, Paul Owens, who'd separated the two boys who were fighting behind the shed at Hepburn. Owens, a 21-year-old and the oldest in a family of four, had reportedly been horrified that his act, which was designed to keep the peace, had led to an almighty brawl. He lost form in the weeks after the incident and played in the reserves against Newlyn. I later tried to interview him by phone several times without success.

Dunnstown president Barry Sheehan and former president Gary Bridges were also wary of interviews. Before the Newlyn match, I rang Bridges to tell him of my plans to watch his club. Bridges said Dunnstown would never stop anyone going to the football. His words fell short of an embossed invitation, but they were no more or less than expected. When I appeared beneath the shelter of the Dunnstown rooms, Bridges was non-committal and Sheehan, whom I'd met at Bungaree, looked surprised. Tension filled the air. We said nothing in particular and turned hesitantly towards the game, just in time to see Damian Wood spin on a penny to redirect the flow of play. It was brilliant, in the simplest and most efficient way, and I was moved to gush my admiration. "Who is that bloke?"

Bridges, hands clasped before him, replied: "We like to think in our own modest way that he could have ended up in Melbourne." He said Wood had won the past six best-and-fairests and North Ballarat had tried to lure him to the Northern Oval since he'd played in the Geelong Falcons pre-miership team in 1992. From the corner of his mouth, he added: "He's the best player in this league by a mile."

Sheehan chipped in with the news that Wood was the nephew of Bridges, who in turn redirected the flow of the play by saying that the rover indicated the strength of Dunnstown in more ways than one. He said nobody who was recruited from Ballarat left after their first year. He pointed towards midfielder Dale Learmonth, who'd played in six con-secutive grand finals since leaving Golden Point. Dunnstown was success-ful, stable and proud. I was happy for the club, but I was happier with Damian Wood. His wizardry had broken the ice.

Enough of the ice remained, however, for discussion of the brawl to remain a touchy subject. Sheehan admitted the gathering on Holy Thursday had been emotional but kept further details to himself. "I hope one day we can get together with Hepburn and just get on with life," he said. Bridges added that it was a shame that Hepburn had been rubbed out. "Nobody wants that." But after a few more questions and a few more minutes, a chink in his diplomatic armor emerged. "They say it takes two to tango – well, it didn't." It was the only concession to bitterness to be heard for the day.

Stephen Howard then took a strong mark in the last line of defence. The 32-year-old was among the band of locals who formed the backbone of the club. In the 1950s, the Howard family was one of eight or so that comprised the Dunnstown team. The rest of the list reads like an Irish assembly: Hartigan, Kiely, Lenaghan, Leonard, Murphy, Sheehan and Britt. The decade was noteworthy because the club won three consecutive premierships and upgraded their ground. Until the mid-'50s, they played in a potato paddock.

I looked over the railway line, past the trees to the paddock. It was difficult to believe that footballers had trampled on potatoes as recently as the '50s. Dunnstown was then in competitions based around Ballarat and Bacchus Marsh. In 1979, the Central Highlands league was formed. In the subsequent two decades, Dunnstown played in a dozen grand finals and the names on the team sheets barely changed. Every successful Dunnstown team has members of the old families. Barry Sheehan led me inside to meet some of them.

Straight away, Ray Murphy had a dip at me for devoting most of the article about the brawl in *The Sunday Age* to Hepburn. But the former defender, who played at North Melbourne in the '50s, was scolding me with a grin. He said he was more concerned about the league than his club. He didn't want the reputation of the Central Highlands to suffer. It was an attitude I was to strike all season, especially among the minor leagues in the bush, where the clubs rely on each other to survive. Murphy was one of many to comment on the damage that the brawl had done to the Central Highlands league.

Nobody else seemed too fussed about the article on the brawl. They wanted to talk about their club, about the premierships and Ian McBain kicking 100 goals in nine consecutive years. But they took special pride in their rooms, which had been built with $100 donations and voluntary labor. Daniel Leonard, known to all as Digger, talked about the painting on the cover of the club's centenary history, *From Saplings to Goalposts*, a copy of which was encased in glass on the wall. The artist, James Egan, had made sure to include the Dunnstown ground, the old sheds and Mount Warrenheip. Most supporters believed the old sheds should have been a subject in the painting and that was it. Ray Murphy said he was annoyed during the week when television crews had arrived in helicopters and filmed the old sheds because they liked the peeling paint. He thought the camera crews should have filmed the new rooms and showed the club's best face.

Paddy Leonard, who is no relation to his namesake who was trying to win kicks in the drizzle, agreed. His father, Paddy Leonard senior, had found time in between raising 11 children to help build the new ground in the '50s, and he believed the club should always be portrayed in the best light. Leonard said he'd been coming to the football at Dunnstown as long as he could remember. He wasn't much of a player but he'd served in many roles, including 18 years as the timekeeper. "My heart and soul's in this, so it is."

So it is? His addendum reminded me of Ireland, where in 12 months working as a journalist in Dublin and Cork I became used to hearing lyrical conclusions to sentences. A regular example was: "You Australians sit on the beach all day, so you do." Less common was: "I'm really fond of Vegemite, so I am." The trait was pronounced in some towns and villages more than others, but never did I expect to hear it in Victoria, no matter how many potatoes grew in the paddocks nearby. Until arriving in Dunnstown, I'd believed that the most Irish town in Victoria was Koroit, near Warrnambool, but I'd scoffed at the notion that Irish accents continued to drift across damp paddocks in any part of the Western District. After hearing Paddy Leonard, I revised my opinion. The Dunnstown life member didn't have an Irish accent, but Irish idioms had certainly passed through the generations of his family. Mickey Bourke, the well-known publican in Koroit, could do worse than to invite Paddy down for a beer.

My Celtic reminiscences were interrupted by the offer of a ticket in that night's knockout ballot in the clubrooms. I dipped into my picket for $15 as the siren sounded a 114-point victory for Dunnstown, with Troy Janssens kicking six goals and Damian Wood best afield. The margin was huge but the true victory was the return to comforting routine after weeks of drama. Dunnstown had emerged from the fuss with their honor intact but their souls a little scarred. Paddy Leonard shook his head. "It knocks you around, so it does."

Dunnstown were beaten in the first semi-final by Springbank, which rose from fifth place to win the premiership. Ruckman Luke McKee won the Dunnstown best-and-fairest and Damian Wood finished second after missing nine games with an ankle injury. Paddy Leonard the footballer was cleared to a club in Melbourne. Jarrod Bickley and Craig Jenkins played on at Dunnstown. Newlyn's season continues in the next chapter.

7

OUT OF THE FRAY

Newlyn v Hepburn
the Cats and the Burras

"It's always been that way with Hepburn: you hit one, you hit the lot.
They stick together."

Newlyn supporter Rob Mizzeni

Two weeks after the decision to ban Hepburn for the best part of three
years, the Burras were granted an appeal. The lifting of the ban during the
appeal enabled them to take the field against Central Highlands league
rival Gordon. Lack of fitness cost them any chance of victory, but the real
battle began the following Monday night. The Burras presented their case
before an appeals board on the 14th floor of the Herald and Weekly Times
tower at Southgate. On the following Thursday, Hepburn returned to
Southgate to hear the verdict.

They were told that the findings of the tribunal – whose members were
independent of the Central Highlands league – had been upheld and the
club remained guilty of bringing the game into disrepute. But the appeals
board considered the penalty unjust. The club was to be fined $5000, with
a good behavior bond of $5000 to remain effective for two seasons. A ban
of almost three seasons, from seniors down to under-14s, had been reduced
to a manageable fine and a good behavior bond.

Central Highlands league president Jim O'Keefe was ashen-faced as he pressed his mobile phone to his ear to begin informing umpires and officials of the news. In the foyer, O'Keefe was still shaken but he composed himself as hand-held tape recorders and microphones were thrust in his face. "We've never been against Hepburn at all," he said. "Something happened, we investigated and we accept the umpires' decision."

He added that the league would have trouble finding volunteers if their decisions were to be cast aside. "All these people do it for nothing … I don't know how we'll get people to sit on our tribunals any more." The camera flashes continued as the lift doors closed.

Hepburn president Gordon Torrance hesitated before walking into the barrage of cameras and microphones with vice-president Eddy Comelli and Comelli's wife, Malinka, beside him. He said he regretted the judgment that the guilty verdict would remain, but his face was alight with success. "The main thing is, we're back on the ground."

The Hepburn drama began far away from a plush office tower at Southgate; it began with two boys fighting behind the Hepburn clubrooms. Dunnstown player Paul Owens broke from his team's warm-up to separate the boys. Owens didn't hurt, or threaten to hurt, the boys; he simply placed his hands between them and urged them to separate. One of the boys, Mitchell Elderfield, then sought out his father, who was about to run on to the ground for the senior match. Darren Elderfield was taken aback at the red welt across his son's face. The defender, who'd never been reported in 297 senior games, jogged from the rooms believing that Owens had laid a rough hand on his son.

On the ground, Elderfield broke from the Hepburn warm-up to give Owens a piece of his mind. The Dunnstown player was on the ground doing stretching exercises in the goalsquare. Elderfield bent on one knee and warned him against touching his son. The Hepburn defender didn't touch Owens but his gesticulations earned the attention of two Dunnstown players, who grabbed him. This in turn drew the attention of Hepburn players. The brawl then erupted.

Suggestions that the brawl was premeditated are wrong. Hepburn's only plan had been to try new tactics to curb Dunnstown's scoring power; Jamie Grant studied the flooding that the Western Bulldogs were practising in training. The aftermath of the brawl is well documented: three

Dunnstown players were taken to hospital – one with a fractured cheek-bone, one with a broken jaw, and the third with severe concussion – and the match was abandoned. Three players were reported – for assault and misconduct against "unknown" Dunnstown players – but the charges were dropped because of the failure of umpires to follow correct reporting procedure. Hepburn issued a statement in which they said they regretted their actions and acknowledged the seriousness of the injuries, but they wonder whether the backlash would have been as strong if one of their players had been badly injured.

After the brawl, Hepburn believed that the world turned against them. They endured the negative media coverage despite their belief that Dunnstown had pressured the league and the police, breaking the code of silence that was requested by the league. Eventually, they invited me to interview them. Around this time, the league rescinded its decision to fine both clubs. Hepburn believe the decision was made under pressure from Dunnstown, but it seems reasonable that the league pulled back because it decided to hold an investigation.

Dunnstown president Barry Sheehan later denied that his club pressured the league or police. He said Chief Inspector Bob Barby, the head of police in Ballarat, went to Hepburn to watch his son Michael play for the Dunnstown reserves. Barby ran on to the ground during the brawl to try to separate players. The police chief instigated police action after seeing the brawl at close quarters. Three Hepburn players – Matthew Brown, Darren Harris and Shane Collins – were charged with intentionally and recklessly causing serious injury.

A day and a half after the ruling in the Southgate office tower, the media converged on Newlyn, halfway between Ballarat and Daylesford, to gauge reaction to the lifting of Hepburn's ban. My first interview was with two elderly women, who merrily offered opinions for 10 minutes before swerving at the last question. "Oo, no, we don't want to give you our names." They did give me an Anzac biscuit, which was scrumptious.

Further along the fence, a newspaper bearing the headline "Burras back on the field" was spread across a passenger seat window. I reasonably expected that this might be a show of support, but Allan Briggs put me straight. "It keeps the sun out," he said. Briggs added that his grandson, 28-year-old Michael Courtot, would have retired if the Burras' ban had remained in place. "He wouldn't have gone anywhere else. Most of them wouldn't have, especially when their fathers played for Hepburn, and their grandfathers. The brawl's past. Let them get on with it."

Leanne Bolton, the sister of Darren Elderfield, shook her head when thinking about the impact of the ordeal on her family. "It was too close," she said. "Everybody sort of tried to keep quiet. That's how we dealt with it."

Newlyn supporter Andy Prendergast questioned reducing a ban of almost three years to a fine and a bond. "One laughs at the other," he said, before tacking through the issues. "Those blokes put in hospital must have been beaten pretty badly … I think the ban was tough on the juniors … I've got mixed feelings." His friend Ross Dimond was more certain. "I'd have given them a year. It would have been enough to punish them, but then they could have kept playing."

The match proceeded like any other match in the Central Highlands after a few showers, with players clamoring for the ball in the bog, but the crowd was largely silent. The aftermath of the brawl overshadowed the regular pursuit of kicks and handballs until it seemed almost ghoulish to be screaming for the defenders to man up, or for the umpire to open his eyes. Newlyn supporter Robin Cawthorn sought to break the tension when he strolled past the Hepburn huddle at quarter-time. "Look at the thugs," he said. "Look at them." Cawthorn was amusing himself greatly but Burra fans drew their coats in tighter. They looked dead ahead, trying to ignore Cawthorn, as co-coaches Matthew Brown and Jamie Grant addressed their players. Brown had been banned until he agreed to face the tribunal, but his legal advice was to stay away. He was unwilling to appear before the tribunal in case his evidence might be used against him when he faced the courts.

The 30-year-old ruckman had shoulders as wide as the goalsquare but he looked worried and drained. He'd won a league best-and-fairest with the Burras, and after the season it would emerge that the umpires had given him best on ground in the opening two matches. The brawl erupted before the third game and now he was reduced to coaching from behind the fence. David Rhys-Jones, when he was coaching Frankston, once circumvented a ban by addressing his players from a cherry-picker that lowered him towards the huddle, but Brown had none of the showman instincts of the former Carlton defender. The Hepburn players and fans crowded along the fence but Brown was faltering. The crack from Cawthorn completed the farce.

Jamie Grant sensed Brown's discomfort and stepped in. His first move was to divert the address from general encouragement to specifics. He wanted the forwards to clear out and give Dave Thompson space to lead. "Tell them to arsehole … tell them to get right out of there." He corrected himself in deference to the media microphones that were draped over the huddle. It was the only time he dropped the ball all afternoon.

Back on the sidelines, Robin Cawthorn said there was no problem calling the Burras thugs. "I went to school with half these blokes. They should never have been rubbed out in the first place." He did, however, encourage Hepburn to introduce a code of conduct. He also believed they should have suspended the three players on charges, with the aim of appeasing opposition clubs and the parents of juniors. His manner had none of the bluster of quarter-time, when his irreverence had increased the Burras' edginess.

Rob Mizzeni, the umpires' escort, was as considered as Cawthorn was brash. He said the Burras were no angels but it was unfair to punish many for the actions of a few. "Maybe they've got a reputation," he said. "Their supporters have been pretty tough over the years – everybody will tell you that." Through it all, he admired their loyalty. "It's always been that way with Hepburn: you hit one, you hit the lot. They stick together."

The siren sounded for half-time and a Cats supporter reminded Mizzeni that he had to escort the umpires. A handful of the supporters had listened to my interview and I gained the feeling that some were uncomfortable. Mizzeni made one last point: he said nobody in the competition had any experience in dealing with a statewide controversy. "No one knew how to handle it," he said.

Newlyn president Greg May was reluctant to comment on his club's closest neighbor but he provided a neat summary of wider views. His main points were:

"There's no doubt what they did was a disgrace and it brought the league and country football into disrepute – but the kids were the innocent party.

"It's such a pendulum swing, from a three-year ban to a no-year ban.

"They've decided to convert it into a fine as opposed to a ban. Putting on my diplomatic hat, we've got to abide by that decision."

Barry Clohesy was one of the few Newlyn supporters to put his full support behind the Burras. After acting as the timekeeper for 40 years, he'd seen too many ups and downs to get excited about the brawl. "In my time, we've always got along with Hepburn," he said. "These things pop up. I don't know why. They just seem to happen." His Hepburn colleague in the timekeepers' box, Garry Rodoni, said he was relieved that the ordeal was over. All up, it had taken two months. "We can't believe it went as long as it did."

Rodoni played for the Burras for 10 years. His brother, father and grandfather also played for Hepburn. Rodoni spelt the family name. "R-O-D-O-N-I. Good Swiss-Italian name," he said.

The Swiss-Italian heritage of many Hepburn people had been mentioned during the appeals hearing on the Thursday to demonstrate the Burras' close bonds. In the 1850s, about 2500 Swiss-Italians responded to work bans in their home land by heading for the goldfields in Victoria. Most of them settled in Hepburn, where they helped to establish the football club in 1867. The Swiss-Italians maintained traditions from their home land, with production of grappa and spicy sausages known as bullboars among the practices that helped maintain a strong and proud community and, as a byproduct, set them apart from their neighbors. In a sea of British and Irish influence, the Swiss-Italians would have been forgiven for feeling like outsiders. More than 130 years later, their descendants were described as outsiders during the brawl saga.

While the footballers are considered outsiders in the Central Highlands league, many townsfolk in Hepburn increasingly feel like outsiders in their home town. The rise of tourism and the decline of traditional industry in the spa country has alienated blue-collar workers from those running the cafes and bed-and-breakfasts. People in Melbourne failed to understand how violence had erupted amid such beauty in the ranges of central Victoria but, in doing so, they failed to understand the problems beneath the sheen of beauty. Hepburn has a chronic shortage of blue-collar jobs. Division and anger are to be expected in such conditions.

It was apparent in the match against Newlyn that the ban denied Hepburn, which won three premierships in the '80s, the chance of a place in the finals. The previous week, Gordon had overrun them but, against Newlyn, weight of talent was enough to overcome tired bodies. Jamie Grant and Jaffa Torrance ruled the midfield and Dave Thompson was one of three marking targets in attack. Grant threw himself into everything. At 183 centimetres, the former Footscray utility can play in a key position at this level of football but, in his determination to be at the heart of his team's performance, it was only right that he played in the centre. He broke tackles, dived under packs and directed his team with authority. Grant had been stunned by the brawl. But after the initial shock he steeled his resolve. Against Newlyn, the 29-year-old had control. He was a strong leader.

Newlyn, by contrast, had little going for them. The Cats last won the premiership in 1992. They just happened to be drawn against Dunnstown and Hepburn when I wanted to watch those clubs, but in both matches they looked unlikely to push for a premiership for a long time. I knew a bit about the club from a friend who described Greg Faull playing one game for Collingwood then winning games for Newlyn on his own in the '90s. And a family friend, Vin O'Neil, had described an auspicious match at Newlyn in the '60s, when he lined up on a 16-year-old defender who was playing his first game. Vinny's expectation of an easy afternoon turned to dismay when David McKay jumped all over him. A few seasons later, McKay played in his first of four premierships with Carlton.

Against Hepburn, Newlyn showed no signs of soaring but they never gave up. They battled in the mud, but the Burras kept grinding further ahead. Both sides could be commended for their commitment, if not their finesse.

Hepburn officials were watching their first winning performance in the two months since the brawl when I approached Gordon Torrance and his vice-president Eddy Comelli. "You again," Comelli said. "What more is there to say?"

I asked whether the club would have done anything differently given their time over again. Comelli said no.

Were the preparations for this match different to any other match? They were the same.

Was there a rule to prevent Matthew Brown coaching?

"He's not coaching," Comelli said.

Would the Burras have saved a lot of trouble by suspending the three players whose reports were thrown out of the tribunal? At least until after the investigation had been completed?

"We never considered suspending those players," Comelli said. "They were never found guilty of anything. We hope the truth comes out one day: they didn't do anything."

His answer on Brown was disingenuous, as the ruckman was coaching 20 metres away from us. His answer on suspending the players was consistent with the line the Burras had taken throughout the ordeal. Many Central Highlands people believe the decision of the umpires and opposition clubs to shun Hepburn would have been avoided if the Burras had sacked or suspended players. But Hepburn maintained that they weren't the only club in the fight. They also failed to understand why the tribunal hearing was rushed through in one marathon hearing when more nights had been set aside.

The feeling after the 33-point victory was satisfaction rather than triumph. Many players looked exhausted, including Darren Elderfield, whose face showed the strain of the ordeal. Elderfield's son Mitchell sat close by his side as Jamie Grant congratulated the Burras before whipping into the Newlyn rooms to thank the Cats. Eddy Comelli wandered through the room and, speaking for the committee, urged a strong finish to the season. "We've done our bit. Now it's up to you to do yours."

The next week, a Hepburn under-17 player refused to show his number when the umpire tried to report him. The umpire abandoned the match but Hepburn and Waubra appointed their own umpires and the match continued. The next day, the Hepburn committee resigned and Terry Rodoni, the brother of Garry, was appointed the new president. "The committee felt things were working against them," Terry Rodoni said after the season. "They'd done everything possible to get things going along the right lines."

Rodoni's first act was to arrange a committee meeting at which two juniors and their parents were interviewed. The juniors were suspended from the club indefinitely. Rodoni's next act was to respond to prompting from the league to give up the season. Hepburn withdrew from the final six matches in all grades. The president then looked ahead to the next season, beginning with the appointment of Jamie Grant as the sole coach.

"That was our first step forward." He appointed committees to oversee areas such as player management, marketing and junior development. All players were interviewed to gauge their commitment and their reaction to the turmoil. The club lost 15 players, including half a dozen to Daylesford, but Rodoni was happy with the core that remained. "We're a tighter bunch because of this."

Jim O'Keefe, the Central Highlands president, resigned after six seasons. He said he was due to step down but the drama over the brawl convinced him the time was right. "It was very upsetting. There's no doubting that. It was a complete muck-up of a year." He believed the league had handled the brawl to the best of its ability. "We followed due process and everyone got a hearing." He was proud that the competition had rebounded and record gates were recorded at every final. In the end, he was also pleased that every club wanted to retain Hepburn in the league. "Time's a great healer," he said.

The Hepburn claim that they'd done nothing wrong rang hollow when two of the three players on criminal charges heeded the advice of barristers and pleaded guilty in the Ballarat Magistrates Court. Matthew Brown was sentenced to jail for four months after pleading guilty to intentionally causing serious injury. The *Herald Sun* reported that the magistrate described Brown's attack on Jarrod Bickley, whose cheekbone was fractured, as an attack of "naked brutality". Brown was released on bail before going to an appeal and having the punishment reduced to a two-year suspended sentence. Darren Harris was fined $1500 after pleading guilty to recklessly causing serious injury. Paddy Leonard was severely concussed during the attack by Harris. Shane Collins, who pleaded not guilty to assault and intentionally causing serious injury, was fined $1500.

Hepburn point out that Chiltern player Paul Hodgkin was arrested for alleged offences in three matches in the Ovens and King league but his arrest failed to attract anywhere near the scrutiny that they received. Hepburn also point to the lack of media coverage of the brawl that blackened the Castlemaine and Maryborough district league grand final in 1998, when a victorious Talbot player offered his hand to his opponent after the siren and the Maldon player punched him. Spectators piled in from everywhere.

The Burras are right to question the media snowball effect, in which a newspaper or television station runs with a story and the rest follow, but no amount of pointing out the misdeeds of others takes away from their part in a shocking brawl. They fought the punishment for the brawl through the correct channels, but the process had its cost. The under-17 player who refused to show the umpire his number had seen the senior footballers tangle in an ugly brawl and the club fight to untangle itself from the ramifications. He could be excused for thinking that he might be able to escape the allegations against him. Juniors learn from the example of their seniors.

During the season, I asked an official from Vermont, whose record is unparalleled in local football, the secret behind the club's success. The official replied by describing an incident in which a prized recruit was receiving niggling attention from an opponent. The recruit kicked a goal, turned to his opponent and head-butted him. He was a centre half-forward, the rarest bird in the aviary, but the Eagles sacked him on the spot. The official was making the point that Vermont had become one of the best clubs in local football because it demanded quality of character as well as talent. Vermont is in the heart of Melbourne's eastern suburbs, the most populated region in Victoria, and can afford to be choosy, whereas Hepburn is a small community in central Victoria. But the record shows that successful clubs show responsibility for players' on-field actions.

The final word goes to Jamie Grant. The coach was smiling broadly after the match against Newlyn. His side had won and he was clearly best afield but, most of all, he was delighted simply to be playing again. "Life's been hollow without football," he said. "I just didn't feel right without it."

Hepburn played only five games but, rather than wipe the year from the records, they held a best-and-fairest count, which Jamie Grant won. Midfielder Adam Tippett won the Newlyn best-and-fairest. Matthew Brown returned to the field for Hepburn the next season, but Darren Harris and Shane Collins retired. A back injury was threatening to end Darren Elderfield's career. The case of Paul Hodgkin was listed for hearing at the time of publication.

8

DEVILS' WORK

North Footscray v Central Altona
the Red Devils and the Tigers

"I would sell my soul to play league football again.
You train hard, you get fit with a whole bunch of your mates,
you go to war in front of 70,000 people."

Former Richmond and Footscray ruckman Justin Charles

Hansen Reserve is a world away from the glamor of league football. The unfenced oval bleeds into a soccer pitch. On the other side is a cycling track that looks unused since the days of Hubert Opperman. Graffiti shrieks from factory walls and smokestacks pile waste into the dull sky. In the middle of all this, North Footscray were preparing for their match in the second division of the Western Region league. They fidgeted and fumbled as the club's most famous son wandered around beaming, stopping here and there for a quiet word, exuding confidence that set him apart from the rest of the room. The brown-brick rooms were modest, as far from the carpeted rooms at the MCG as could be imagined, and the air was cold, but former Richmond ruckman Justin Charles was relishing his first year as coach. He called his players around him for the pre-match address. He was interested to see their reaction.

Charles had made seven changes to the side that laid down the week before. Some of his inclusions stared up at him in wonder. They'd never been considered anything more than seconds players. The air crackled with nervous revolution as Charles reminded every man in the red and white stripes of his right to be considered a senior player. He fixed his eyes on individuals and urged them to trust the man inside. Others he advised to work harder. In addressing each player before the group, he wanted them to feel special. The word "terrific" was tossed around like confetti. Everyone needs to be valued, he said.

The 29-year-old pointed his marker pen at the whiteboard, where he'd outlined his three platforms for success: desire, discipline and responsibility. It was responsibility that provided the most telling indicator of the man who shouldered the blame when he became the first AFL player to be banned for drug use. In 1997, Charles cried when he explained to his Richmond teammates that he'd tested positive for the veterinary drug boldenone. His teammates were angry. None of them had used a drug to get over injuries, but they got over their shock and rallied around him. Charles finished his 16-match ban and was never the same player again. In 1996, he finished four votes behind James Hird and Michael Voss in the Brownlow Medal. After the 1998 season, he retired with an arthritic hip injury similar to the injury that finished the playing days of Dermott Brereton. The main lesson Charles had learned on his rollercoaster journey through football and life was responsibility. He instructed the North Footscray players to join hands and gather tight. Then he repeated the question that serves as his mantra.

"Who's responsible?" he said.

"I am," the players yelled.

"Who's responsible?"

"I am."

"Who's responsible?"

"I am."

The answers became louder and louder until Charles gave the word and the Red Devils roared. The circle broke up and players dived for the toilet or rummaged in their bag for chewing gum or tape. Some jogged on the spot. All were killing for the energy to be released. Finally, they fell in behind the captain, Chris O'Halloran, and entered the dreary afternoon. On the way out, I asked Charles the regulation question: do you give yourselves a good chance? "Always," he said, beaming again. Somehow, the answer didn't seem so "regulation" coming from him.

Justin Charles is among the most positive men on earth. He knows it's a trait that brings energy to some and annoys the hell out of others. He said himself that only 15 per cent of people in the world are truly optimists, and in the end they give the world the shits. He accepts this, but it won't change his ways. At Footscray, where he began his AFL career in 1989, he was renowned for breaking into song. At the Florida Marlins, the United States baseball club he joined in 1994 after Footscray said they would try to trade him, he turned a rusty opening into a concerted push up the ranks. He felt he might be getting somewhere when a simmering feud with a manager erupted and he was sacked. Charles returned to Australia and the game that was first in his heart, and Richmond drafted him at No.46. In time, Tiger officials would try to keep him off his bike because they feared he was pushing himself too hard.

In his positive outlook, Charles lived by the belief that hard work brought just reward. His belief failed to consider the effect of injury and misfortune. Former Richmond coach Robert Walls wrote in *The Age* that, after Charles's stellar season in 1996, he tore a hamstring before Christmas and was unable to run for a month. In January, he picked up hundreds of scratches when helping his father put the boat in at Altona. Severe infections kept him off his feet for another stretch. He played only one practice match, in which he planned to scare Wayne Campbell's tag at the opening bounce but knocked out himself and Campbell. He managed a couple of games early in the season before the tribunal rubbed him out for two matches for head-butting Melbourne onballer Alistair Clarkson, who denied that Charles had head-butted him. The final straw was aggravating an achilles tendon injury. In his attempt to overcome setbacks and regain his form of the previous year, he decided to try something extra. He wanted to be a leading AFL footballer so much that he injected a drug. The AFL made no announcement after the first test. But an announcement was made after the second test was positive.

"The reason I took steroids was to get back doing what I loved," he told me. "I wasn't doing it and it was hurting. It was going to take six weeks and that was not acceptable to me."

Charles got over the drug ban but found dealing with retirement a bigger issue. In attempting to restock the adrenalin that surged through him when he pulled on a black and yellow guernsey, he went to as many Richmond games as possible, including interstate games, and worked out regularly in the Punt Road gym. He wanted to work as a ruck coach but nobody on the staff under Jeff Gieschen asked him. After a year, the unspoken rejection forced him to leave the Tigers behind and re-emerge in the world. He'd gone back to plumbing but was unsatisfied. Later he would say that plumbing left him spiritually bankrupt. Through Paul McKessy, his eyes had been opened to a holistic approach to life after football.

They met when Charles gave a speech at Breaking the Cycle, a national program that helps youth emerge from dependency on welfare. Charles undertook McKessy's personal development course and the pair became friends. The course helped Charles regain belief in his worth away from the bright lights of the AFL. A large part of his self-redemption included forgiving himself for resorting to a drug. Three years after his ban, he was still being reminded of his mistake whenever he stepped outside his house, but the questions, and taunts, failed to daunt him. "I fucked up. However, I'm not a bad person," he said. "I'm a good person. I'm an outstanding human being." The drug issue was other people's problem.

McKessy taught him a lot about acceptance, and even celebration, of himself. Charles realised he thrived on applause – it's fair to say he was addicted to applause – but he accepted that he didn't need it any longer to validate himself. He realised he thrived on fitness and discipline, and it wasn't such a bad thing. He missed the gladiatorial element of entering the MCG before the baying thousands, but he accepted it would never happen again. His goal became to explore new avenues of life, to find out about himself as a man of many parts rather than a man who once was a footballer. It took courage to alter his thinking but, with McKessy as his mentor, he did.

He was reluctant to hurl himself back into football when Aldo Pagano rang after the 1999 season. The North Footscray president knew the Red Devils held a special place in Charles's heart, which was sentimental at the best of times, and he wanted to milk it. John Charles, Justin's father, coached North Footscray after his short career at the Western Oval. The club theme song, beginning "Cheer, cheer the red and the white", was etched in Justin's brain by the time he went to the Western Oval as a promising junior. Pagano thought he might be able to convince Charles to complete the loop of his father. Charles resisted for months before Pagano nailed him to the lesser commitment of assistant coaching. The appointment lasted minutes. "I hung up and thought, 'What good is me being assistant coach when I'm going to take over anyway?'," Charles said. "My knowledge and experience would undermine the coach. So I rang Aldo back and said, 'All right, you've got me'."

His father believed it was the right decision. "He goes, 'Yep, you've got to do it at home first'. That just sent goosebumps down my spine."

But Justin Charles took over a different North Footscray to the club his father knew. Back when John Charles coached, Melbourne's inner west had young families. By the time the Red Devils were enjoying their golden years under leading western suburbs coach Ron Brown, winning three premierships in division one from 1979 to '82, the drift to the outer suburbs was gathering momentum. West Footscray, Seddon, Spotswood, Kingsville and Albion were fighting North Footscray for the same pool of juniors. Finally, in 1993 the Red Devils were unable to field juniors and two years later the senior club was relegated.

The regeneration began in 1996, when the club formed an under-10 side. The next year it fielded an under-12 side. Now, the club again has the full complement of junior sides. The Red Devils advertise coaching clinics in the schools but the biggest boost to recruiting in the 2000 season was Justin Charles. Pagano said children mobbed him as he walked the boundary at junior matches, and some took his hand. He was like a 198-centimetre pied piper, smiling in that winning way, with a trail of young admirers. It's been like that for most of his life. Charles has never lacked the ability to charm.

He also has an eccentric streak. For the match against Central Altona, he stood on the boundary in jeans and Blundstones, which could be found at any ground on any given Saturday, and a black, shin-length coat, which wouldn't be out of place in London or New York. Somehow he got away with it. Next to him, Paul McKessy wore a red and white bomber jacket. He was as short as Charles was commanding. Their relationship had the air of the old trainer guiding the young boxer, whose power was matched only by his lack of worldliness. It's a relationship that has had its place in sport, literature and life throughout the ages.

Behind them, the two interchange players zipped and unzipped their flimsy jackets in an attempt to ward off the wind. Once or twice they got up from the thin strip of wood that served as a bench and mingled with friends from the reserves. Normally, they would have played in the reserves and watched from the boundary with these friends. This was a very strange week. Jason McCluskey, a passionate Red Devils advocate, said Charles had united a club that had been split into two camps: seniors and reserves. "He's not afraid to change the side around," the defender said. "If you're in form, he'll play you."

He added that Charles had gained respect by overcoming discomfort to play three matches early in the season. Charles had bone scraping on bone in his right hip. He took the centre bounces before dropping back into the path of opposition attacks. "I would only say my performances were handy," Charles said. On Sunday mornings, he woke up in fearful pain.

McCluskey said nobody at North Footscray was interested in Charles's episode with a performance-enhancing drug. He dismissed the question with a wave of his hand. "He's over that. It's in the past."

Cleaning the slate is an act that Charles encourages. Before the season three players from Newport were apprehensive about looking for a game at Hansen Reserve. The previous season, their club had been banned after a vicious brawl with the Red Devils. The Newport trio arrived at training during summer and several senior Red Devils took them aside to pledge their support. Aldo Pagano followed up by taking them to see Charles. One of the former Newport players, Sam El-Houli, spread his arms like a preacher when describing the coach's reception.

"Mate, he had his arms wide open and he said, 'Gentlemen, you're fucking welcome'. If you're down and out, he knows how to pick you up. He gives you confidence."

During the reserves match, El-Houli's teammates took bets on whether he would be sent off, as he had been the previous two matches. On arriving at the ground, my first sight was El-Houli running through an opponent whose head was bent over the ball, but he lasted the game before bringing a light touch to the seniors match. Early in the first quarter, he dispensed advice to centre half-back Jano Matar in Lebanese.

"What does that mean, Sammy?" a spectator asked.

El-Houli was urging his friend to play hard. His delivery made the crowd laugh. Charles swivelled around to join in the fun. The babble continued behind him throughout the game, with the coach giving no thought to curbing his own thoughts or the advice from the spectators surrounding him. It's egalitarian to a degree rarely seen at football clubs, which thrive on hierarchy. It's also vastly multicultural. In a league represented by 43 nationalities, North Footscray has Greeks, Italians, Yugoslavs, Albanians and Scots, with Muslims and born-again Christians thrown into the mix. "We've got all sorts," Aldo Pagano said with a shrug.

There was one thorn. Lee Undy was tall and lean with a handy leap. He had cropped, blond hair and tattoos that blazed down his legs. His talent was clear but he was prone to distraction. He was the classic full-forward who could do with a season on the half-back line, just to learn the team game, and Charles was unsure how to handle him. He tried the firm hand, he tried the soft touch but, whatever he tried, it didn't work. In the third quarter, Undy was penalised for petulance and jogged off the ground. Charles concealed a frown and tried to look as if he knew what was going on. Jason McCluskey curled his lip before piercing the air. "See you at training on Tuesday, Lee."

A few minutes later, Undy returned from the rooms and explained that he'd run off the ground because he had to fetch something in the rooms. Red Devils fans were unsure how to approach this twist in the afternoon and Charles was more confused than anyone. Undy had joined North Footscray because he wanted to play under him. Charles had thought he could reach the wandering spearhead by showing that he cared. "You've got to feel loved," he said. "You can get more out of someone if there's respect there." At three-quarter-time, he tried massaging Undy's confidence before encouraging the rest of the team to continue the hard work. Then he instructed them to hold hands.

"Who's responsible?"

"I am."

"Who's responsible?"

"I am."

"Who's responsible?"

"I am."

In the rooms was one thing, but on the ground in the drizzle was another matter. I found it moving and unnerving. If Steve Biddulph's book *Manhood*, about men dropping the façade and expressing their feelings, were to be made into a film, this would be a scene. It had everything: moody sky, graffiti on walls and footballers girding for combat by holding hands and yelling like warriors. They went on to express their trust and reliance on each other with an 18-point victory that was as gritty as the surroundings. Chris O'Halloran, the undersized centre half-forward and veteran of 300 games, was best afield, and his brother John, who also had played 300 games, worked hard in the midfield. The match had failed to feature a single memorable incident apart from Undy's exit. It was a victory for the purists, for those who prefer an arm wrestle to a parade of skills.

In the rooms, Charles was proud and happy and he wanted to share the feeling. He pointed to his whiteboard and the word TEAM, the acronym for "together everybody achieves more". Charles had always intrigued me in this sense: he was the ultimate individual, one out of the box, the Tiger who celebrated every goal like there'd never be another, and yet he was one who gave his all for the team. There was something in his highly individual soul that needed the common cause. He's probably like most of us, but more open about it.

Then he returned to a path that has never thrilled me: he addressed every player individually in front of the group. Before the game, I'm dubious. After the game, I believe it's usually a function of frustration, and sometimes of vanity, performed by coaches who should talk less. Charles wasn't frustrated; this was his way of sharing his joy, boosting his players and, it should be said, keeping the spotlight switched on for that little bit longer. The Red Devils were nervous but soon relaxed and lapped it up. "I have an affection for the cheeky blokes, and you're one of them," Charles said of onballer Mark Lakkis. "With your hardness at the ball, you give us something." He made special mention of the seven promoted from the reserves, including Jano Matar. "Arab magic," said one of the players. The mood was light and breezy before Charles came to Undy and was forced to measure his words. "We can't afford to have you on the bench. Channel your aggression at the footy and you'll have a stellar season." The mood was punctured. The coach wound up his address with a plea for everyone to get along to the ugly shirt night in the social rooms.

Charles and I adjourned to a stark bench seat underneath a tree in the gathering gloom. We spoke about his years at Richmond, the drug ban and his retirement, and the intoxicating allure of the limelight. He described league football as his perfect existence. "I would sell my soul to play league football again. You train hard, you get fit with a whole bunch of your mates, you go to war in front of 70,000 people."

His downfall was living for the war and finding no peace. He came to recognise that, beyond the bluster about courage under fire, footballers are vulnerable and scared. He asked his players to hold hands to enable them to draw strength from the collective will. It also was part of his plan to push the boundaries. He believed there was a lack of confidence in the western suburbs that curbed development. Promoting seven players showed he was prepared to smash preconceptions. "What is really satisfying is seeing people do things they think they can't do," he said. "I'm always surprising myself by doing things that previously I thought were beyond me. I didn't know how hard coaching was going to be but I think I'm doing a pretty good job."

After the season, he said some players embraced his ideas but most rejected them. They were unwilling to let go of the loser tag because, in their experience, positive messages were hot air. They all ended up being wrong. Charles said he grew to appreciate that confident people take initiatives and, as it was, he grew tired of leading. He gained from his first experience of coaching, and after finishing in the finals he would like to think he did a good job, but the battler mentality of the western suburbs had worn him down. He resigned after the season to concentrate on his business with Paul McKessy. Their company, Lift Your Game, takes young footballers, including AFL players, through personal development programs.

One of his final comments was that he sensed he was growing out of his mentor relationship with McKessy. The journey of Justin Charles was about to take another fresh turn.

This match was Lee Undy's last for North Footscray, which went on to score 13 consecutive victories. In the last round, Sam El-Houli was suspended for pushing the umpire in the reserves and Jano Matar was suspended for striking in the seniors. In the first final, Charlie Pagano, Aldo's brother, played his 500th club match but Chris O'Halloran injured his knee and fellow key forward Jason Barry tore his hamstring. The next week, the Red Devils were eliminated by Central Altona. Central Altona went on to lose the preliminary final to Glenorden by a point. Jason Barry won the North Footscray best-and-fairest after kicking 80 goals. Matthew Frank was second and Brian Izzard finished third after starting the season believing that he was a reserves player. He was later invited to train with VFL club Werribee. Midfielder Paul Sardi won the Central Altona best-and-fairest. Justin Charles was thinking about a hip replacement when he saw a Chinese doctor and found himself able to do spring squats for the first time in two years.

9

PRIDE OF THE YORTA YORTA

Rumbalara v Benalla All Blacks
Rumba and the Panthers

"It took a while for the other clubs to get used to us,
and we were certainly not used to them."

Rumbalara president Paul Briggs

On the eve of Rumbalara's first home game, in April 1997, Aboriginal people from across Victoria and the Riverina converged on their ground on the industrial northern fringe of Shepparton. Women made banners and decorated the clubrooms and men applied oxywelders to last-minute tasks until three o'clock in the morning. The next day, their hearts swelled when the footballers from Rumbalara, an Aboriginal word that means the place at the end of the rainbow, ran on to the ground wearing jumpers that featured the red, black and yellow of the Aboriginal flag.

Clive Atkinson, an Aboriginal graphic artist in Echuca, had designed a jumper on which the red, black and yellow looped in waves around the players' ribs, suggesting the confluence of white and black people, and the Murray and Goulburn Rivers that are lifelines in the Yorta Yorta nation. The royal blue background represents the wide sky of the Goulburn Valley. Only North Ballarat, whose away guernsey features the Eureka flag, has anywhere near the significance of the Rumbalara jumper. Victorian clubs increasingly adopt AFL colors in an uninspired attempt to save money, but Rumbalara had invested too much energy in getting their club off the ground to shy from investing in a jumper with strong symbolism.

Rumbalara president Paul Briggs was in a small party that had tried to form an Aboriginal club in Shepparton for 15 years, only to find that resistance ran deep. Prejudice and misunderstanding had been in the way of Aboriginal football since Cummeragunja won their first premiership in the Nathalia district league in 1898. In the decade from 1921, the club from the mission on the NSW side of the Murray River won six premierships, with Selwyn Briggs, Paul's grandfather, playing in three. Other descendants of Selwyn Briggs include David Wirrpunda and Sean Charles.

After Cummeragunja's decade of dominance, their rivals in the Picola league tried to limit them to players under 25 years of age because they were too strong. The club was outraged and quit the league. In 1946, the Cummeragunja All Blacks bobbed up in the Central Goulburn league and won the flag, only to be expelled again.

In the era that Briggs and his co-workers tried to resurrect a team from the Yorta Yorta nation, which stretches from the south of the Goulburn Valley into the Riverina, Aboriginal clubs fought losing battles around Victoria. In 1987 the Purnim Bears won the Mount Noorat league flag in the Western District and were kicked out, for reasons never officially explained. In 1993, Coomealla were voted out of the Millewa league, based around Mildura, because some players failed to turn up for tribunal hearings and because opposition supporters complained about their swearing. In 1998, after a bitter and protracted battle following a brawl at Buchan, Lake Tyers were expelled from the Omeo and district league.

In Melbourne, the Fitzroy Stars enjoyed success and strong support in the Aboriginal community but became stranded when the YCW competition folded in 1986. Since then, the Stars have applied for entry to many competitions without success. Paul Briggs said of Rumbalara: "We're not the first, but our infrastructure is stronger."

I found Briggs in a white coat behind the goals during the reserves. In the previous three matches, the 46-year-old had come out of retirement to kick 22 goals but this week there were enough players, so he was goal-umpiring. In 1978 he was captain of the Fitzroy Stars side that defeated Collingwood Districts to win a grand final, but most of his career was spent in the Goulburn Valley. In all, he played at 15 clubs, such as Tallygaroopna, Wunghnu and Dookie United, always with the same story. Clubs with little money and few players would recruit a dozen Aboriginal players as a bloc. Often the numbers and talent of the Aboriginal recruits would push the club up the ladder. Inevitably, the chance of a premiership would entice several hometown players to return. Sometimes, so many returned that noses were put out of joint, especially if hometown players were unable to make the team. Grumbles began surfacing about the Aboriginal recruits denying favorite sons a game. The grumbles would rarely be hostile, but they would be enough for the Aboriginal players to feel uneasy. They would push on to another club, where their talent and numbers would begin another climb up the ladder. The cycle lasted one or two years.

Through it all, Briggs never lost faith in his vision for Rumbalara. "We always knew that we'd soon have our own team," he said. His dream was realised after the 1996 season when the respected administrator Keith Wellman asked whether Rumbalara would join the second division of the Goulburn Valley league. After years of applying without success, a phone call had been made to invite them aboard. The Aboriginal community set to work. "We were running on adrenalin the first six months," Briggs said.

Players descended from Swan Hill, Echuca and the Riverina. Some made the weekly journey from Melbourne. None were paid. The lure was the opportunity to play with their people every weekend rather than at annual carnivals. In the first season, they made the finals. In the next two years, they played in the newly formed Central Goulburn league and won two premierships. Briggs said the early seasons were successful but uncomfortable. "It took a while for the other clubs to get used to us, and we were certainly not used to them."

Rumbalara were always going to be under scrutiny. Briggs said rivals wanted to beat the new club, especially because it was an Aboriginal club. He said Rumbalara had more reports than their rivals because umpires were extra vigilant. When asked whether Rumbalara had rough players, Briggs replied: "Not really."

Off the field, Briggs was keen to dispel the stereotype that Aboriginals are "not that strong on the work ethic". Part of destroying this perception is managing the funds from sponsors such as Rio Tinto and the North

Melbourne Football Club. The main benefactor has been the Victorian Government, which contributed $900,000 towards buying the land for the ground and developing facilities such as the tea-rooms and dressing-rooms, whose curved, modern design marks them apart from the no-frills rooms to be found at most grounds. The City of Shepparton pays half the water bill but the Rumbalara Co-op, of which Briggs is a director, is responsible for all other financial affairs.

As well as his leadership role at Rumbalara, Briggs is a leader with the Aboriginal and Torres Strait Islander Commission and, in the week before the match against the Benalla All Blacks, he was in Perth helping to set up an Aboriginal credit union. He's a busy man, and highly respected. During our interview over a cup of tea in the tea-rooms, it seemed that those setting up the half-time coffee and cakes reserved a special courtesy for him. His answers were clear and thoughtful, with no hint of rancor or triumph. He had an almost dreamy evenness. He believes all humans, no matter what their race, have graces and flaws. His ability to handle several tasks was evident when he delivered patient responses to many questions and kept an eye on the game. At one point, he was noting the inclusion of paintings from Yorta Yorta artists in the planned new social rooms while observing that Rumbalara had rebounded by kicking the last six goals.

Rumbalara needed those goals. The club was struggling with numbers after losing a dozen from the premiership side, including the best-and-fairest winners from their first three seasons. Darcy Ronan, who won two, went to Tocumwal, and fellow midfielder Brett Lowe went to Mooroopna. Briggs described them as good footballers and good blokes. "We were disappointed but you can understand that they are using football, in the short term, to feed their kids," he said.

To my suggestion that Rumbalara must be doing something right if raiders wanted their players, Briggs turned up his nose. He had no interest in being a feeder club to the major leagues and, more to the point, it upset the Rumbalara leadership program. The scheme relies on visibility of leaders, to curb the hurt that children feel after the departure of someone to whom they've become attached. He believes AFL players are not necessarily the right leaders. Michael Long, for example, is a hero to children and might do a fine job when giving a footy clinic but, just when the children are becoming attached, he must return to Melbourne. Continuity is a leading theme.

Another theme, encouraged by Briggs, is inclusiveness. The first indication that Rumbalara aims to reach beyond the Aboriginal population came at the entrance to the ground. I admit that I pulled up and wondered whether the two men selling raffle tickets and programs at the gate were Aboriginal. Briggs explained that they were members of the Reconciliation Group, which does voluntary work at Rumbalara. He was also proud of the contribution of men such as Dallas Terlich, a white teacher who is a leading player for the club, and added that his vision for the new social rooms included visitors from everywhere. "We're not just here for Aboriginal people," he said.

At half-time, members of the Reconciliation Group drank tea with the Yorta Yorta. The atmosphere was polite rather than jovial. Attempts to bridge the cultures were earnest and respectful, without the banter that comes with familiarity. Linley Walker, a co-ordinator of the Reconciliation Group, explained that members of the group had manned the gate because Aboriginals find it difficult to take money from their people. She herself had found volunteering difficult. "I'm a shy person," she said. "It was the experience you have if you're a shy person and you walk into a crowded room." But after three years at the football club she felt more comfortable. "It's great to do something practical."

Walker said the Reconciliation Group had 160 members in Shepparton. Their meetings usually include a guest speaker who explains an aspect of Aboriginal culture or politics. Walker joined the group after returning from Portland and feeling shock at the racism in her home town. She told me she felt also guilty about the treatment of Aboriginals, before reminding herself that guilt was a negative emotion. "They say compassion is the word," she said, bringing the cup of tea to her mouth. I filled the pause by suggesting that guilt, although negative, was natural. Why call it by another name? Walked knitted her brow. It was an issue that vexed her. "I'm not worried about using the word guilt. I think there should be a national guilt."

Her fellow co-ordinator, Tammy Lovett, was as sunny as the sky was steely grey. The 28-year-old was a member of the Gunditjmara tribe in the south-west of Victoria who'd thrown herself into life with the Yorta Yorta since moving to Shepparton. She hosted an Aboriginal affairs show on public radio and worked on the family preservation program of the Rumbalara Co-op. She made the point that Aboriginal people rarely volunteered at non-Aboriginal football clubs but, among their own, they were more likely to come forward. She said watching the Rumbalara footballers run out for their first match in 1997 was among the best days of her life. "We were so excited. We were sitting at the first home game and we couldn't believe it. We said, 'Look at it'."

This, however, was not one of the best days for Rumbalara. In his first game for the season, Brad Boon went down in a heap. The former Diamond Valley forward had won the Rumbalara goalkicking award the previous year but travelling costs had prevented him playing early in the Central Goulburn season. As he was helped from the field, a blatant free kick to a teammate was left unpaid in the goalsquare he was forced to leave behind. Rumbalara fans strained at the fence to scream abuse at the umpires as the siren signalled three-quarter time. Paul Briggs greeted the decision with phlegmatic silence.

The loss of Boon left Rumbalara with few options on the bench. Neville Atkinson, the 38-year-old defender who also served as football manager, had broken his arm in the first half. The formation of Rumbalara had given Atkinson a new lease of life, with two premierships as a bonus, but the father of six spent the second half of the All Blacks game in the back of his family van contemplating life after football.

Leadership duties were left to another veteran, Eric Egan, who came down from Mildura to round off his career. The 37-year-old ruckman had long limbs and a paunch that hung over his shorts but failed to stop him reaching contests all over the ground. His deft ball-handling backed up the word that he was a top basketballer. His brother Alex was a wiry wingman whose chiselled features, ponytail and goatee beard suggested a sensitive artist. But there was fire in his eyes when he attacked the ball.

Alongside the veterans, coach Jason Briggs, a former Robinvale midfielder who went on to St Kilda, was keen to blood teenagers. Gangly Quentin Tass took the occasional knockout but fellow 17-year-olds Nathan Moran and Norman Baxter were barely tall enough to play as rovers. Before the game, Moran had been distraught at the prospect of playing in basketball shorts that stretched down to his knees. Jason Briggs, who was more relaxed than most coaches, had a great laugh as his young rover sprinted from the rooms to demand the footy shorts of a reserves player.

I spent the last quarter of the match doing a slow lap of the ground. The first stop was the All Blacks' bench, where I asked president Wally Armstrong, a 34-year-old full-forward who was out injured, about the nickname. The club was named the All Blacks when it began in 1934 because, after the president's wife had mustered every jumper she could find, black was the only color that would take when she dyed them. In the climate of the time, few batted an eyelid at the nickname of the Niggers. The nickname continued to be part of the fabric of the club until Rumbalara became a rival. Rumbalara supporters were unhappy when the All Blacks defeated them and belted out "Oh, we're from Niggerland" in place of "Oh, we're from Tigerland", the opening lyrics in the Richmond theme song.

After two seasons of playing Rumbalara, the All Blacks committee led a fierce debate on whether to adopt a new nickname. Some of the members had been put out when asked to remove their "Go Niggers, go" banner from the MCG during a one-day cricket match against the West Indies, and they saw no reason to drop the nickname now. Armstrong was among them. "We were Niggers and that was tradition to me," he said. "But it's a time of change." The club emblazoned a panther across the front of their guernseys and changed the first line of their theme song to "Oh, we're from Pantherland."

Next to the scoreboard, a dozen Rumbalara supporters gathered around a 44-gallon drum, taking in the warmth of the fire. One of them became rowdy and aggressive as he tried to break a piece of wood to push into the flames. A Rumbalara official emerged from the scoreboard and warned him to hold his tongue. Further along, Rumbalara women spanning three generations screamed abuse at the umpire, screamed support for their players, and screamed at the All Blacks when they came too close to the fence. Their knowledge of the game was questionable but their passion was astounding when it was considered that Rumbalara were eight goals down with five minutes to go. During the day, it had been whispered to me that Rumbalara supporters were a problem and I could see why their volume would upset some. But, as far as I could gather, it was only noise. It's what footy's supposed to be about. The problem was the difference in culture – what was regular behavior for some was too robust for others. Besides which, the greatest din came from the patch of dirt behind the dressing-rooms, where the young Rumbalara fans held the noisiest scratch match in the world. Dozens of boys were scrambling after the ball when I arrived around lunchtime, and they were still scrambling when the sun went down. Their number and delight suggested the future of Rumbalara was rosy.

On the ground, the only sign of tension came when a Rumbalara play-er lined up an opponent from metres away and crunched him as he bent over the ball. It was crude and unnecessary and might have started a brawl if it were the first quarter of a final. But it was the final quarter of a regu-lation match in which the All Blacks were gathering steam. The groggy Panther thought about remonstrating before going back and taking his kick. Panther forward Tony Reaper kept taking marks above his height and Darby Morrison controlled the half-back line. The All Blacks ran out winners by 45 points.

For Rumbalara, Eric Egan earned the best player award after showing his younger teammates how to fight out a game. After the siren, the sup-porters by the scoreboard slipped two chunks of wood through holes in the 44-gallon drum and carried it towards shelter on the other side of the ground. The flames climbed into the dusk as the drum made its way across the centre square.

Rumbalara continued their habit of previous seasons and came home like a train before losing the preliminary final to Yea by three points in a mudbath. Centreman Michael Chisolm won the best-and-fairest. Eric Egan, who was appointed coach for the new season, finished second. Paul Briggs won the reserves' goalkicking with 39. Neville Atkinson decided to play on. Darby Morrison won the best-and-fairest for the All Blacks, who missed the finals. The league was consumed in controversy after a brawl erupted following the siren in the thirds grand final between Rumbalara and Thornton-Eildon. The Wangaratta Umpires Board refused to officiate in further Rumbalara matches before rescinding after several months of talks. At the end of the season, it was announced that an Aboriginal club from Healesville called Worowa would begin playing in the Yarra Valley Mountain District league.

10

THREE'S A CONTEST

North v Currie
the Bulldogs and the Robins

"One day I rode my pushbike to Grassy for a game. Not far from Grassy,
at Gentle Annie, I saw some cattle on the road. I couldn't stop and
rode straight through the hind legs of a calf. The calf was all right
but I lay there till a lad from Grassy came to rescue me. I still
played in the match, and we won."

Tom Sullivan, In the Path of the Roaring Forties

Kevin Grave, the secretary of the King Island Football Association for 27
years, was telling me about Ben Hassing, the ruckman who cracked jokes,
and the fleecy-lined jumpers that the Grassy Hawks wore to insulate
against the cold when the siren rang for half-time. "Time to put the
kettle on," he said. A minute later, the umpires marched in looking red and
puffed after a windy first half. "Phew," said Mark Jones. "It's enough to lose
your toupée." The man in white made his way to the small table in the
corner of the room and reached for a cup. He plopped the tea bag in the
water and jiggled it up and down. Then he leaned forward, placed one
hand on his hip for balance and, taking care not to poke his eye out with
the whistle on his fingers, he raised the cup to his lips. "Ah, that's better,"
he said.

King Island is that sort of place: where a strong cup of tea is always preferred to a Gatorade. Jones sipped from his brew and wondered aloud
about the weather. The wind and rain that had created a racket overnight,

pounding a tattoo on our roof and threatening to blow the island across Bass Strait to New Zealand, had died by late morning. The sun had come out and the under-16s had played their match in relative calm. But Currie coach Rod Graham was on to something at quarter-time in the senior match when he gave the usual advice to run hard and kick long before adding some special advice for the conditions. "Boys, you'd better kick your goals this quarter," he said. "Before that wind springs up."

The wind did pick up and the match declined. On the sidelines, thick jackets with oily surfaces were pulled on and the teenager walking around in a Hawaiian shirt was forced to take stock of his latitude. King Island, which was named after Philip King, the Governor of New South Wales, in 1801, is not in the tropics; it's a sliver of land halfway between Cape Otway in Victoria and Cape Grim at the north-west corner of Tasmania. It's also in the path of the winds known on the Roaring Forties, which race across the Southern Ocean before slamming into the King Island coast. King Island footballers know to expect trouble with the elements but Kevin Grave said he could remember only one match in which the weather had kicked the final goal. In the '50s at Yambacoona, in the north of the island, players tired of scrambling under box thorns to escape fierce hailstorms and the match was cancelled. In the '70s, Grave said, the owners of the scheelite mine at Grassy invested in the satin jumpers with fleecy lining to protect the footballers in their workforce. "Christ, they were pretty," he said. Mostly, the conditions are accepted as part of life, like the change in seasons, or a cup of tea at half-time. The kettle boiled again. I declined a second cuppa and Chris Barnett, the president of the competition, led the way into the North rooms for the final minutes of the break.

The atmosphere was relaxed, with several players standing around like they were in the front bar of the pub. Most seemed more interested in telling gags than discussing the match, although one player did raise his voice to rally his teammates. "C'mon, boys, we've got to run harder." His teammates ignored him and continued talking about Worm Watson's 40th birthday celebrations to be held in the sheds that evening. Worm is a noted card. At the end of half-time, he giggled more than he stretched. Barnett said the half-forward, a deckhand on the cray boats whose real name is Peter, had retired every year since he was 26. His fellow half-forward, Tony Alexander, a cray fisherman, begins most seasons as an umpire. "He's having a strange season," Barnett said. "This year he started playing straight away."

Worm Watson was less convincing on the field than in the rooms. His choppy gait carried him to contests but he fumbled the ball like it was a frog in his hands, and his lack of fitness left second attempts out of the question. In the rooms he was at the centre of the action but on the field he looked worried, as if he was in danger of damaging himself before the main event. It seemed to me that he wanted the match to finish, so he could begin the party, but Snow Williams took another view. I spent the third quarter with Snow, whose real name is Cyril, in his four-wheel drive on the fence at the half-forward line. The farmer from the north of the island said Worm Watson looks like his father. "He walks like him; he does everything like him," he said. "His father would put his arms up playing football and you'd have to run around him." The 86-year-old cocked his elbows and performed his impersonation of Jack Watson, the father of Worm, then grabbed his steering wheel in laughter.

It was instructive, and entertaining, to watch the game with someone who'd been born not long after the island was settled by anyone other than lighthouse keepers. Snow's father had moved from Tasmania to take up grazing land in 1911. When Snow was seven, he bolted into the paddocks after seeing his first car because he thought it might shy at him like a horse. At 19, he took his maiden voyage from King Island when he caught a boat to Burnie, on the north-west coast of Tasmania. "I went to Wynyard to see an auntie then I came back to milk the cows," he said. By the time he was 30, he'd fought with the Australian army in Egypt, New Guinea and Borneo. He'd also met his wife Vera at Puckapunyal. Vera was a New Zealander, so the dampness of King Island was never a problem.

Williams said his family was lucky because none of his brothers had died in the war. Seven Williams brothers returned to King Island. Most of them pulled on the boots for North and, with the toughness of combat behind them, they played until ripe ages. Splinter Williams, whose name was Lindsay, kicked 12 goals in a match at the age of 40 and played until he was 44. Snow pointed at the goalsquare as if the spirit of Splinter was still there.

When his football career ended, Snow Williams concentrated on his other sporting passion of trotting. Even now, in his late 80s, he continues to rise at 5am to train his trotters before tending his farm. He prepares the horses for the summer meetings on the track just outside Currie, where the gallops continue to be alternated with the trots and the highlight is the King Island Cup on New Year's Day. Williams said the mild climate encourages sport. "Dad always said King Island was the overcoat on Tassie." But his words seemed hollow when the wind began tearing in from the south and the rain fell sideways. Williams explained that it was an unfortunate spate of Grassy weather that had found its way to Currie. "It's pretty close to Tassie down there."

Grassy is about 30 kilometres from Currie, on the south-east tip of the island. The town emerged in 1952 to service workers on the scheelite mine. The football club soon followed, with another club formed at Mount Stanley, five kilometres away, when Grassy became too big for one team. The population of Grassy reached 1200 before plummeting after the mine closed in 1990. The town is now a collection of empty houses, with a small supermarket and an RSL club to serve the remaining residents and the tourists who come for a sticky-beak at a ghost town. It does well by continuing to field a football team, although Chris Barnett said selection was rarely a problem. Whoever turned up during the 2000 season got a game, with only one Hawk, Gerald Sartori, living in Grassy. The rest lived in Currie. My regret was arriving a week too late to see Grassy host a rare game at their traditional ground.

Most Currie and North players also live in Currie, the island's main town. When I asked Barnett what North referred to, he said north of the Catholic church, which is on the outskirts of the town. His smirk suggested he designated the boundary on the spot but, in a competition whose three clubs have come to draw from the same pool, at least it contributed a notion of place. North players traditionally were farmers from the north of the island. Their land produces the beef and dairy products that are renowned around Australia but their farms are unable to provide work for their sons. North players are now more likely to work on the cray boats than on the farms, but they play for the Bulldogs because their fathers and grandfathers did. North coach Craig Crawford was one of the three policemen in Currie, a task that appears straightforward when King Islanders consider locking your door an insult.

The original clubs in the King Island Football Association were North,

Currie and Pegarah. The competition has evolved over the decades but it has never had more than four clubs at the one time. In the three-club competition, the season begins with a meeting to work out the training schedule for the Currie oval. In 2000, North had Mondays and Wednesdays and Currie had Tuesdays and Thursdays. When one of those teams had the bye, Grassy slotted into their nights. One match is held each weekend, with one club having the bye. The clubs play each other five times, after which the top team moves straight into the grand final. The other two play in the preliminary final.

All players on King Island tend to know each other, which would be difficult to avoid on a plot of land 60 kilometres by 20 kilometres, but if a player is new to the island, he quickly gets to know his opponents because he plays them so regularly. Barnett said matters do become heated despite the blurred line between friends and foes. "We have our blues, don't you worry," he said. "It's football. It's an emotional game and you wouldn't have it any other way."

The problem is numbers. Even without wings, Grassy was touch and go to field a side; before the season Currie looked unlikely to field a side at all. The return of Duncan Clemons after a pre-season with Glenorchy in Hobart enabled the Robins to cobble together a team but Barnett said fears were growing that one team would drop out and the competition would die. "It's a struggle every year and it's getting harder," he said.

Before the season, the dwindling population forced the decision to scrap the under-17s and under-13s and combine them into the under-16s. The danger in this decision was exposing primary school students to a battering from mid-teenagers. One solution was to force boys over, say, 12 years of age to wear black shorts and restrict them to tackling each other, while boys under 12 would wear white shorts and tackle each other. In the under-16s match that served as the curtain-raiser before the senior game between Currie and North, it appeared that tackling restrictions were unnecessary. The larger boys were mindful of their smaller opponents and left them alone. As one slip of a boy lined up for goal, the gentle defender on the mark crouched to the ground and barely put his hands above his head, to give his opponent a better look at the big sticks. Some of the young ones became cocky with their preferential treatment and flew for marks with no fear of being crushed.

Around the ground, senior players emerged from mud-spattered four-wheel-drives with small bags slung over their shoulder and their boots in hand, which was a nice touch. In most parts of Victoria, footballers carry footy bags that would serve them well on a three-month tour of Europe. There would be no thought of exposing your boots to the rigor of the walk to the dressing-rooms. The King Islanders were comparatively modest, in keeping with a three-team competition on the edge of Bass Strait. They received no pats on the back as they walked to the rooms. They had a chat as they changed into their gear and ran on to the ground in dribs and drabs.

The amazing thing, for me, was that they didn't run on to a swimming pool. I realise the wonders of sandy soil but I did expect a few puddles, maybe in the goalsquare or on the edge of the cricket pitch, after overnight rain that would have filled Lake Eyre. Geoff French, who's been writing match reports for King Island newspapers for 25 years, said the Currie oval is never muddy. "I've seen this ground under water at 11am and they were marking overhead in the game."

My expectation that the football would be blown into the sea was also wrong. Not only did the wind have a rest during the juniors and the first quarter of the seniors, but the ground's sunken elevation – "it's in a dish," said French – and protective ring of macrocarpa trees and tea-trees kept out the little breeze there was. It was mild during this interlude, like an overcast autumn day in southern Victoria, without being quite mild enough for a Hawaiian shirt. Spectators thought this was no big deal. "Inland Victoria is freezing compared to here," one said.

The mildness surprised me only because the night and morning had been so wild. The force of the conditions reminded me of facing into winter gales on the Dingle Peninsula in Ireland, at the western tip of Europe, where waves thundered on to the rocks and there was an invigorating feeling of being at the edge of the world. It was the same feeling on King Island, where there was nothing between our cottage overlooking the cliffs on the west coast and Argentina, which was 24,000 kilometres away. The southern view took in Currie harbor, which churned like a washing machine for the best part of three days. Cray boats heaved up and down on the harbor suds and it was apparent why none of them had headed out to sea for a month. It was also apparent why our cottage,

Blencathra, was named after a shipwreck and why King Island was Australia's marine graveyard. The rhythmic, pounding rain and the wind driving up from Antarctica brought to life the history of our worst shipwrecks. It was exhilarating to be on King Island during the fiercest storms for several years.

The storms held off during the senior match until late in the second quarter, when the wind started gathering force. Currie defender Nathan Kirby, a Victorian who joined his family on King Island after scoring a job in the cheese factory, tried to keep pace with the wind, scrambling from pack to pack. He made quite a sight, with his bushy beard, red boots and knee-length shorts, tumbling the ball forward with bursts of energy, while his coach, Duncan Clemons, provided ballast. Clemons was steady and assured. He marked strongly and tried to place his kicks to advantage, a detail that eluded most of his teammates.

For North, Kerry Towns kicked three goals before injuring his ankle and Tony Alexander revealed the soundness of his decision to give up umpiring by roving the packs and kicking five goals. The dreadlocked Kurt Sullivan was steady in defence and Shane Johnston gained his share of possessions after returning home from Assumption College, in the cold interior of Victoria, for the weekend.

Finally, with the wind and rain lashing at the players, and news coming through that it was snowing at the MCG, the siren rang to signal a 42-point victory to North. David Summers, gatekeeper, raffle ticket-seller and spruiker of King Island steaks, cleaned up the leftover salads as news came through that snow had failed to reach the MCG after all. But, we were assured, inland Victoria was one big blizzard, which turned out to be true. After a trying afternoon in shipwreck conditions in Currie, players and umpires trudged from the ground in near darkness. Worm Watson looked like he could do with a birthday drink; Mark Jones looked ready for a nice, hot cup of tea.

North went straight through to the grand final after finishing the season on top. In the grand final, North and Grassy were level at three-quarter time before North pulled away to win by 67 points. The wind was reportedly gentle. Midfielder Andy Summers won the North best-and-fairest. Key position player Jamie Synott won the best-and-fairest for Currie. Worm Watson was appointed coach of North for the new season. Tony Alexander was torn between umpiring and playing.

HARD YARDS

11

HEAVY CROWDS AND PURPLE REIGN

Vermont v East Ringwood
the Eagles and the Roos

***

"We have a pride to be number one."

Vermont football manager Lee Bidstrup

***

In 1991, the North Ringwood Saints were still finding their feet in division one of the Eastern league when a magic moment stirred the Saints into finding their voice as well. Five minutes before the siren, a handful of supporters began a rendition of the club song. *"Oh when the Saints, Oh when the Saints, Oh when the Saints go marching in ..."* The supporters alongside them joined in, and the supporters next to them. Pockets of Saints fans picked up the song as it made its way around the ground. "It was like a Mexican wave in voice," said Ted McCarthy, now the club president. Before long, every North Ringwood supporter was singing up a storm. Their club, just up from division two, was about to topple the invincible Vermont. For a club without a division one premiership, it was the biggest moment in their history. The song was repeated over and over until finally the siren rang. Saints fans burst on to the field. Their team had ended Vermont's unbeaten run at 61 games. The photos on the walls in the North Ringwood clubrooms continue to commemorate the day.

Former Vermont players confess that they were relieved at the end of their undefeated run. The pressure to keep winning after three undefeated seasons had become a yoke around their necks. But these same players recognise that they were in a privileged position. Vermont established their national record for consecutive victories during an era that installed the club as the most successful in senior competition in Australia. The record was set in the years in which the Eagles won four consecutive flags. From 1982, the Eagles won 12 flags in 17 years and missed just three grand finals. Their winning touch was emphasised in the 1986 preliminary final when an official recognised that a Vermont goal had been given to Scoresby. He protested to the goal umpires at half-time, three-quarter time and when the final siren rang to signal a loss by less than a kick. After the match, he banged on the goal umpires' door before police advised him to stop. A Scoresby official offered to toss a coin for the match but Vermont fought through two hearings and overturned the result. East Ringwood were brushed aside in the grand final. At the past players' reunion on the day that I went to Vermont, midfielder Steve White looked sheepish when admitting that he'd left the Eagles because they win so much. "This might sound silly, but I needed another challenge." Since moving to Blackburn in the second division, he'd gained a new appreciation of his home club. He mentioned that medical staff were always on hand and that every detail seemed to be covered. "Vermont is very well-run. They put a pretty good package together."

White had returned to the club for which he played in seven premierships. Next to him, former wingman Steve Tudor had also played in seven flags. Tudor is tall, about 188 centimetres, and lean. The fact that a player of such height was able to play on the wing was a measure of his club's depth and talent. Next to him, Mick Winter had played in three flags. Winter made his senior debut at 15 years of age in the Riverina before leaving for Sydney to try his luck in the AFL. From the Swans, he went to Hobart. He said the professionalism of Vermont ranked with that of any club. John Brinkkotter also played with Sydney before joining Vermont. His old teammates laughed when he said he played in two premierships with the Eagles. Two was considered a paltry tally. Then former rover Craig Coghlan walked past on his way to the bar. Coghlan played in 10 senior flags. Nobody ribbed John Brinkkotter any more.

The banter came to a halt as the former Eagles tried to put their finger on what makes the club so strong. Steve White's point about staff was valid. The club has six trainers at every session, with a doctor and a physio dropping in twice a week. The word "professional" was mentioned several times but, in five minutes, this was all the former Eagles could suggest. The answers were characterised by their lack of punch, which somehow comes across as an endorsement of efficiency. The Eagles don't do anything remarkable; they just do everything better than the rest.

Vermont raised the stakes in doing everything better when they appointed Lee Bidstrup as football manager. It was the early '90s, when few football clubs had full-time employees. Bidstrup was born for the role. He's the son of Viv Bidstrup, the president who was known as Mr Vermont. At 21, Lee followed his father's footsteps and became treasurer. He continued voluntary work while setting a club record of 221 senior games. He was the official who badgered the goal umpires in the '86 preliminary final. The only reason he stopped being treasurer after 25 years was that the role was included in his job as football manager. "Vermont has been my life," he said. "It's my passion, I guess."

Bidstrup played in Vermont's two premierships in the first decade of the Eastern league. Nobody at Vermont had played in more than two flags until the club began its rise in the '80s. Bidstrup said the emergence of outstanding juniors and the presidency of John Gunn had enabled the rise. In a decade under Gunn, Vermont won seven flags. "John was a fantastic organiser and a real people person," Bistrup said. A series of excellent coaches and strong recruits completed the recipe for success.

The Eagles are geared entirely towards success. Most clubs in suburban and country football have many players in the reserves who have no chance of playing seniors. They are too old, too fat, or they have less talent than the goalpost. In many cases, these players are the backbone of the club. The absence of their names in gold letters on the honor board fails to limit their enthusiasm; lack of skill or fitness fails to impede their performances in the bar or on the committee. Vermont has none of these players. Their reserves team is a feeder team. If a seconds player has no chance of making the seniors, he's rotated out of the club. The competition for places in the senior team is maintained by the annual influx of recruits. Vermont recruit less aggressively than some, but their record ensures player interest. Match payments could be improved elsewhere but potential recruits are attracted to Vermont's record and their reputation for taking care of players. The Eagles, for their part, demand that recruits must have more than talent; they must be of sound character. "If we're going to pay good money, they've got to be good people," Bidstrup said.

The only question mark over the club in the 2000 season was a reputation for softness. "But we keep winning," Bidstrup shrugged. His honesty suggested another reason behind success. Most football people would rather scrub the social rooms after a boozy function than admit that their club's brawn was under question. Bidstrup loses no sleep worrying about the "soft" slur. He said the efficiency of the club's running game was behind the reputation.

The running game is so good that the club's home ground is a disadvantage. The ground is small, almost cosy, tucked off a busy road in an area that, not so long ago, was planted with orchards. Now, large gums form a canopy over the grid of streets and houses. The trees at either end of the ground reach towards the goalposts, trapping the roars of the crowd and adding spice to contests in the teeth of goal. Spectators jostle around the fence and in front of the social club along the wing. The ground might stifle the Eagles but it doesn't seem to stop them performing on larger grounds during the finals. For a regulation match, the Vermont Recreation Reserve is a great place to feel part of the fizz and bubble of a lively crowd and be entertained by slick football an arm's length away.

The standard of football is among the reasons for the growing crowds in all four divisions of the Eastern league. A record 3200 attended a Vermont match at Bayswater before the loss of Waverley Park gave the suburban competition a further kickalong. Vigorous promotion from full-time media staff ensures that the Eastern league benefits from disillusionment with the AFL. Reams in local newspapers and hours of coverage on public radio and television are capped by a website that attracts more traffic than most AFL sites. Guidance from former league umpire Kevin Smith ensures a high standard of umpiring, with men in white appointed for every game at every level. Then there's the population. Eastern league clubs are based in a wedge that diverges, roughly, from Doncaster to the Dandenong Ranges. More than one and a half million live in this area. In such a population, the football should be good. On what I saw, other local football competitions would be hard pressed to beat it.

Vermont players went into the game with sore ears after a draw against the old nemesis, North Ringwood, prompted team meetings after the three nights of training. "We weren't happy with our players," Lee Bidstrup said. "We have a pride to be number one." East Ringwood also had their eyes on the top rung and threw everything at the Eagles. The Roos controlled the early part of the match for minutes at a stretch but their assault was founded more on hope than belief. Vermont held their nerve. Brad Neil, a throwback to the era when big men were directors rather than athletes, began to shape the game for his rovers. The ruckman looked out of place with the sleeves of his purple guernsey cut off at the elbow. He had a soft body but he played hard. By contrast, Jason Smith was gleaming and taut. His sorties from the back pocket were showy and effective. The Eagles broke the deadlock with three late goals. Their flurry was the sign of a side with belief.

I watched the second quarter with East Ringwood president Peter Baker, a member of the most devoted breed in football: the midfielder who anchors the team before becoming the coach and then the president. Baker analysed the match with a fury. His side was working hard, building momentum with several possessions, before handling the ball once too often. At every turnover, he threw up his arms in exasperation. In appearance and manner, he bore a striking resemblance to Terry Wallace, another intense former centreman. Baker played in five losing grand finals, including four against Vermont. In three years of coaching, he lost one grand final to Vermont. It was no wonder his club struggled to believe that it could push the Eagles from top spot.

Then, showing more heart than poise, the Roos rebounded. Midfielders persisted until they emerged with the ball and the coaching staff went on the attack, shifting the talented Paul Grayling from defence to the forward pocket. Baker nodded. "I thought he should have done it before." Grayling struggled to lay his hands on the ball but he diverted attention from James Gerstman, the full-forward who'd kicked six goals a game since his late start. "He missed the first part of the season because he's a rowing coach at Scotch," Baker said. For a period in the second quarter, Gerstman drew the ball like a magnet. He led straight and the ball landed in his hands. Spectators strained at the fence to hoot him but the 20-year-old kept smiling. He was dominating in an unobtrusive way and his side was showing signs of belief. The game had heart, vigor and one individual bucking the weight of the system. It was a pity his kicking was astray. By half-time, Gerstman had kicked 4.4, almost the entire East Ringwood score. His impertinence had humbled full-back Andrew Dwyer, an opponent with seven premierships behind him. Dwyer would break the club games record in weeks to come but, on this day, he went into the break with plenty to think about. His former teammates had plenty of premierships to talk about. The reunion was in full swing.

It was like a premiership convention. Anyone without a flag to his name would have felt like a goose. I interrupted the reminiscences of Steve White and his friends to ask the whereabouts of Rod Dux, the president. Dux had risen through club ranks since his sons had joined the juniors. Watching him in action, it was easy to see why. He buzzed around the rooms like Kevin Bartlett near goals. He had a million tasks to complete, largely because the reunion had been timed to coincide with the opening of the Perry Fletcher Room. Dux wanted me to meet Fletcher. "He's a very artistic person."

Upon our introduction, Fletcher didn't say a word. He showed me a golf ball, put it in his ear and retrieved it. "He's very artistic," Dux said. I'm not one for magic tricks, but Fletcher's exploits with an engraving wand deserve mention. The Perry Fletcher Room houses all the engravings that the former defender promised after returning from the Vietnam War. When he first returned, Fletcher spent six months cowering alone in his room. The football club helped him get back on his feet. The Eagles won the 1969 grand final by a point and Fletcher was again filled with the possibilities of life. He promised an engraving for every flag to follow. It was his way for thanking the club for welcoming an erratic soul back into the fold. "All my life I've been an enigma," he said.

The 54-year-old has a neatly trimmed moustache and grey hair that curls towards his shoulders. He was dressed in black from head to toe. He estimated that, over three decades, the engravings had taken 4500 hours. He said he felt honored at the club's recognition. His tour of the Perry Fletcher Room began with the American eagle bearing the inscription, "The year of the Eagle", entwining his experience in Vietnam with his place in the flag side. The room was teeming with engravings. Every shelf in the glass casings held memories of success. Fletcher believed his artwork was a small price to pay for the club's part in his recovery from the trauma of Vietnam. Football clubs are conservative. They struggle to cope with mavericks, but they do recognise a good heart. Fletcher had been welcomed back like any Eagle with a good heart.

I left Fletcher the Etcher, as he describes himself on his business card, and retired to my car in the bottom corner of the recreation reserve to write a story for *The Sunday Age*. The crowd of 2500 had supported the claim that crowds were thriving in the Eastern league. The performance of Vermont supported their reputation for excellence. Cheers rose through the trees with increasing regularity as the last quarter progressed. The Eagles broke the Roos' resistance to glide to a 58-point victory. Jason Smith was the popular choice for best on ground, with almost the whole backline named among the best. Andrew Dwyer kept James Gerstman to one goal after half-time.

The Eagles filed into the rooms and belted out their song. Coach Mick Kennedy, wearing a modest woollen jumper, jeans and brown shoes, looked almost too self-effacing to join in. Kennedy had grown up in the tough northern suburb of Fawkner before battling through six years at Carlton. His reward was a place in the 1987 premiership side, but he said it was the battle that defined him. He relished the resources at Vermont but was perfectly placed to keep his feet on the ground. In the brief periods in the first half in which his side had played at full throttle, I thought the Eagles had shown a blend of height, skill and pace that would be envied at every local footy club in Victoria. Kennedy sang with the same gusto as he would have done whether the victory was at Vermont, Carlton or Creswick. Lee Bidstrup sang with gusto entirely because the victory was at Vermont. After almost four decades and a tower of premierships, victory at a home game in early June still made him grin like a teenager and give the air a little punch. "Suburban footy," he said. "There's nothing like it."

In the last game of the season, East Ringwood kicked 10 unanswered goals in the last quarter to defeat Vermont by two goals. The next week, the Roos lost the first semi-final to Bayswater. James Gerstman kicked 102 goals to win the league goal-kicking. Midfielder Kane Fraser won the Roos' best-and-fairest. Vermont's season continues in chapter 22.

12

SHOOTING STARS

Doutta Stars v Aberfeldie
the Stars and the Two Blues

"We washed in a puddle outside. There was no hot or cold water.
It was rough."

Doutta Stars stalwart Nipper Jordan

The career of Simon Minton-Connell ebbed and flowed at Carlton,
Sydney, Hawthorn and the Western Bulldogs. In the Essendon district
league, he was flying high. The nephew of the former Hawthorn champion Peter Hudson went into the match against Aberfeldie with 67 goals
from seven games, including several returns of five goals a quarter. In the
match against Aberfeldie earlier in the year, he kicked nine goals in the first
half.

In the first quarter of this match at Buckley Park, deep in the grid of
streets in which leafy Essendon drifts into modest Niddrie, he barely got a
touch, not that it bothered him. The 31-year-old was simply lapping up
footy away from the pressure of the AFL. "The grass roots stuff is really
good," he said. "I haven't enjoyed my footy like this since Tassie days."

Minton-Connell played in a premiership with North Hobart in 1987
and then joined Carlton. Throughout his AFL career he tried to keep football in perspective, working in the pub game and maintaining friendships

from various strands of life. Even his friendships within football maintained a broader view. It could be no other way when he lived with Carlton forward Luke O'Sullivan, who spent as much time in the café as in the gym, and, later, Sydney forward Dale Lewis, who remains the antithesis of all that is uptight about the AFL. In the end, though, the grind of pre-seasons and endless rehabilitation from injury wore Minton-Connell down. The prospect of a season in the Western Bulldogs reserves was the last straw. He played a bit of golf and was ready to head overseas when Bulldogs coach Terry Wallace asked him to become the forwards' coach. Minton-Connell thought about it for a day and accepted. The overseas trip would wait.

His coaching commitments, while requiring him to be with the Bulldogs every match, left the odd Saturday afternoon free. He joined former Hawthorn teammates Anthony Condon and Jason Taylor at Balwyn, where his five games included the Southern league grand final. Balwyn won their third successive premiership. After the season, Minton-Connell joined his friend Paul Harrison at Doutta Stars, who'd just won the Essendon district league premiership. The spearhead's only plan was to enjoy himself.

His enjoyment included no pre-season, plenty of golf and never going near a barbell. His weight in his last year with the Bulldogs was 95 kilograms; at Doutta Stars it was 88 kilograms. "I'm as fit as a fiddle," he said. "I've put a spring back in my step." Some full-backs tried to curtail that spring by stepping on his toes but Minton-Connell said his concern at reports that the league was on the rough side proved largely unfounded. Most full-backs appreciated the chance to try their hand against an opponent who'd kicked more than 300 AFL goals. "Every now and then you might get someone who wants to make a name for himself," Minton-Connell said mid-season. "But it's been OK."

Against Aberfeldie, he spent most of the first quarter applauding as the ball sailed over his head. Teammates had a picnic further out, especially midfielder Paul Docherty, who played the most casually dominant quarter I'd seen since Damien Houlihan loped all over Lavington two months earlier. Docherty strolled through the centre, shimmying past opponents while weighing up his options in attack. His forays sometimes met an untidy end, with a tackle from behind as he searched for holes in a crowded forward line, but they never failed to entertain. Twice he kicked goals from the point where the arc meets the boundary line. Not to be outdone, Leigh Tudor, the former Geelong forward, sailed past a pack and collected the falling ball before chipping to Ashley Hicks at the point where the arc meets the boundary. Playing in his first game for two years, Hicks rounded his opponent and slotted a goal, reminding younger team-mates of his powers.

In the second quarter the Stars began looking for Minton-Connell but the 194-centimetre forward was unable to hold the ball to his chest as frequently as he would have liked. He led strongly but his lack of strength overhead and the number of opponents in his path proved frustrating. In body duels in the goalsquare, Aberfeldie full-back Dean Gray would get a fist to the ball at the final second.

The scraps were left to Hicks, who scooped them up with amazing skill considering his absence from Buckley Park. Hicks coached Doutta Stars for two years after a decade on the forward line at Port Melbourne. But after the Stars had failed to play to their abilities in the B-grade finals, he was sacked. Paul Harrison coaxed Hicks back to the club after hearing that he was burning in super-rules matches. Harrison pestered the 35-year-old because he wanted Hicks at the feet of Minton-Connell. "I copped a bit of flak for bringing Ashley straight into the side," he said.

Hicks's brilliance, which defied the laws of ageing, brought to life a few memories. I recall him as one of the two best players in the Essendon district league from my days as an over-awed junior. Strathmore forward David Mangels was built like a man at 14 years of age and ruined games by crashing through opponents like a car through a fence. Often I played the part of the fence. Hicks, on the other hand, was among the slightest players in the competition. Where Mangels was brutishly effective, Hicks was balanced, skilled and quick. In one match in the under-18s, he took the ball from the centre bounce, ran around his opponents – at least I didn't feel like a broken fence – and kicked a goal. Every footballer of any age dreams of roving the ball from the centre bounce and booting a solo goal, but this remains the only time I've seen it done. In the same quarter in the under-18 match, Hicks hurled his scrawny frame back into a pack to take a courageous mark. After that game, I followed his career as much as a career can be followed through pub talk and in the newspaper results. He trained at Windy Hill but the coaches told him he was too small. I saw him play once for Port Melbourne, in a televised match during which Phil Cleary swooned in the commentary box after Hicks rounded another opponent to kick a goal. It didn't look so different from the under-18s.

His crumbing partner in the match against Aberfeldie, Leigh Tudor, had the cleanest foot skills I've seen in junior football but, like Hicks, his skinny body was against him. Essendon said he was too small. He managed eight games at North Melbourne before adding 60 at Geelong, where his accuracy around goals earned him a game in two grand finals. He then spent a year at Glenelg but chronic back problems forced him into retirement. On returning to Melbourne, he sought fresh advice on his back. Halfway through 1999, he returned to the Doutta Stars line-up for his first game at Buckley Park since he was a teenager. He said afterwards that he felt like a teenager again. Surrounding him were members of the families with whom he'd grown up playing scratch matches in the streets of Niddrie. It put some pep in his game, and he added polish to the Douttas' forward line. At 29 years of age, the bonds that Leigh Tudor formed in childhood played a large part in his first senior premiership.

The close bonds at Douttas contribute to the club's charisma. The Stars fascinated me when I was a teenager. My link to the club began when my uncle moved down from the country and took his eccentricities, such as a furry hat of the type worn in Moscow, down to Buckley Park. Then I was put through a course in Doutta Stars folklore by the brothers of my first girlfriend, Cathy Hogan. Cath and I drifted apart after two years but, in the meantime, her brothers provided a thorough grounding on the intricacies of their footy club. The Stars seemed so close; they did everything together. And they had a hint of menace. I played junior football at St Bernard's, where there was no menace. Even our tattooed defender, Anthony Johnstone, was more likely to smile his opponent into submission than he was likely to sort him out. This would all change when I left school and played with St Bernard's in the Amateurs association, where all of a sudden we were as hard as many clubs, but as a battered junior in the Essendon district league I wondered what it would be like to play for a team with might. I wondered what it would be like to play with Douttas Stars.

Eventually I was a teenager no longer and I rarely gave a thought to Doutta Stars. They were known to everyone in the wedge between the

Maribyrnong River and the Moonee Ponds Creek, but my football world was now the Amateurs, a competition that stretches across Melbourne. In time, I even stopped looking up the Douttas results in the newspaper. Yet something always nagged at me. Throughout the years, I recognised the Douttas charisma. Not only were they proud and close, they wore a silly yellow star on a navy jumper and got away with it. They belted out a theme song based on the tune from the *Mickey Mouse Fan Club* and nobody thought twice. Their ground was completely without distinction apart from its exposure to every breeze that curled over the thistle plains beyond Keilor. But they continued to pop up here and there in my life. When I played at Golden Square, the team manager was an old Douttas man. He reported with pride when the club won another grand final, with Damian Hogan, one of the brothers who'd put me through the course in Douttas' folklore, best afield. When I was living in the Northern Territory I also heard about the Stars. The club with the funny name was known way beyond the wedge between the Maribyrnong River and the Moonee Ponds Creek, after all. Maybe it was the funny name that provided recognition.

The reason became apparent when former Douttas president Don McIntosh took me through the club history. In 1946, returned soldiers and the North Essendon Presbyterians formed the club and took the name from the Aboriginal words Doutta Galla. There are several versions of the meaning of Doutta Galla. Some claim it means treeless plain, which is plausible. Others claim Doutta Galla was the wife of Jika Jika, John Batman's native servant when Melbourne was founded in the 1830s. Justin Madden, after his election as the member for the state province of Doutta Galla, which stretches from Niddrie across to Melton in the outer west, claimed the translation is "star warrior". Madden played more than 300 AFL games, so no one disputed him. In any case, he's lived in the area all his life and he might just be right. As far as the football club goes, any trifling disagreement over the origin of the name fails to hinder recognition. Don McIntosh described end-of-season trips to Tasmania and Adelaide where the locals twigged about their visitors. " 'Oh yeah,' they say. 'Doutta Stars in the Essendon district'."

The path to recognition began three years after the club was formed. The Stars won their first premiership. The next year the Stars went through undefeated, and on it went. From 1948, Doutta Stars won 12 premierships in 17 years and established the reputation that carried their name to distant places. The phenomenon was to be repeated decades later, when Vermont won 12 premierships in 17 seasons in the Eastern league, but Douttas were the original suburban glamor club.

The Stars were less successful from the mid-'60s before returning to the premiership list in 1980. A decade later Douttas won two more premierships to bring their tally to 17, more than double the tally of their closest rival, but then the unthinkable happened: Doutta Stars were relegated. A batch of stalwarts had reached retirement together and the dwindling numbers of families in North Essendon and Niddrie depleted the junior sides. Outside the club, the news was greeted with shock and delight. It was like Collingwood or Port Adelaide crumbling under the weight of proud histories. Older Douttas supporters found the decline hard to accept. Some members of the teams that won premierships during the '50s wanted to stop the club adding the names of B-grade trophy winners to the honor boards.

It was noticeable how many older former players were at the match against Aberfeldie. The area near the social club featured several stars from the club's early years, confirming the power of premierships as a binding force. I spent the third quarter with Nipper Jordan, who, at 76, continues to introduce himself with the nickname his older brother gave him as a child. Nipper Jordan followed his brother Jack to the club after returning from army service in Japan. He said the discipline of the returned soldiers was behind the club's early success. Hardships such as relying on a tilley lamp for lighting were accepted without complaint. "We washed in a puddle outside," he said. "There was no hot or cold water. It was rough."

The former coach rattled off the names of greats from the undefeated 1949 side. Ruckman Jack Wade should have gone to Essendon. Tom Rawlins was a champion key forward. "Tom was brilliant," Jordan said. "And he did the best rendition of *Mammy* you ever saw." Members of what Jordan insisted was the greatest half-back line in the history of local football were listening a few steps in front of us when John Kirk, himself an old premiership player, suggested that Rae Evans should be at the top of the list. Jordan concurred. "Better put him in. He's my wife's brother."

The former players watched Douttas lose their grip on the match. Injury had forced two defenders from the ground before half-time. The problem was compounded in the third quarter when Paul Docherty took a nap and the Aberfeldie midfielders took over. The Two Blues hauled the home side in with six goals, before Scott McLaren kicked two running goals to restore Douttas' advantage at the last change.

Aberfeldie continued their fightback in the last quarter, with Leigh Woods and Jason Casey leading the charge from the middle. Douttas continued looking for Minton-Connell but, with Aberfeldie coach Jamie Madigan dropping into the hole and Darren Gray continuing to get a hand on the ball, finding Minton-Connell was difficult. I wondered whether attempting to find him was counter-productive. Douttas had won the premiership the previous season with Sam Tankard kicking almost 70 goals from a forward pocket and three players kicking 30 goals from further upfield. Concentrating the attacks on Minton-Connell seemed limiting.

The Aberfeldie challenge was gathering pace when – what do you know? – I bumped into Cathy Hogan for the first time in almost 10 years. As a teenager, I used to negotiate the thistles along Rose Creek before walking up the hill to Niddrie to see her, often to be greeted by a houseful of siblings. In adult years, the family has remained close. She was here with two brothers and two sisters, and two children of her own. We chatted about our lives and the scattering of friends before I settled into a long chat about footy with her brother Damian, just like the old days. It was unfortunate to hear that a back injury had cut short his brilliant sporting career.

The siren went with the Stars nine points ahead after an unconvincing afternoon. Midfielders Ben and Chris Tankard were the best players and Minton-Connell kicked three goals. "It was good to only get a few goals and we still won," he said later. Ashley Hicks booted five goals but his teammates were in no mood for the Mickey Mouse theme song. The Stars trudged into the rooms, where coach Paul Harrison locked them behind closed doors. Harrison had shown a penchant for long and intense speeches, so I deferred the interview plans. Deadlines for *The Sunday Age* also forced me to defer the Hogan family's offer of a beer in the clubrooms, which was a shame. I've never had a beer with the Hogans at

Douttas. Given the links and memories and their part in a football life, it was probably about time.

Doutta Stars entered the finals missing half a dozen leading players through injury. They lost the first semi-final and finished fourth. Aberfeldie finished fifth. Simon Minton-Connell kicked 108 goals and finished third in the club best-and-fairest; none of his teammates kicked more than 20 goals. Paul Harrison won the best-and-fairest but quit the club for work reasons. He was later appointed playing coach at Aberfeldie, where Minton-Connell joined him. Ashley Hicks retired after a season interrupted by hamstring injuries. A knee reconstruction forced Chris Tankard to retire before the finals. Jason Casey won the Aberfeldie best-and-fairest.

13
MATTER OF FAITH

Ajax v Prahran
the Jackas and the Two Blues

"A footy club's a footy club whether you're Jewish, Chinese, Arabic, Catholic, whatever. It's still a footy club."

Ajax coach Wayne Harmes

In the 1950s, long before Richard Pratt became a leading businessman and benefactor of the arts, he was a young hopeful in the Carlton reserves. When it became clear that he would struggle to make the seniors, the Melbourne Jewish community hoped he would ruck for the new club called Ajax, which takes its name from the Associated Judaean Athletic Clubs. Pratt informed Ajax that he would heed another calling. He would miss their inaugural season because he was to act in London in the new play *Summer of the Seventeenth Doll*. The play ran for seven months, a huge achievement for an Australian production. Ajax supporters were delighted. Many football people would shy in fright if one of their number became a success on the stage, but flying high in the West End of London is just the type of achievement to make Jackas fans proud.

Pratt returned to Melbourne and won a competition best-and-fairest in the Victorian Amateur Football Association. His name is on Ajax honor boards alongside many others whose achievements stretch beyond football.

Best-and-fairest winners at Ajax include a Queen's counsel and a Federal Court judge. Surgeons and captains of industry also feature in gold lettering. Players and officials from rival clubs often spend one or two beers scouring the names and faces on the walls in the Ajax rooms, which are named after David Mandie, a former Richmond patron. The Ajax oval, at the start of the finishing straight in Albert Park, is named after Gary Smorgon, from the famous business family. Many Amateurs clubs boast former players of high standing, but few clubs have as many notable former players as the Jackas.

In taking me through a list of Ajax greats, long-time clubman John Brustman noted achievements in the professions as well as on the field. Not only was Michael Zemski a leading midfielder who played a handful of games at Hawthorn, he went on to become a successful architect. Brustman looked proud when noting that Mark Blashki would miss the game against Prahran because he was studying in Israel. Blashki is the leading ruckman at a club with a chronic lack of height, but Brustman was unperturbed. It's a Jewish club and the ruckman had his priorities right.

Brustman is a balding man in his early 60s, stocky, with pale colorings. On the day that I met him, he was dressed tidily in white runners and casual pants. Four decades ago, he played 20 undistinguished games before a dislocated shoulder persuaded him to serve the club off the field. Since then, he's served in almost every role on the committee, waved the flags as goal umpire, and written the match reports for the *Australian Jewish News*. His highlights include watching the sons of former players pull on the Ajax guernsey and the club's achievement in playing in A-section in the early '80s. Reaching A-section was an enormous achievement for a club that draws from a small population. Melbourne's Jewish population has risen to 50,000 with the influx of South Africans over the past decade, but Brustman doubts that Ajax can reach A-section in the near future. The team that took Ajax through the grades in the glory years was full of rare gems. To return to those heights, every talented Jewish footballer would have to pull on the Ajax guernsey and play at his peak. I mentioned that a few outsiders might help the club on its way. Brustman looked ahead with a blank expression. "You have to be Jewish," he said. All members of every Jewish sporting club in the world must be Jewish. It's a stipulation of the

Maccabi association, to which every Jewish sporting club belongs. The exclusion policy maintains strong ties in the Jewish community and limits the chance of marrying outsiders. The ties are strengthened with the Maccabi Games in Israel every four years, though Australian football is not part of them.

Sport has been a binding force for Melbourne Jews since families began shifting from Carlton to the south of the city after the Depression. The annual football match between teams from the Jewish communities north and south of the Yarra River was one of the biggest events on the social calendar. In 1956, the footballers had the idea of expanding on the annual match and forming a club called Ajax, to play in the Amateurs. St Kilda president Reuben Sackville organised jumpers with the Star of David in place of the Saints' emblem and the Jackas made their home debut at the ground behind Luna Park known as the Peanut Farm. The symbolism of the Star of David was lost on Amateurs secretary Jack Fullerton, who, at the Jackas' first presentation night, congratulated the club on its season and reminded everybody that the important thing in life was to be good Christians.

Misunderstanding was common in this era, as Melbourne grappled with the addition of bagels and baklava to its cultural palate, but it was preferable to racism. In 1959, Port Melbourne Amateurs captain Joe Harrison told his team that anyone uttering an anti-Semitic remark would have to deal with him. The two clubs had several spectacular brawls but Ajax appreciated the absence of racism. The next year, Joe Harrison was killed in a car accident and several Ajax players and officials went to his funeral. Against other opponents, the Jackas just tried to ignore the racist remarks. Every so often a player would crack but, for most Jackas, who were more attuned to books and study than pugilism, retribution was not an option. Before a game against Coburg, two players decided to do something about the club's lack of intimidation and applied bubblegum tattoos. The effect was lost when rain fell and the tattoos ran down their arms. Ajax have always had a nice line in self-deprecation.

Soon afterwards came the incident that John Brustman described as the lowest point in the club's history. It was the 1972 season in E-section. Ajax explained to the Amateurs executive that the Jewish New Year was to fall on grand final day and asked for a change of date if the seniors or reserves made the decider. The Amateurs executive rejected the request. The reserves won the second semi-final by 10 goals and Old Ivanhoe won the grand final by forfeit. In the rematch between the clubs the next year, the seniors and reserves games disintegrated into spiteful brawls. Hostility continued between the two clubs for several years.

In 1975, the Amateurs realised their insensitivity and moved the grand final away from the Jewish New Year. Ajax won the flag and unlocked their golden era. More and more high-quality players returned as the club moved up the grades. One season, Mordy Bromberg returned from St Kilda for six games and almost pinched the best-and-fairest. The club rose four grades in five years to achieve the unthinkable. The bookish Jews were in A-section.

I remember seeing Ajax once in those lofty years, on a sunny day at St Bernard's when I watched from the logs on the hill. I never thought to listen for racist remarks but I do remember thinking that Ajax had many players with dark, curly hair and most of them were short. From memory, St Bernard's were about to be relegated but they managed to scrape out a win. A few years later, I ran on to the Ajax oval at Albert Park and I couldn't believe how short their players were. By this time I was fully grown, which at 180 centimetres was unimposing, but my opponent barely reached my shoulder, which was unnerving. It was a windy day and the ball was often on the ground. Ajax players scampered everywhere but we controlled the match without incident. The match was so totally without incident that I remember watching the ball in the forward line and wondering whether I'd ever met a Jew. To my knowledge I hadn't, but most of my teammates had. St Bernard's spent the previous few seasons under Michael Ritterman. The coach had won four competition best-and-fairests in five years at Ajax but he failed to turn the fortunes of St Bernard's. The gap in culture was large.

In that one match in which I played against Ajax, I don't remember racist remarks. But at 18 years of age, I had no concept that anyone would bother. I defer to John Brustman, who said racism was rife 20 or 25 years ago. "It used to be every week – very anti-Semitic." He added that it had dropped off in recent years. "It's almost non-existent lately. I just think people are more educated, more tolerant."

The Amateurs, following the lead of the AFL, have done their bit to stamp out racism. In 1997, a St Bernard's player was found guilty of racially vilifying a Jewish midfielder from Old Scotch. The St Bernard's player was suspended for four matches and the club was ordered to get a speaker from the Human Rights Commission. For the Scotch player, the controversy was another chapter in a tumultuous season. Phil Goldberg and his twin brother Brian had created a storm in Jewish circles by playing at Scotch rather than Ajax. They said they wanted to play in A-section rather than D-section. Debate raged in the *Jewish News*, with several correspondents taking the decision as a snub. It was questioned why the twins would aspire to the top level of the Amateurs when they'd played with the Melbourne reserves and in the VFL. They'd achieved to their best and now it was time to return to their community. John Brustman was among those who believed that their community needed them. "In fairness, they came back," he said. "They all come back in the end."

Phil Goldberg was named Ajax vice-captain in 1999, another season in which the grand final had been scheduled on the same day as the Jewish New Year. Ajax notified the Amateurs of the clash before the first round. When it became clear that the Jackas would reach the finals, other potential finalists were asked to nominate alternative grand finals dates. The Jewish New Year is celebrated every September, and occasionally on a Sabbath, which is from dusk on Friday to dusk on Saturday. Alternatives ranged from Monday night under lights to the Saturday after the Jewish celebration. Monash Blues nominated Friday afternoon. By the time the Blues had won the preliminary final, their nomination was the Saturday after the Jewish celebration. The delay meant Ajax had three weeks off after winning the second semi-final. Their lack of match fitness took its toll late in the game, but their 13 goals in the second quarter proved enough to secure the club's first flag for two decades.

Phil and Brian Goldberg retired before the new season but Julian Kirzner returned. The high-leaping spearhead was struggling to overcome the injuries that had curtailed his career at Essendon and North Melbourne. He was in and out of the side as Ajax struggled to settle down. Against Prahran, he was the strong option in attack but a howling wind down the home straight of the grand-prix racetrack made it a difficult day for marking forwards. Kirzner's match ended when another knee injury forced him from the field. A broken hand also forced rover Michael

Konsky to the bench. Konsky had been best on ground, with frenetic work at the foot of the packs. Ajax coach Wayne Harmes took the blow in his stride. The former Carlton defender saw no reason to get upset about things that he couldn't change.

Harmes was as relaxed as his Prahran counterpart, former Richmond captain Tony Free, was intense. The pair had represented their clubs in the back pocket but that's where the similarities end. Free had tried to lift a struggling club, Richmond, towards success; Harmes had played in three Carlton premierships by his early his 20s. A knee injury had forced Free to retire in his prime; Harmes played until he was too slow. Free learned the ropes of coaching as an assistant at Richmond; Harmes helped his old teammate Des English at Airport West. Free was intent on game plan and structure; Harmes urged his players to attack the ball. Even their appearances were poles apart. Free was neat and crisp in fashionable jeans and shirt-sleeves rolled to his elbows; Harmes looked like he'd been watching television all night.

Harmes wore tracksuit pants, a bulky parka and a peaked cap. He had a goatee beard and he worked his jaw over his chewing gum. He might have started by helping Des English at a blue-collar club in the suburbs but within a few years he was at Old Scotch. After the match, he revealed that different clubs are all the same.

"Is it fair to say you're a knockabout bloke?" I asked him.

"Oh, shit yeah."

"How did you cope at Old Scotch?"

"I get asked that question a lot, but it doesn't matter where you come from. A footy club's a footy club, whether it's Old Scotch or Essendon or Oak Park."

"What about Ajax? It's a very tight community … "

"It's a different culture when the players have to be Jewish and the coaches obviously aren't – Harmes being of German extract – but a footy club's a footy club whether you're Jewish, Chinese, Arabic, Catholic, whatever. It's still a footy club."

Prahran is not the same as most footy clubs. It's a merger of the former VFA club Prahran, which was forced from the field by debt in 1994, and a conglomerate from the Amateurs. The original parties in the conglomerate were the Commonwealth Bank and State Bank clubs, which became Southbank. After the 1998 season, development around the Melbourne Park tennis centre forced Southbank to look for a new ground. Prahran had traded out of debt and were looking for players. The Prahran Amateur Football Club was formed.

The club spent its first season doing well to avoid relegation from C-section. The unavailability of Prahran's traditional ground, Toorak Park, which has been the home of Old Xaverians since the mid-'90s, forced it to train at Royal Park, which is in Parkville, and play home games all over Melbourne. Before the 2000 season, the club pledged to continue to fight for Toorak Park and continue with plans to set up a multi-sports complex. Junior development programs were put in place using funds from the club's Tabaret in Chapel Street and the Two Blues set themselves the ambition of reaching A-section in five years.

Tony Free described the aim as aggressive but achievable. Strong recruiting would be vital. The native of the Mallee hooked into his country networks. He invited friends from Swan Hill and he recruited David Gallagher, the Prahran captain, from Bendigo. His prized recruit, Travis St Clair, was also from Bendigo. Free recruited him by chance. The coach had rung a share house looking for a potential recruit when St Clair answered the phone. A conversation began. St Clair told Free that he was tiring of his weekly journeys from Melbourne to play in the Bendigo league. Free persuaded the key forward to come down to Prahran. The only problem was reinstatement. St Clair had been drafted by two AFL clubs and had played at several leading country clubs. Prahran went to many lengths to earn his permit, so Free felt let down when St Clair was reported against Ajax.

The teams were level with five goals each at half-time. Scoring had been difficult but the match was absorbing because of the contrast in styles. Ajax were mercurial and relaxed, reflecting their coach, while Prahran were edgy, also reflecting their coach. Prahran attempted to overwhelm Ajax with physical force but their efforts were in vain. Their frustration wasn't helped by their fear of making mistakes. The match was taut. Something had to give. St Clair provided the release when he was reported for striking. His send-off marked a turning point, with big men trying to make up for his loss by throwing their weight around. Prahran supporters let out shrill cries when a collision was imminent. The Ajax players kept battling for the ball, neither retaliating nor even acknowledging that the tempo had lifted.

The visiting supporters became more vocal with each heavy clash. Tempers became heated when a Prahran water boy mouthed off at the crowd. Ajax fans gave him an earful in return. The water boy was cocky because he had an official band around his arm. He strutted around the boundary and invited the heckling. His charade became ridiculous when he started pulling faces. There was something about his belief that an official armband and water bottles made him untouchable that annoyed me. I dropped the façade of the neutral observer and yelled that he must have something better to do than pull faces, an innocuous suggestion that prompted him to stop and stare, the cuffs of his white overalls tumbling over his runners and a water bottle cocked in each hand. We must have looked pretty stupid, me with a note book and a red face and him with an opinion of himself that was as big as his overalls, but distraction intervened in the form of a melee inside the boundary. It was one of those moments when emotions on the field and in the crowd feed off each other. The performing water boy trudged around the fringe of the melee, chuffed to be close to the action but miffed at becoming a sideshow. The main event was harmless, with Prahran pushing and shoving in the role of the schoolyard bully and Ajax playing the part of the brothers under siege. "Watch out, they're all family," said one Prahran supporter. His friends tried a combination of nervous laughter and searching for a hole to swallow them up. The Ajax supporters said nothing. The sudden silence disturbed the players and the melee melted away. Ajax kicked three goals with the wind and the Two Blues were held scoreless.

In the Ajax huddle, the players looked quizzically at their coach. Wayne Harmes was excited. He crouched low and exhorted his playing to continue attacking the ball. He made much of the fact that it was a close game, a scenario that seemed to bring out the best in him. In the dying moments of the 1979 grand final, Harmes was central to one of the most famous incidents in football history when he retrieved the ball from the second row of the grandstand and belted it to Ken Sheldon, who kicked the winning goal. This one incident has given Harmes an aura in close games. The Ajax huddle didn't seem worried in any case. The players relaxed with their backs to the wind.

Tony Free took the modern approach. He was calm and instructive, urging his team to channel their energy at the ball, but I couldn't help feel the players wanted to get excited. They wanted a pep talk, if only to break the tension. Free spoke of using their hatred of Ajax to advantage. Apparently, one or two incidents had happened in the Southbank days. Ajax supporters later said they never thought about it, but Prahran seemed intent on making it an issue. "Be aggressive, but be smart about it," said Free. It was a neat summary of his playing career.

Early in the last quarter, the Prahran coach had cause to regret one phone call in his recruiting campaign when Travis St Clair was again reported for striking, sending him straight back to the bench. His team-mates soldiered on, and looked a chance when Aaron Rhodes used the wind to kick a goal from way out near the boundary. "He's kicked it from St Kilda Road," said one fan. But Ajax were revelling in the loose man. Defenders flew over packs and back into packs to take a series of courageous marks. A feature of the Jackas' game was the players of medium height who outwitted taller opponents in the air. Among the best players in the air was Grant Samuel, the son of AFL commissioner Graham Samuel. Samuel senior was an ordinary Ajax player who became one of the most powerful men in football.

In attack, Marty Halphen sealed the match with a captain's goal. Nobody else had been able to find the goals against the wind unless they were about to trip over the goal-line, but Halphen nailed a banana from the pocket. His execution was matched only by his timing. Ajax steadied and held on for victory by 10 points. The match had been compelling, a contest of wills and a contrast of styles. It was significant that, when the match was in the balance, the side drawn from the tight community, whose players had known each other since childhood, came through. The side drawn from all over Victoria was left to ponder its ambition.

In the rooms, the Ajax players were content rather than jumping up and down. Michael Konsky nursed his hand and Julian Kirzner revealed the frustration of too many injuries. He would require another knee reconstruction. Outside the rooms, Wayne Harmes pulled a roll-your-own out of his packet and praised his side for its best win of the year. If only the players could stir themselves to be consistent, he said. Harmes expressed concern for Kirzner but he kept smiling. He knows that footy is a roller-coaster ride.

The Prahran rooms were tense. Tony Free was fuming. He hunched over his match details as players moved in and out of the showers in silence. A proud man who expects a lot of himself, the drop from AFL to C-section Amateurs seemed to frustrate him. On the phone during the week, Free was personable and articulate. He said the indiscipline of Travis St Clair had cost his side the match, which was true, but I wouldn't say it was the sole reason for defeat. The Prahran upheavals were still settling down and the recruits were yet to click.

At Ajax, there would never be any such problem.

Ajax lost the preliminary final to Therry-Penola Old Boys, who went on to win the grand final. Prahran finished seventh. Wayne Harmes left Ajax to coach Therry-Penola. Tony Free remained coach of Prahran. Gabriel Dukes, the 19-year-old centreman, became the youngest player to win an Ajax best-and-fairest. He then left Melbourne to live in Israel. Rover Tim Murphy won the Prahran best-and-fairest from centre half-back Dave Gallagher. The next season, Prahran began training at Como Park in South Yarra, sharing the ground with Old Geelong, and drew up plans to develop training facilities at Gardiner Park, off Malvern Road. The Two Blues would share the facilities with Old Xaverians. Both clubs would share Toorak Park for home matches.

14

MARCHING ON

Echuca v Shepparton Swans
the Murray Bombers and the Swans

"I always thought there was some unfinished business."

Echuca coach Ken Sheldon

In 1993, St Kilda's promising season went off the rails around the time that Nicky Winmar went on strike for higher pay and Tony Lockett was injured. The Saints finished 12th and Ken Sheldon was sacked, despite having coached the Saints to two finals series in four years. "You go into the coaching business knowing these things can happen," he said at the time. "I'll sit back and have a good think about what's on offer. I'll be fine."

Seven years later, as he prepared Echuca for their match against the Shepparton Swans, the former Lemnos Football Club, Sheldon maintained his grace about his ejection from St Kilda. "You can't be bitter," he said. But there was resignation in his voice, rather than acceptance. He'd left St Kilda ranking behind only Allan Jeans, who coached for 16 years, as the longest-serving coach in the club's history. At the age of 33, he had reason to believe that an AFL rival would dismiss his sacking at St Kilda as the work of a club beset by instability and offer him a job. But the opportunities failed to appear. Sheldon moved to South Australian National

Football League club South Adelaide, where the Panthers came within percentage of the finals in successive years, but again he was sacked. He stayed in Adelaide to work in the media while his prospects of returning to the AFL as a coach ebbed away. In the rooms at Echuca, he admitted his regret at not having another chance to coach in the AFL. "I always thought there was some unfinished business," he said. Then he paused. For a moment the scar was exposed.

It was to be his only pause in an interview that began with a one-hour phone interview on Friday night and resumed in the rooms before the match. The 41-year-old was cheeky and likeable. His agenda was to push his youth policy at Echuca. My agenda was to interview him in the wake of Tim Watson's resignation at St Kilda. The prospect of talking about another Saints coach on the scrap heap failed to thrill him but Sheldon took care to answer my questions. On the curly matters, he creased his brow before emitting one forthright line of reply. Other times, he was the cagey rover who played in three Carlton premierships by the age of 23.

The previous night, St Kilda had rebounded from months of insipid performances to defeat Geelong. Sheldon said it was a shame that it took Watson's resignation to spark the Saints into action. He hedged, however, at the question of whether Watson should have resigned; he said that only the inner sanctum truly knows what goes on in a match committee. "As Tim said, you go into coaching with your eyes open."

Sheldon was more prepared to comment on another announcement of that week: that Rodney Eade, in his fifth season at the Swans, was about to pass the games record for a coach at South Melbourne or Sydney. He was emphasising the records of the Swans and St Kilda compared with Essendon under Kevin Sheedy and Carlton under David Parkin. "Rodney Eade is now the longest-serving coach at a club with a history of 112 years," Sheldon said. "How ridiculous is that? It's a reflection of the club."

Sheldon grew up west of Echuca, in the wheat town of Mitiamo. As a teenager I followed his league career because my father had mentioned Mitiamo in his stories of chasing rabbits in his school days, and because the town sounded like the name of an Indian chief in a dodgy western. My great-grandfather, Mark Daffey, is in the front row in the photo of Mitiamo's 1900 premiership team, arms folded, moustache bristling. The Daffeys ran a pub in Mitiamo but the business dwindled and they moved to Kangaroo Flat. The mention of Ken Sheldon used to bring to mind the little family history I knew.

At 16 years of age, when he left Mitiamo, Sheldon wanted to play in a premiership, notch 100 league games, play for Victoria and return home. Four years later he kicked the goal that sealed Carlton's victory over Collingwood in the 1979 grand final. Around this time, he gained the nickname of Bomba on a footy trip to Fiji. To win a bet, he scaled a palm tree in a disco and was named after the character in *Jungle Book*. Three years later he was a member of three flag sides, a Victorian representative, and on the verge of his 100th game. Injuries filled his next few years and he lost focus.

The Blues stocked up before the 1986 season, with Craig Bradley and Steve Kernahan among the recruits, and some premiership heroes were superseded. Before the finals, coach Robert Walls told Sheldon he was not under consideration for the senior side. Sheldon remains proud that he was captain of the reserves side that won the premiership. He then considered a move to East Fremantle as assistant coach before St Kilda swooped on him and Alex Marcou. He played another three seasons at St Kilda, mainly in the back pocket, before turning up to his coaching interview with a dossier outlining his scheme to change a club he believed had failure dripping from the brickwork. The cover was the famous photo of him kicking the goal that sank Collingwood in the 1979 grand final, a photo that depicted success. Inside he listed overhauls in everything from dress and behavior to the heating in the boot-room. His point was that a freezing boot-room would never be tolerated at a club with attention to detail. The job was his.

Sheldon said midway through his reign at Moorabbin that he thrived on the pressure. When reminded of this comment in Echuca, he laughed. "There was never a shortage of challenges."

His return to northern Victoria had nothing to do with the challenge of coaching in grass-roots football. He was simply fulfilling his teenage pledge to return home. But after settling into a job in financial planning and real estate, the challenge of coaching was offered and he was happy to take it on.

Echuca had paid big money for one premiership in the previous five years. In 1999, the Bombers were knocked out of the finals in straight sets and Sheldon, perhaps wishing to distinguish himself from his predecessors, was unequivocal about blaming high-priced recruits. "They didn't produce in the fat time," he said.

The Bombers retained a couple of big-name recruits, such as Brad Smith, a full-forward from the Diamond Valley league, and Jeremy Smith, a wandering Tasmanian, but the emphasis was on youth. Sheldon talked up Kristan Height, Scott McGlone and Rhys Archard, who were Year 11 class-mates at St Joseph's College, the school in the grand old convent around the corner from Echuca's ground, Victoria Park. Coaches who ramble on about youth are sometimes safeguarding against failure – nobody expects too much of a young side – but Sheldon did seem to enjoy the prospect of moulding a team. At the same time, he was canny enough to retain a core of experienced players so that he wouldn't have to sink to the bottom before rising.

I had a fair knowledge of his side's make-up – more knowledge than I had about his feelings on Tim Watson's resignation – when I turned up in the cavernous dressing-rooms below the old stand. I was taken aback, however, when Sheldon asked me to reveal my knowledge to his team. One minute he was rubbing his hands together and addressing his players about the importance of keeping in touch with the top six; the next minute, like a Greg Williams handball from nowhere, he switched the direction of the game on to me. "Tell the boys what we talked about last night, Paul."

About 30 heads turned in silence, making me distinctly uncomfortable. As well as preferring to stand at the back of the room and mind my own business, I squirmed because Sheldon had told his players I was there to write about the club. That was part of my reason for being there. Sheldon knew my main mission was to write about him and the St Kilda Erstwhile Coaches Club, but his plan worked perfectly. Instead of stating to the Echuca people that Tim Watson's resignation had cast a topical light on their leader, I told them that their club had recruited heavily in recent years, with the 1997 premiership its reward. Two years later it finished on top of the ladder but missed the grand final. Under Sheldon, the club had resisted recruiting big names. Retirements, clearances and injuries had forced a rebuild. Almost a dozen players had made their senior debuts. Echuca were about mid-table.

Sheldon looked at me with his hands clasped and his mouth agape for a few unsettling seconds. I was worried I'd somehow dropped a clanger, or missed his intention, but the coach returned his gaze to his players. "There you go," he said. "We're in a rebuilding phase."

I was off the hook, and Sheldon was off on his favorite tangent: counting the teenagers who'd made their senior debuts. Then he grouped together veterans Patrick Pellegrino, Troy O'Brien and Tim Edgar. The trio had recently played their 150th games and were vital in his scheme to balance experience with youth. Ashley Byrne, the centre half-back who was drafted by Fitzroy in 1987, was also vital in this scheme but the main plank was Glenn Fitzpatrick, who the previous week had gathered 48 possessions.

Sheldon had been forced to work hard during the pre-season to persuade Fitzpatrick to play one more year. The 35-year-old had played at clubs throughout Victoria and in the Amateurs in Perth. I knew him when he was at teachers' college with a friend of mine in Ballarat. In those days, he played reserves at East Ballarat because he was devoting a lot of energy to the social side of teachers' college. But he obviously found his focus because the next I heard he was coaching Woorinen, outside Swan Hill, and he was selected in the Victorian Country squad. He'd also become a responsible, if nomadic, teacher, with his stint at a school in Kuwait coinciding with the beginning of the Gulf War. Sheldon said Fitzpatrick's leadership had been vital to the club's improvement. After winning only two of the first seven games, the Bombers had notched three victories in a month. "Our performances in the past few weeks have been as enjoyable as anything in footy," he said.

The coach paced in slow circles. The soles of his RM Williams boots made a gentle clomping sound on the floorboards and he crouched, seemingly ready to pounce. His eyes danced when making every point, and he gave me a lesson in the lexicon of football. I'm still getting used to "process" as the buzzword for adherence to a game plan but Sheldon has moved on to "methodology", which has too many syllables for a pre-match address, and other words such as "springer", which I quite like. It's the term for the forward who leaps over the ruckmen at throw-ins. Sheldon later explained that he's in constant touch with his football contacts throughout the cities. He coaches at a ground in a bend of the Murray River, but the language of the big stadiums is never far away.

After the address, Sam Sheldon, the youngest of the coach's four children, shuffled through the room with reluctance written all over him. The 11-year-old had been lined up with his cousin Tom, also 11, to be a water boy, but Sam was wondering whether he might have a day off. Ken Sheldon looked at his son. "Not hungry enough," he said.

Behind them, Simon Eishold looked like he hadn't gone hungry in months. The former AFL midfielder was bulging beneath his fluorescent yellow runner's uniform, not that it worried him. At 33, he was enjoying his first year of retirement. Eishold arrived in Echuca after his father-in-law, Doug Crow from Kyabram, left a message on his phone that he was mad to be slushing through the mud in the Richmond reserves when the sun was shining in the Goulburn Valley. Eishold agreed, and applied for the Echuca coaching position. In five years, he led the Bombers to four grand finals and won a league medal. In his final year, he relinquished the coaching role and won his fourth club best-and-fairest. Sheldon was keen for Eishold to remain around the club as a role model and, in his fluorescent get-up, he looked as content as any man I've seen in retirement. His last words to me were to try the kebabs from the caravan in front of the grandstand. "They're nice and fatty," he said.

As the reserves siren rang out, Sheldon sidled up to Glenn Roberts, the Bombers' secretary, and muttered from the side of his mouth that a goodwill gesture for the Swans reserves might be an idea. He wanted to give them drink vouchers to reward their efforts in avoiding a forfeit. With only 10 players available, the Swans had brought up a dozen under-18s and fixed a ring of tape to their arms. Echuca players agreed to go easy on the teenagers with the armbands but it made little difference to the result. The Bombers won by 21 goals before embarking on an exercise session in the rooms to make up for their inexacting match. The Bombers' seniors ran on to the ground as the reserves ran from one end of the room to the other and sang the theme from the movie *Stripes*.

Both sides kicked five goals in the first quarter and Sheldon was livid. He believed the Bombers were coasting after their easy victory over Mooroopna the previous week. "You kick 20 goals in a half and your heads go boof," he said, making the gesture for big heads. Sheldon had already made it clear that he hated coasting. In the previous month, he dropped Allan Corrie, the assistant coach, and Jeremy Smith, who played one game for Carlton in 1993. Smith responded by kicking nine goals in the reserves and 13 in his return to the seniors. It was all part of Sheldon's policy of changing the culture. The coach had even threatened to drop Mark Heritage, the captain, at the final break in a match against Tatura, but the red-headed defender saved him the trouble by breaking his ankle in the last quarter.

Heritage was a brilliant prospect at Golden Square when I played at Wade Street. In half a season, he graduated from being a cocky schoolboy who hung around training in his Catholic College uniform, having a kick on the boundary line and pestering the coach for attention, to being a senior wingman who kicked raking goals on the run. He had the left-footer's knack of running 20 metres, as smooth as glass, and booting the ball long and low. He seemed to me to have the talent to emulate another Golden Square product, Wayne Campbell, even if their games were completely different, but he failed to grow quite tall enough or strong enough. After bumping into him on the sidelines at Echuca, I guessed he would be about 180 centimetres.

He still had the cheek of his school days. When Sheldon arrived in Echuca, Heritage warned him against delivering any tirades. He was referring to a practice match when he was a teenage hopeful at Moorabbin and Sheldon turned the air blue. "He tore everyone to pieces," Heritage said. "He just degraded everyone. When he came here I said, 'You've got to relax, and acclimatise. You're from the country and you've got to get back to that'." Sheldon believed his tirade had been positive. He wasn't degrading anyone; he was challenging the Saints to take the responsibility of becoming premiership prospects. Back at Echuca, he said he was looking forward to the return of Heritage at centre half-back.

In the grandstand, teenagers vied for the attention of former thirds coach Mick Mulvahill. The burly social worker traded quips with his young friends in between answering my questions. All the while he was chuckling. He said Sheldon had struggled to readjust to the different demands of country football, but he admired him for stepping back. "He relates terrifically with the young blokes," Mulvahill said. "They know that if they're good enough they'll play seniors."

Behind the bar, Jay Galvin became worked up when I asked whether Sheldon was good for Echuca. He said Sheldon shouldn't have been coaching there. "He should be coaching the red, white and black. He had one ordinary year, and that's got to happen." Galvin leaned over the bar and raised the sleeve of his flannelette shirt to reveal a St Kilda tattoo. His great passions were the Saints and Echuca. "The club tried to buy a premiership last year and failed," he said. "Sheldon's got the kids going well."

The half-time siren sounded as Galvin pulled another can from a large tub of ice. He slid the can over the wooden bar that stretched across the length of the tin shelter. A few metres away, the footballers trundled into the rooms beneath the historic grandstand. Echuca were down by three points but home fans appeared unworried as they leaned back on the bar, ignoring the chill of the dull afternoon. Sheldon sensed a similar nonchalance in the dressing-rooms. "I've been in games like this," he said. "You blokes think you're going to win."

He dropped the aggressive goading of quarter-time but complacency remained his concern. He attacked the lack of second efforts and lack of thought when kicking into the wind. He scolded some players for wearing moulded soles and, in urging his side to dig deep, he bent down and lifted an imaginary load from the floorboards. His eyes widened and circled the room. "Whatever you've got, pull it out," he said. Then he bent down and lifted another load from the floorboards. "If it doesn't work the first time, keep going the second time."

In the second half, Glenn Fitzpatrick picked up another swag of possessions and Silus Laidlaw, who works in summer as a clown in a touring emu show, came out on top in the ruck duels. Brad Smith was strong and agile at full-forward, but the hero of the day was Rhys Archard, the 16-year-old who was a favorite among supporters because he preferred Echuca to the Bendigo Pioneers. Archard was reluctant to travel around south-east Australia playing in the TAC Cup for under-18s because he wanted to ride trackwork for his father. Staying at Echuca enabled him to work the horses. He kicked eight goals against the Shepparton Swans as the Bombers cruised to a 49-point win.

Sheldon said he was pleased with his side's performance, which brought the ledger to six wins and six losses and left the door open for a finals berth. He celebrated in the clubrooms for a few hours, which was a regular practice. President Bob Martin said Sheldon usually arrived at the ground around 10am for the thirds match and often stayed until 10pm. "He believes a big part of coaching any club is talking to everyone," Martin said. Such a routine wouldn't be possible if Sheldon were shy and retiring. I asked him whether his reputation for social shenanigans in the AFL had been overstated. "Footy's been a lot of fun – put it that way," he said.

At Carlton, he was renowned for working as hard at parties as he did on the training track. Sheldon admitted he lost focus when he was injured, but he also said he was unsettled. He was in his late 20s before he adjusted to life in Melbourne. At St Kilda, he was a useful performer in the social club disco, and he remained social when he became a coach. But it struck me that his distaste for complacency stems from his playing days. He made his Carlton debut in 1977 at 18 years of age and, two years later, kicked 53 goals to be the leading goalkicker in a premiership year. His three flags at a tender age, in a team that is considered among the most exciting in the history of the competition, must have convinced him that football success comes easily.

In later years, he learned the value of hunger. His statement that his son lacked hunger was a gentle prod, but it also contained the nub of his approach to life. Ken Sheldon knows that achieving to the full sometimes requires the hand of fate. He knows it certainly requires stability, but it also requires sustained drive. That was the lesson he was trying to teach his players at Echuca.

Echuca finished outside the finals, with Brad Smith winning the best-and-fairest after kicking more than 60 goals and filling in holes at centre half-back and in the ruck. Glenn Fitzpatrick finished second in the best-and-fairest, bought some cheap skiing gear and went to live in the Ukraine. Kristan Height and Scott McGlone went to the Bendigo Pioneers. Rhys Archard had shoulder surgery after a trackwork accident. Shepparton Swans finished well down the ladder. Centre half-forward Jason Rachele won the Swans' best-and-fairest from midfielder Garry Merritt.

15

LAND OF THE DANIHERS

Ungarie v Girral-West Wyalong
the Magpies and the Bulldogs

"Australia is divided by a deep cultural rift between the north and south
known as the Barassi line. It runs between Canberra, Broken Hill,
Birdsville and Maningrida and it divides Australia between
rugby and 'rules'."

Historian Ian Turner, The Great Australian Book of Football Stories

---

Ungarie might be enshrined in Australian sporting folklore as the home of
the Daniher brothers but, at 650 kilometres north of Melbourne, it's a long
way to drive for a bush footy match. Just as I was beginning to doubt the
wisdom of the journey, about the same time that I began to lose my bear-
ings because there were no Victoria Bitter or Carlton Draught signs on the
façades of pubs, an unexpected bonus presented itself in the otherwise drab
town of Temora.

On my left was an expansive pub of golden bricks, of the type favored
in New South Wales but never seen in Victoria, with Tooheys New signs
in bold, black letters. But on my right, smack in the centre of town, was
the statue of Paleface Adios, the Temora Tornado, whose distinctive white
blaze had failed to cross my mind for two decades. Now it featured in
recollections of Saturday nights at Moonee Valley, when, like many early
teenagers around Essendon, I was too young to go to parties but somehow
old enough to bet on the horses. In one of several farewell races, Paleface

Adios streamed four-wide down the straight to win in typically dramatic fashion, providing one of my earliest sporting highlights. I wasn't sure that Ungarie would provide a sporting highlight but, after seeing the likeness of the lairy chesnut, who often seemed to have luck on his side, I was satisfied that the long journey into a strange land would be worth my while.

The entrance to Ungarie was underwhelming. While Ararat proclaims itself as the birthplace of cyclist Shane Kelly and Inglewood, near Bendigo, asserts itself as the birthplace of Sir Reginald Ansett – even though he wasn't a sportsman – Ungarie neglects to stake its claim on the Danihers. Instead, a sign says: "Welcome to Ungarie." Neither did the main street provide any recognition. The main street was wide, in the fashion of most towns north of the Murray River, but there was no representation of, say, the famous photo from 1990, when the four brothers played their only AFL game together. The street featured a few shops, the stock and station agent and a café, or what southern Victorians would call a milk bar. The main pub consisted of red bricks, rather than golden bricks, and both pubs featured Tooheys signs on the guttering.

The football ground was on the other side of Humbug Creek. I dipped the 1985 Fairmont down the floodway and found the oval, which firmly belonged in the no-frills category. The rooms are concrete and boxy and the canteen is wrapped in corrugated iron. The grass is streaky and a sea of endless plains surrounds the ground, making the urban Victorians in the crowd feel a bit dizzy in all the space. The sky was as endless as the plains. The Danihers come from wide open country.

Chris Daniher was strolling across the old netball court, trampling on the weeds that strained through the asphalt, when I introduced myself. He was polite and welcoming, with unkempt hair and many freckles, and he was taller than I remembered in the No.7 guernsey for the Bombers. In his jeans and runners, he looked lofty enough to be a key forward, yet during his Essendon career he was lucky if he ever played in attack. His career at Windy Hill was renowned for industry, rather than heroics in the forward line. As a teenager, his progress was delayed when he damaged his knee on the Ungarie swings after a few drinks to celebrate the end of the harvest. He had a reconstruction but it took him years before he was considered a regular member of the Bombers' side. He played his 100th game at 30 years of age in a feat that defined his career. His work ethic was so strong that, after scrubbing windows all day for his brothers' window-cleaning business, he sometimes fell asleep on the masseurs' table before training.

After the 1997 season, Daniher took his work ethic back to its place of origin, the family farm, where he gives his father Jim a hand with the sheep and crops. He also took on the coaching job at Temora, whose location as the northernmost club in the Riverina league still leaves it a fair way south of Ungarie. Daniher tired of three-hour round trips for training, and the journeys were longer for matches at Wagga and Griffith. Injuries also took their toll before the 34-year-old resigned after two frustrating seasons and agreed to complete a fabled loop. Terry had played in Wagga until he was in his 40s before returning to Melbourne to join the Essendon coaching staff. Neale had moved straight from playing into coaching at the top level, and Tony had remained in Melbourne to hold up the window-cleaning business. In signing with Ungarie, Chris became the only Daniher to finish his career at the family's home club.

In football circles, the Danihers' home club could hardly be more famous if the Harbor Bridge ran over the Humbug Creek. Ungarie secretary Lyn McGrane said her home town attracts curiosity in all parts south. "It happened when I went to buy a car in Albury. I mentioned Ungarie and the bloke went on and on and on about the Danihers. I said, 'I'll get you an autograph if it'll make the car any cheaper'."

The Danihers' link with Ungarie began when Jim Daniher, the grandfather of the Essendon brothers, moved from Miepoll, near Euroa, to the Riverina under the closer settlement scheme early last century. Jim Daniher had won best player awards at Longwood and Euroa before moving to Ungarie, where he was the foundation president of the football club in 1914. He would also serve as the president of the rugby league club. The closer settlement scheme, which aimed to decrease the size of sheep stations and populate the land, attracted many Victorians and South Australians. The Riverina traditionally had close links to Victoria, because of Melbourne's economic dominance after the gold rush and because of the difficulty of building railway lines over the mountains to Sydney, but the influx of southerners helped to strengthen the hold of the southern game in the region.

In 1924 Jim Daniher played in an Ungarie premiership. His son Jim continues to count the premiership medallion among his prized possessions to this day. In approaching Jim the son for an interview, I was a little daunted. At 74 years of age, he was tall, if stooped, with a half-grin and a stream of laconic wisecracks. He didn't say yes or no to an interview; he just smiled wryly and let the questions come. We began by establishing the family tree. Jim and his two brothers had married three Irwin sisters from Toolleen, a town outside Bendigo. Jim and Edna had 11 children, Jack and Beryl also had 11, and Leo and Dorothy had six. Boys from all three families tried out at South Melbourne as teenagers.

Jim Daniher junior won his first league best-and-fairest in the early years of the Northern Riverina league, which began after the Second World War. Leo won a league medal as well. Within a decade Jim had won three league medals but it wasn't until 1974, almost three decades after he first played for the Magpies, that he put the finishing touch on his career. Terry, the oldest of his tribe, had just won the league best-and-fairest award at 16 years of age. Father and son lined up together and guided the Magpies to an overdue premiership. A few years later Jim was 50 years of age and retired when his second son, Neale, returned from Assumption College for the holidays and played in an Ungarie flag. In all, Jim played for 28 seasons. When I asked how many games he played, he smiled and said: "I never counted them."

Jim was also renowned as a tough rugby league forward. His performances for the Riverina against a touring English side received constant mention during my weekend in Ungarie. Some said Jim was a better at rugby league than "rules", as football is known in the Northern Riverina. Jim prefers "rules". "Well, it's a better game, isn't it?" But his all-round talent was passed on to his sons and daughters, with two of his daughters playing state netball. Neale was considered a leading rugby union prospect when he was at boarding school in Goulburn, south of Sydney, but the word around Ungarie was that Jim made sure Neale transferred to Assumption College because he wanted him to play the southern code. Jim said he had no influence on Neale transferring to Assumption. He said Neale could see that Terry was doing well at South Melbourne and he wanted the chance to follow him. History records that South Melbourne traded Terry and Neale Daniher for Neville Fields in one of the great

Australian sporting blunders. Neale was traded straight out of school without setting foot on the Lakeside Oval.

Jim was self-effacing when asked about his rugby league match against the English. His only comment was: "It's a pretty tough game, league." It was a view I heard many times throughout the weekend. Ungarie sportsmen traditionally played "rules" on Saturdays and league on Sundays. Ungarie now has no rugby league club, which is unusual in the Northern Riverina, but most Magpies have tried their hand at the game and regard its physical demands with a mixture of awe and scorn. Three Magpies travelled into West Wyalong to play league on Sundays but the rest were happy to follow the game in the newspapers and on television, or simply ignore it. In my short time in Ungarie, I noticed none of the chest-thumping that is found in regions where one code has the monopoly. The Riverina is truly catholic in its sporting tastes. It reminds me of the Top End, where rugby league and the Australian game are embraced in roughly equal measure.

While Ungarie is distinctly a "rules" town, it's hardly inundated with footy culture. The newspapers are full of rugby league and it felt strange to be in the golf club, which doubles as the footy social rooms, on the Saturday night with no footy match on the television. A Wagga television station shows matches on Friday nights and Saturday afternoons, but never on Saturday nights, and only on Sundays when Sydney plays. It's possible to order Melbourne newspapers but no one seems interested. Most footy news is gained on the Internet or on pay-television. I had to admit to various Magpies that I'd never seen a football show on pay-television but, by the end of the season, I was beginning to realise the inroads that pay-television is making in football, especially in isolated areas.

The Australian game has made inroads in New South Wales with AusKick and the introduction of the NSW-ACT Rams into the TAC Cup for under-18s, while rugby league supporters are worried about development in their game. A fortnight before I was in the Riverina, the *West Wyalong Advocate* reported that the top two sides in the local rugby league competition were playing their matches before one man and his dog because they imported players; the bottom clubs had the highest gate takings because they fielded local players. It was claimed that Yanco-Wamoon had defeated lowly West Wyalong then approached the two best players from the beaten side with an "open chequebook". The previous season, Narrandera had won the premiership with a side consisting almost entirely of Pacific Islanders. The recruits were given food and board, while the locals were pushed into the background. When the locals did get a game, the Islanders from opposition clubs crushed them. Many Narrandera players drifted from the club and some drifted from the game. At the end of the season, the Islanders drifted elsewhere and Narrandera were left with no one. The club folded within months of winning the premiership.

Nobody in Ungarie was triumphant when telling me the parable of Narrandera, but I heard it several times. My research was hardly extensive but I did gain the impression that rugby league is faltering in the Riverina. Rodney Daniher, one of the cousins who tried out at South Melbourne in the '70s, said the AusKick program was redirecting the flow of talent from rugby league, and to a lesser extent rugby union and soccer, to the Australian game. "We used to get the leftovers," he said. "Now we're getting the goodies."

Rodney Daniher and his brothers Mark and Pat were key members of Ungarie sides in the '80s. Rodney said he and his brothers then left for Girral-West Wyalong because they wanted a challenge, but I understand that a coaching dispute prompted the move. The three Danihers and Kim Block led the Bulldogs to six premierships in seven years, a huge achievement considering the club had no tradition in "rules". West Wyalong, which is 40 kilometres south of Ungarie, is a rugby league town but the population of 3500 enabled the Danihers to piece together a strong "rules" team while their former club drifted down the ladder. Ungarie, for all the tradition lent by the Victorian and South Australian immigrants, has only 400 people, outnumbering only Tullibigeal for population.

The Magpies failed to return to the top of the ladder until 1999, when they thrashed Barellan United in the grand final. Their coach, Jamie Grintell, then headed 100 kilometres south to Ariah Park, the traditional first stop for Ungarie players wanting to try their hands in a higher league, but the return of Chris Daniher ensured that the Magpies remained on top. Daniher was reportedly in outstanding form for his home club, and enjoying his football more than injuries had allowed at Temora. He missed the penultimate match of the season because he went to a reunion at Windy Hill. Before this last match of the season, Daniher told me he'd enjoyed catching up with old Bombers before excusing himself and joining his Ungarie teammates in the shoebox dressing-rooms.

He emerged looking one or two inches shorter than in his street clothes, mainly because of his hunched running style. He wore an un-familiar black-and-white guernsey with the familiar No.7 on his back. His helmet was necessary after suffering repeated concussion during his career. The ball was bounced and the midfielder began a period of domination that would last until the final siren.

The match followed a remarkably regular pattern. Daniher or Lachlan Rowling, midfielders from founding families of the Ungarie football club, would sweep the ball from the centre and the Magpies would score. Steve Henley kicked six goals from centre half-forward in the first quarter and Daniher worked as hard as he would on the MCG. He had a hand in most passages of play but the lingering effects of a long-term virus forced him to labor. A couple of times he sharked the ball from packs with a precision that lent the impression of speed, but was the result of superb timing off the pack, and his ability to deliver the ball brought several forwards into the game. In one instance, he marked the ball, took one step and kicked with his left foot on to the chest of the leading David Zvonaric. At all times he looked to bring young forwards into the game rather than kick for goal himself.

Steve Henley grew so tired of shooting at goal by the second quarter that he kicked a point when he and the goal umpire could have shaken hands. His stumble embarrassed him but, in his more balanced moments, Henley was a raking kick, long and low without the familiar left-footer's grace. He was heavy-set but he was in constant motion, and he marked strongly. With Daniher, he was on another plane to all others on the enormous ground and it was easy to see him in a higher competition. A few years earlier, he'd played in the reserves at Windy Hill in between washing windows for the Daniher brothers. Over the weekend, I met several Ungarie footballers who occasionally wash windows in Melbourne. It emerged that the Danihers effectively sponsor a cultural exchange program, with Ungarie friends washing windows and taking in the city lights for a short time before returning home to the farm. Every player in the Magpies' line-up came from a farm. The Danihers had no choice but to be earthy.

At the breaks, Chris Daniher encouraged the Magpies to keep pushing despite their colossal leads. Ungarie led by 15 goals halfway through the second quarter but, at half-time, Daniher squirted his mouthguard with water and reminded his teammates that this was the last hit-out before the finals. It was hard not to admire his attitude. It was also hard to fathom impending finals in early July, a time of year that Victorians link with the slog of winter. The spectators at Ungarie were wearing T-shirts.

It surprised me that Girral-West Wyalong were also preparing for the finals. Most of their players had little comprehension of what was going on. A handful were built like silos, and had fractionally more pace. They were rugby league forwards who were giving "rules" a go for a bit of fun. But away from the restrictions of a rugby-league pitch, they were lost. The main entertainment by the last quarter was seeing whether Chris Daniher would have a shot at goal, and following the Sydney and Melbourne game on the radio. Neale Daniher was coaching the Demons and Ben Fixter was making his AFL debut with the Swans. Fixter's family had moved to Wagga in his early teens but Ungarie still claimed the teenager as their own. Jim Daniher returned from his car and reported that young Fixter had picked up a few kicks and Melbourne were leading comfortably. The Ungarie supporters on the tiered seating murmured their approval. I asked Jim Daniher whether he supported Melbourne or Essendon. "Probably Melbourne, because Neale's a first-grade coach," he said. When supporters fussed over a player who'd come off with a leg injury, Jim maintained his half-grin. "Nothing a bit of shearing wouldn't fix," he said.

The match took a welcome twist when Peter Gordon, a 35-year-old defender, galloped purposefully around the boundary line and kicked for touch. The unexpected delight at seeing a drop kick on the run prompted laughter, but I must have laughed too hard because the Magpie fans started assuring me that Gordon was a great bloke with a big heart. It hadn't crossed my mind that he was a ratbag; I simply assumed he was a rugby convert. I was laughing because I hadn't seen a drop kick since 1987, when St Bernard's full-forward John Pearson gained many giggles by drop-kicking a goal in the dying minutes of an Amateurs grand final. Pearson was being a showman but Gordon was deadly earnest, which made his cameo all the funnier. "There you go," said Jim Daniher. "You have to come to Ungarie to see a drop kick."

The siren sounded with the Magpies 179 points ahead. Some of Terry Daniher's teammates from the 1974 premiership, such as Red McLintock and Harry Rowling, sauntered towards their sons coming from the ground while Mark McGrane, Terry Daniher's best mate, trudged off in his whites after another fine performance with the whistle. In the airless dressing-room, players climbed over the jumble of bags to reach the slab of beer in the middle of the floor while Chris Daniher leaned on the wall by the doorway. He rated his game as average, although clearly he was best afield. Steve Henley had also dominated, kicking 10.6 before fading in the last half. Daniher pushed up young players such as his midfield partner Lachie Rowling. "These blokes are trying as hard as anyone at Essendon," he said. "They don't like training but once they're out on the ground they have a real dip."

He cradled a sports drink, while most others cradled a beer, and hesi-tated before taking a pie from the tray that was doing the rounds. It was a long way from the post-match bananas and jelly snakes at Windy Hill but Daniher looked at home. "I was brought up to enjoy my footy," he said. The modest midfielder finished his pie, apologised that he had to leave, and headed for a family function at Temora.

The next morning, I was tucking into bacons and eggs in the café and grumbling about the lack of footy in Sydney newspapers when Ungarie president Lindsay Henley found me. On King Island I'd bought Tasmanian newspapers because I wanted to read about the peculiar clubs and compe-titions on the Apple Isle, but the Sydney papers had too much rugby league and no sign of the Australian rules competitions. Henley, a former rover with a spring in his step, suggested an end to the grumbling with a trip to the Four Corners oval, honoring a promise made by Chris Daniher before his family commitment bobbed up. Daniher mentioned that the Four Corners was a great old ground in the middle of nowhere. He said all his brothers had played finals at Four Corners and it was like no other experience in football. "There's only a paddock, but on footy days it came alive," he said. I gathered that it would have a soul like other grounds have a fence, and it would possibly offer an insight into the Danihers' hardiness. There would, however, be a delay: we were to go by way of the league delegates' meeting at the Tullibigeal Hotel. I hopped in the car with Henley, Ungarie delegate Viv Koop and Ungarie supporter

Bryan Stear. The morning was clear and the chill was receding as we headed north.

A delegates' meeting in the Northern Riverina league is like a league delegates' meeting anywhere in Victoria, with bickering over which club is bending the rules and which finals are to be played where. The difference, for some clubs, is the distances. Hillston delegates drove in from the cotton fields out west and Cobar delegates, whose town is closer to Bourke than Tullibigeal, drove 300 kilometres. The delegates convened over middies of lemon squash or beer before filing into the back room for the meeting.

I left them to it and wandered up the street to the public phone booth. My task was to ring around Victoria for the column for Monday's *Age*. Several quirky stories popped up: a stunt pilot had thrilled the large crowd at Tempy, in the heart of the Mallee; a recruit from Macedon had kicked 16 goals in his second game for a club in the bottom corner of the Western District; and Yarram had edged to victory after kicking four late goals in South Gippsland. The weather in Victoria was reportedly grey and wintry, but the sky over Tullibigeal was vast and blue. Over the road from the phone booth, a station hand got out of his ute wearing boots, jeans and an Akubra. He looked like an RM Williams catalogue, but the effect was diminished when he returned from the shop carrying two Paddle Pops and a video. His ute was big and dusty, like the plains. I felt like I was a long way from Victoria.

Back at the pub, I was drinking a lemon squash and pondering whether to bother with the Sydney newspapers again when the Ungarie officials emerged from the back room looking worn but satisfied. Their club would host the elimination final, and they had moved the motion that blocked Barellan United's attempt to qualify a late recruit for the finals. It was a successful start to the Magpies' finals campaign.

The 20-kilometre drive to Four Corners prompted Lindsay Henley and Viv Koop to tell me stories about the club based at the junction of four properties. The stories were about greats such as "Jelly" Ray Preuss, who landed drop kicks in the centre of the ground, and Dudley Ireland, the father of the Ireland dynasty. The Irelands had been the mainstays of Four Corners but, in a reflection of the times, their purchase of the surround-ing land had lessened the number of families on farms. Finally, in 1994, there were too few families and farmhands to sustain the football club.

Henley and Koop spent the last few kilometres speculating on the state of the old school across the road from the Four Corners oval. "She was getting a horrible lean on her last time I saw," Henley said. The pair fell silent when they saw that the school was in ruins, collapsed and rotting in a heap at the point where the four properties meet. The football oval, however, was just as they remembered it. One forward pocket was pock-marked with rabbit warrens, and tree limbs continued to block the path to goal. The grass was coarse and spare. I was scuffing my shoe on the red dirt that separated the tufts when Viv Koop noticed my concern. "You learned to stand up," he said.

The goalposts were gnarled and knotted tree trunks, cut down and placed at either end of the paddock when the competition began in 1946. "I don't think they've ever been replaced," Koop said. The goalposts leaned at defiant angles, with coats of paint that were fading to reveal grey bark. Koop, a 74-year-old with smiling eyes and the stoop of a former ruckman, began playing for Ungarie in 1946. He recalled a match at the Four Corners in the '70s in which Henley kicked 3.11. Henley, a dual league best-and-fairest winner, confirmed the tally. Later, he recalled the sheep that trimmed the grass between matches. "There's no doubt about it – wherever sheep graze, there's always the danger of anthrax or tetanus," he said.

The former ruckman and the former rover reminisced as I went for a walk to get a feel for a ground that might be described as a rough diamond. Henley's family had moved up from the Adelaide hills; Koop's family was from the Wimmera, where many German immigrants had settled. Their histories of migration to the Riverina were among the reasons that Australian football had gained a foothold in the region. Bryan Stear listened to the stories with interest. Stear is a shearer who had no idea of Australian football when he arrived in Ungarie. But, after seeing the Four Corners oval, with its resilient goalposts and rusting shed, he'd gained a glimpse of the soul of the game in his adopted home. It was amazing to think that football had been played on the dirt and tufts as recently as the mid-'90s. We left the rustic charms of the Four Corners oval and listened to the Sydney rugby-league broadcast on the drive back to Ungarie.

The next day I left the warm hospitality of Ungarie and took my time returning to Melbourne. I headed down back tracks to Barellan, the home town of Evonne Goolagong, where rugby uprights compete with goal-posts, and through to Narrandera, the town with the rugby league premiers but no rugby league team. Below Narrandera, the uprights vanish and you re-enter the land of goalposts. Once upon a time, I wanted the Murray River diverted around the top of the Riverina because, in my mind, New South Wales begins where Australian football is off the map. Now I appreciate more about the diversity of the Riverina. It's a diversity that ranks it among the country's most interesting sporting regions. Let's just be thankful that the Danihers were born into a family and a town with a leaning to Australian rules.

Ungarie finished the season with a percentage of 405. Chris Daniher won the league best-and-fairest with 28 votes; Steve Henley finished second with 14. Girral-West Wyalong defeated Cobar in the elimination final before losing to Barellan United the next week. In the grand final, Ungarie defeated Barellan United by six goals. Daniher won the club best-and-fairest with 187 votes; Mal Williams was second with 80. Three Magpies kicked more than 50 goals for the season: Steve Henley kicked 58; Chris Daniher 54; and David Zvonaric 53. Blake McGrane, Mark and Lyn McGrane's son and Terry Daniher's godson, played in the Ungarie premiership as well as a junior rugby-league premiership with West Wyalong. Centreman Michael Rees won the Girral-West Wyalong best-and-fairest.

16

BATTLE OF WILLS

Moyston-Willaura v Streatham-Mininera-Westmere Rovers
the Pumas and the Rovers

"He lived at Lexington station, Moyston, while playing as a child with Aboriginal children. In this area, he developed a game which he later utilised in the formation of Australian football."

Inscription on the Tom Wills monument at Moyston

In Aboriginal legend, bunyips haunt swamps and billabongs. In Victorian rural mythology, pumas slink around the Grampians. The story goes that American servicemen left a handful of big cats behind after the Second World War and their extended families still prowl the sandstone ranges. Some wander over towards Central Victoria, where one goldfields publican kept a tab on sightings. He said it created interest in his bar.

In 1995, the Moyston Football Club harnessed the interest in big-cat sightings by holding a puma hunt in the Grampians. About 80 hunters gathered at the football ground on Good Friday and prepared for their quest with a bush dance. The next morning a parade was held in the main street, with a caged puma, hired from a Maryborough farmer for the regular fee, leading the parade. The football club held a training session for the Melbourne camera crews and enjoyed its biggest turnout for the year. The town of Moyston holds sheepdog trials at the football ground in March and a rabbit-skinning competition on Boxing Day, but the festivities surrounding the puma hunt surpassed anything seen in the district for years. Dave Hermans, the chief puma tracker, led the hunting party into the hills amid great excitement.

A few hours later, the excitement was washed away by torrents of rain. Hermans insisted he was on the trail of a big cat when the conditions forced him to abandon the night to drinking stubbies by the campfire. "I lost the tracks out in the Londonderry," he said.

The venture raised money for the football club but it failed to stave off decline. Moyston began the '90s by winning the premiership and ended the decade by winning one game in their last few years. During the dark years, half the reserves side had to double up and play seniors. Down the road, a shortage of players forced Willaura into recession. Neither club had much to lose when they formed the Moyston-Willaura Football Club, but the merger did offer a twist.

Most mergers combine the forces of two neighboring clubs with a history of rivalry. The merger is always resisted because supporters hold grudges over the clearance of a star forward between the wars, or the goal that was disallowed on the siren in the 1965 grand final, but animosities settle down when supporters realise that their neighbors are remarkably like them. Moyston and Willaura shared no animosity because they'd never played each other. Only 20 kilometres separate the towns but their clubs played in different leagues with different cultures. Moyston played in the Ararat association, which featured a large proportion of workers from the mills and factories. Moyston itself had become an outpost for policemen. Declining population forced a succession of mergers until the Ararat association ran out of clubs. Willaura played in the Mininera league, which stretches the length of the Western District. Recruits are drawn from larger towns such as Ballarat and Hamilton but the flavor of the competition owes more to farms than provincial cities.

Moyston-Willaura arranged to play early matches at Willaura, where the superior social rooms gave everyone the chance to start on the right note, and later matches at Moyston, where the drainage would offer a superior surface in the boggy months of winter. The location of the towns in the shadow of the Grampians lent the nickname of the Pumas. A jumper was designed in the black, white and teal of Port Adelaide, with claw marks in place of the Power's lightning strikes. The merged club celebrated like it had won a final after defeating Glenthompson in an early match. Defeat was the expected order of things, but Pumas supporters regarded the club's success in fielding full seniors and reserves sides as victories in themselves. "We saw the writing on the wall and the merger's worked out well," Dave Hermans said.

Football supporters across Australia have an interest in ensuring that the merger continues to work. If football dies in the Moyston area, part of the history of the game will die with it. Tom Wills, the acknowledged father of Australian football, grew up on a property outside Moyston in the 1840s. His playmates were Aboriginal children who taught him the game of marn grook, a form of keepings-off that was played with an inflated possum skin. Marn grook required dash and daring. When Wills went to Rugby boarding school in England, he learned about honor and bravery. Historians believe that Wills had such traits in mind when he wrote a letter to a Melbourne sporting weekly urging "a game of our own" in 1858. But historians fail to agree on whether the main influence in his vision was the Aboriginal game or the manly virtues encouraged in English public schools. Geoffrey Blainey, in his book *A Game of Our Own*, believes the imperial vogue for muscular Christianity was the biggest influence on Wills. Col Hutchinson recognises the place of marn grook in the origins of Australian football and, as the AFL statistician, it was his opinion that held sway when the Moyston Progress Association sought AFL approval of the town's standing in the game.

In September 1998, Hutchinson was the main dignitary at a ceremony on the outskirts of Moyston. The ceremony also featured Bill McMaster, the Geelong recruiting chief and history buff from Lake Bolac, south of Moyston; Scott Turner, the Richmond defender from Ararat; and Martin Flanagan, the *Age* journalist who wrote *The Call*, a novel based on the life of Tom Wills. A monument commemorating Wills was unveiled and Moyston was declared the home of Australian football. A year later, signs were erected alongside the five roads that lead into Moyston. The signs confirmed the town as the home of Australian football.

As a home for an obsession, Moyston is humble. The town is approached after a 15-kilometre drive from Ararat, through undulating grazing country and past one or two vineyards off the main road. Churches and houses sprawl gently over the hill and the Grampians brood in the background, 20 kilometres from the edge of town. Street names such as Campbells Reef Road hint at the hubbub of the goldfields, and Morocco Hills Road lends a whiff of exotica. The only shop is low-roofed and busy, and there is no pub.

The road to the Grampians wraps around the football ground before the AFL-approved monument invites drivers to stop. The monument stands 2.5 metres high and features an inscription praising the vision of Tom Wills. "He lived at Lexington station, Moyston, while playing as a child with Aboriginal children. In this area, he developed a game which he later utilised in the formation of Australian football."

Lexington station is a few kilometres out past the ground. The homestead was derelict and abandoned for 20 years before being restored in the '80s. The wonder was that the Wills family lived in temporary digs, including the barn, for a decade. The house had barely been finished when the departure of shepherds, who were unwilling to remain on the station when gold was flowing down the streets of nearby towns, prompted the family to sell and move to a property outside Geelong. This detail fits the life of Tom Wills. Little in his life was conventional. He lived in a barn and played keepings-off with children whose spirit was in the land. His own spirit thrived on the rough and tumble of physical games. Wills became an alcoholic and died at the age of 44 after stabbing himself in the chest with a pair of scissors. But standing at the homestead where he grew up, overlooking the gorgeous valley in which he chased the possum skin, it was plain to see why the young Tom Wills was inspired to run and jump. It was also evident that he might have spent the rest of his life trying to recapture the freedom of the valley.

Over the road from the monument, a Kentucky fried chicken sign jarred the eye at the entrance to the historic football ground. Cars inched through the mud and supporters made their way to the canteen. The clubrooms were worn and grimy, with heavy beams and panelling that block out the light. Flames crackled from the hearth. The rooms had a sad foreboding, like a Henry Lawson story.

Spirits were lifted when the Moyston-Willaura reserves earned a draw with Streatham-Mininera-Westmere Rovers, the top team. The Pumas' seniors then ran out with 21 fresh players. However, all optimism departed soon after the first bounce. Moyston-Willaura were outclassed in every position as the Rovers kicked 12 unanswered goals. The Pumas looked more likely to spot a big cat than kick a goal but coach Tom Stapleton was determined to put a shine on the bleakest prospects. At the quarter-time huddle, he urged the forwards and backs to keep their heads up. He wanted them to plug away and see what happened. Then he fiddled with his clipboard before finding the words for his onballers. "In the midfield, not everything went as we would have liked," he said. In terms of understatement, it was a premiership performance.

When an invitation came to join Stapleton on the bench, I was hesitant. I'd never been in a coach's box on match day and I thought I would cramp his style. But the coach put me at ease with his opening gambit: "What do you reckon about Colonial Stadium?" His style wasn't cramped at all. I said I have no great warmth for Colonial Stadium but I prefer it to Waverley Park. Stapleton said he thought Colonial Stadium was fantastic. He was an AFL member and he headed down to the new ground all the time. He was on for a chat about a range of football issues. We talked about the AFL, the state of football journalism, and his role as full-forward in two Moyston premierships. I began wondering why it had taken me so long to sit in a coach's box. Then I truly entered into the spirit of things and suggested it was about time for a couple of changes. Stapleton looked at the ground and sighed. "Haven't got the resources, mate." The Rovers kept piling on the goals.

We were sitting at either end of the Pumas' bench. Between us, two skinny teenagers waited on their call for the big adventure. They smiled away as their team sank deeper into the mire, before another teenager wandered around in front of the coach's box to ask his brother how he was getting home. The teenager on the bench was unsure. He didn't know whether their father was picking them up or they should walk. Drinks in the bar after the match never entered the conversation. It was unusual, but heartwarming, to watch two teenage brothers try to work out their travel arrangements as one of them waited to go on to the ground. The younger brother shrugged and returned behind the fence. The senior footballer swathed himself deeper in his tracksuit top to keep out the cold. Tom Stapleton looked on with fatherly care. All kinds of strategies must be worked out in the coach's box.

A few minutes later, a young girl with plump cheeks paraded around the boundary line with a whiteboard announcing "winning ticket black D75". Stapleton dug into his pocket and pulled out his raffle tickets. "Ah, well," he said. I also had no luck, but in another sense I'd hit the jackpot. My quarter on the bench at Moyston was a reminder of the humanity of football away from the palaver that surrounds ambition. At half-time, the Pumas wandered past the crackling fire and into the dressing-rooms to await the oratory of their coach. They were trailing by 18 goals.

Stapleton's stocks failed to improve after the break. The Rovers surged and the Pumas battled but the Rovers kicked the goals. Shaun Smart and Shane Jenkins, the Pumas' on-field leaders, tried to rally their side but their only teammate of talent was Les Brennan, the centre half-forward. Brennan had played with Collingwood reserves and at Williamstown under Barry Round. At Avoca, he won two league medals playing alongside Richmond legend Jim Jess. Now 33, he was past his best but he was the only Moyston-Willaura player able to take the ball cleanly. In one passage of play, he met the ball, turned on his right foot and sent a thumping kick towards the goalsquare. He was the only Puma capable of kicking a reasonable distance but supporters were reluctant to praise him. They referred to his record of moving from club to club. "He's got a few jumpers behind him," one supporter said.

Brennan has played at a dozen clubs since he was an early teenager in Ararat. He arrived at Moyston-Willaura at the invitation of Daryle Baldock, who began the season as coach, and who was once denied a St Kilda membership because the Saints refused to believe his name. At Moyston-Willaura, Baldock fell out with the committee after a few rounds, leaving Tom Stapleton to fill the breach. Before long, the club had its third president for the season. Brennan stuck with the Pumas despite the departure of Baldock and the club's instability, but supporters were unimpressed.

Amid such instability, large losing margins must be expected. But faced with my second successive match in which the margin was approaching 30 goals, I could stand it no longer. My solution was to stand at the bar and drink cans. The steely afternoon passed with a degree of pleasantness as I leaned on the pine with Dave Hermans and progress association president Lindsay Peacock. Hermans' mother, Marie, would later give me a potted history of Tom Wills and his years at Rugby but, during the match, the talk was of the new social rooms and the rotunda to be erected behind the Tom Wills monument. A few Pumas fans gathered around a 44-gallon drum in front of us and watched the smoke curl from the fire. Behind us, the Grampians turned a deeper shade of blue as evening closed in. Tim McKay kicked his 11th goal and the Rovers drew to victory by 169 points. At the siren, I swirled the dregs of my can and read the list of Moyston premierships on the latest addition to my club stubbie-holder collection. The list illustrated a decade of decline.

On what I saw, the future for Moyston-Willaura looked grim. The feeling was compounded the next morning when a handful of teenagers played basketball in the valley where the Djabwurrung had played marn grook, but there was not a football to be seen. If hope was to drawn, it was in Martin Flanagan's book *The Call*. Flanagan describes Tom Wills as Australia's Icarus, the man who flew too close to the sun. Maybe Moyston-Willaura would rise, after all. Maybe pumas would slink down from the Grampians and watch the football from behind the goals. Anything's possible when the spiritual father of your club has flown within kicking distance of the sun.

Moyston-Willaura ended the year with one win. Centreman Matt Hutchinson won the best-and-fairest and the Pumas' committee showed good signs of settling down. Les Brennan left the club to become assistant coach of Dunolly. The Rovers lost the grand final. Centre half-forward Gavin Nash won their best-and-fairest and full-forward Tim McKay kicked 92 goals.

17

UPS AND DOWNS

Marcellin Old Collegians v Melbourne High School Old Boys
the Eagles and the Unicorns

"This sort of game can make or break a club."

Marcellin president Chris Mason

The contrast was stark. At Moyston the previous week, drinks were served from a shed. I leaned on the bar as the flames from a nearby 44-gallon drum licked at the fading light. At Marcellin College, drinks were served in an expansive room with full-length windows and a view of the ground. I sipped white wine as the president made special mention of the school principal, who'd been behind the $5 million upgrade of the facilities. Football is a great leveller but, to paraphrase George Orwell, some clubs are more level than others.

Moyston-Willaura and Marcellin Old Collegians did have something in common: they were both towards the bottom of the ladder. But their responses to their fate had as much in common as their facilities. Moyston-Willaura, the club struggling under the weight of the rural decline, accepted their position with stoicism. Marcellin, the club from the aspiring eastern suburbs, accepted their position with the grace of a cornered cat. The Bulleen club was prepared to thrash at anything that tested its survival in A-section of the Victorian Amateur Football Association. Their response was a clear illustration of why the relegation system works.

The relegation system is one of the great strengths of the Amateurs competition. With two clubs going up and two going down in every section, it ensures that competition remains hot until the last game. Sometimes survival or demotion is decided in the last breath of the season. In such moments, we are reminded why sport grips us like it does. The other main strength of the Amateurs competition is the rule against player payments. While failing to prove that Amateur players love the game any more than their paid counterparts, the shunning of money does limit the greed and envy that divides football clubs. Contravention of the payment rule in the Amateurs can set hearts racing as much as relegation dramas.

Marcellin had been trying to escape the jaws of relegation all season. The battle began when Tony Paatsch was forced to resign as coach because St Joseph's College, Geelong, had appointed him vice-principal. The club cast around for a replacement before appointing Garry Connolly because, after coaching in four grades, he had wide experience of the idiosyncrasies of the Amateurs. The problems with a late coaching appointment were compounded when the renovations on the college grounds forced the Eagles to train without lights at Bulleen Park. The club played home matches here and there until the renovations were completed about a month into the season. By then the Eagles were relegation candidates.

Melbourne High School Old Boys had earned promotion to A-section for their first season since 1972. They'd recruited former Melbourne High School student Cam Eabry, who'd played in A-section with Ormond and Old Melburnians, but little was expected of them away from their tiny oval beneath the grand school building in South Yarra. Yet they travelled to the Marcellin College grounds needing only to win to ensure safety in A-section. Marcellin had to win or they would be demoted. Relegation talk filled the room as lunch guests tucked into their meat and salads.

At lunch I joined Marcellin president Chris Mason, a 33-year-old fruit wholesaler whose knockabout ways fail to mask his sharp mind. His parents, their friends and an injured senior player were also at the table. Paul Herrick, the college principal, was the guest of honor. Mason said in his speech that the football club was grateful that it was benefiting from the renovations. The school had covered the cost for the upgrade of music and sporting facilities; the only cost to the football club had been the inconvenience of a nomadic few months. Mason said it was a small price to pay for the best facilities in the Amateurs. Guests nodded as sunlight streamed into the room. It was a long way from the grime and darkness at Moyston.

Former coach and president Ray Walsh had another reason to praise Herrick. Walsh said the Eagles had suffered when Marcellin College principals failed to encourage sport. Since Herrick became principal in the early '90s, students were encouraged to play sport. Walsh said if the students enjoyed football in the higher years at school, they were more likely to join the old boys' football club when they left school. Parents offer support and the club improves on all levels. Walsh said the Eagles' rising fortunes from the mid-'90s could be traced back to Herrick. "He got the school going. He made the students proud to be Marcellin students."

When Walsh completed his schooling at Marcellin College, there was no old boys' club to join. He played 150 games with De La Salle before becoming Marcellin Old Collegians' captain-coach in 1970, when the Eagles were in their third year in the YCW competition. The acronym stands for Young Christian Workers but the behavior of some clubs was a fair way removed from Christian teachings. "We didn't do any good in the YCW," Walsh said "It was hard and tough but it was good training."

The Eagles were admitted into the Amateurs in F-section the next year. At the first training session, Walsh counted nine players who were good enough for A-section. He said they were "confident young kids". The club sailed through the grades in seven years. Walsh stepped aside to coach the under-19s after the club reached A-section.

The Eagles moved between A and B sections for the next decade before reaching the A-section preliminary final in 1988. A month later the club was in disarray. The coach, Mick Petrie, taught at the school and several players held grudges from the classroom. Ray Walsh, by now the president, wanted to reappoint him, but moves were made to unseat Walsh and his committee so that a new coach could be appointed. In most years, a dozen supporters attend the annual general meeting; in the year of the falling-out, 80 turned up. Walsh was retained as president but he decided against reappointing Petrie because he wanted to avoid losing key players. Some of the players left anyway. Walsh stuck out another year but he had a sour taste in his mouth. He said at the Melbourne High match that Marcellin committees have tended to be weak. "We're not an organised club." He later amended the description from "weak" to "well-meaning but casual". He sometimes looks ruefully at the administrative rigor of clubs like Old Xaverians, a club that was poorly run before becoming the benchmark in Amateur football.

In the year after Petrie was replaced, the Eagles held on for another season in A-section. In the next two years, the club went down two grades. Cynicism replaced the sense of adventure that had underpinned the club in the '70s. It took the Eagles almost a decade to return to the top flight. "Once you're in C-section, it's hard to get back up," Walsh said.

In the light of their recent history, the Eagles knew the difficulty of clawing back to A-section. It was why they were willing to fight like cornered cats to stay there. The 2000 season began with a series of thrashings but margins lessened when the club settled back into the college grounds. Then players returned or recovered form and the Eagles began to steal victories. The most notable players to return were Steve Thiesz and Bernie Dinneen. Thiesz was working on building sites on the Solomon Islands when a military coup forced foreigners to evacuate. He returned to Melbourne, greeted his family and headed down to the footy club. Dinneen missed 12 matches after tearing his quadricep muscle in half early in the season. Chris Mason was open in his admiration for the relentless midfielder. "He's the youngest of eight. He's had to fight for everything."

Mason was indulging in a little presidential licence – Dinneen is the sixth of eight – but his admiration was well-founded. Dinneen is one of those players who lines up for the opening bounce with a grin from ear to ear because he's about to put his body in extreme danger for the afternoon. His first touch of the cherished leather was delayed when ruckman Mark Browne thumped the ball 20 metres. With the wind muscling in from the forward pocket, it was as good as a kick. In the winter months, the wind at Marcellin has a habit of tearing across the school grounds and then diagonally across the main oval. The Eagles harnessed the wind, scoring the first goal within two minutes. Home advantage was going to be a factor.

The advantage wasn't nearly enough to still the nerves of Chris Mason.

The former defender was of the breed of president with a preference for removing himself from the crowd and yelling himself hoarse. Mason was in no frame of mind to be interviewed but he was candid when asked what relegation would mean for his club. "It wouldn't mean the end of the world," he said. "We're financial and we've still got our supporters around the club. We'd lose better players who want to play A-grade …"

Just then, Matthew Chun bulldozed out of defence. The back pocket had played for De La Salle before returning to Marcellin when the club returned to the top flight. Mason continued: "We'd lose better players but you'll always get them back if you're in A-section."

The Eagles' early advantage was wiped out when Cam Eabry, the Unicorns' prized recruit, worked himself into the game. The centreman had been reluctant to play for Melbourne High School Old Boys when they were stuck in lower grades. But the Unicorns extracted a promise that he would join them if the club reached A-section and Eabry made good his promise. Against Marcellin, he constantly found space in the centre square. His side became angry after an early goal was ruled a behind. Marcellin were unable to gain any advantage with the wind until Leigh McMillan, the 18-year-old son of former Richmond forward Marty McMillan, snapped a goal from a tricky angle like he was having a kick in the street with his neighbors. The breakthrough heralded a fightback and the Eagles led by a point at half-time.

Marcellin full-forward Andrew Treganowan, a Lygon Street publican, opened the scoring after the break. In both halves, the Eagles had struck early against the wind. Melbourne High rover Peter Sherry replied but an umpire ruled that the ball had been touched. An incensed Sherry argued until he was sent off, leaving the Unicorns with 17 men. The wind dropped markedly but Melbourne High fought on to lead by two goals at the final break. With no wind, it might be enough. Former Collingwood champion Peter Daicos conferred with the Melbourne High coaching staff. Daicos had planned to come out of retirement and play with the Unicorns before his weekend employer, radio station 3AW, strongly advised him to drop the idea. The Unicorns were left to hope that a little magic would rub off on them from the coaches' bench.

In the Marcellin huddle, Garry Connolly was calm. "Don't panic," he said. "Stick to the game plan and believe in yourselves." The players were too tired to panic. Their way of coping was to retreat into their heads. Around them, supporters roared fighting words and clenched their fists. Players nodded at the fists but failed to hear a word. Players like tense games because the contest is reduced to blood and sweat. Theories go out the window and instinct remains. It's a liberating feeling.

In these matches, many players leave the final huddle with a good instinct whether their side will win. I looked for signs in the Marcellin faces and the players seemed cool enough, even if a few supporters were so tense that they risked injury. At this point, I admitted to myself that the match had turned out perfectly. It had confirmed that A-section relegation battles provide theatre to match anything in local football, and the score enabled a small experiment to test the theory that Catholics win close matches. Such an experiment might sound out of whack with these secular times, but old divisions thrive in the Amateurs. In my early years in the competition, I was taught the dubious lesson that everything comes easily to Protestants, which is why they have no heart for the battle. While still at an impressionable age, a fellow student told me that Catholics always win finals and every Amateurs club knows it. His words echoed those of the St Bernard's coaching staff. It was like having the Holy Trinity confirmed. "It means more to Catholics," my informant said. For the record, he was from Old Caulfield, a Protestant club.

In later years, I shared a house with a woman who had a condition she described as "Catholic envy". She was convinced that all Catholics remained friends with everybody from their primary school. It was part of the great conspiracy to exclude Protestants. The conspiracy was exemplified at Mount Pleasant Football Club, where her brothers did all the work but failed to get a game in the finals because the Catholics marched in. "They were always better players, the bastards." She said Catholics were tribal and she felt left out. I believed she was a mad rambler but I've since read about Catholic tribalism and she's turned out to be wise.

Author Edmund Campion has written that Catholics have a ghetto mentality. In the past, banding together was a way of dealing with the blows of life, as it is for any minority group. The ghetto mentality was evident in the Catholic propensity to run exclusive sporting competitions. An example is the regular church tennis competitions. In Melbourne, the YCW football league, which folded as recently as 1986, is the obvious example. Campion probably never meant his writings to be used for speculation on Amateur football, but his descriptions of a ghetto mentality can be useful in illustrating why Catholics might win close matches. Poverty is no longer the inheritance of Catholics, but the strong bonds that formed a shield against the blows of life continue to exist. It would be interesting to see how the last quarter at Marcellin panned out.

The Eagles hit the lead when Andrew Treganowan received a handball and kicked his sixth goal. I spoke briefly to Melbourne High president Colin Green and he cursed his side's luck. The Unicorns scored a stroke of luck when Marcellin ruckman Mark Browne was reported and sent off for tripping with 15 minutes to go. Then a Melbourne High forward was tackled on the line. A Melbourne High shot for goal was marked on the line. A rainbow burst from the sky and arched over the wing. This match had everything.

I walked around the top end of the ground, where the crowd amounted to a few stragglers. Along the wing, the crowd thickened. Many spectators had dogs at heel, terriers and hounds engrossed in the duel like their masters. They watched as the ball burst free of its moorings, propelled by a knock-on or a hurried handball, only to be dragged back into a sea of arms and legs. Neither side seemed capable of scoring. The logjam was too much for Chris Mason, who in joining the crowd became the fulcrum of several arguments with Melbourne High supporters. "This sort of game can make or break a club," he said. Then he turned to the timekeepers up in the scoreboard. "How long to go?"

Less than a minute.

Mason threw his cigarette to the ground and raised his arms to the rainbow in the sky. "We've got it," he said. Marcellin had kicked three goals to one behind for the quarter. Melbourne High had been denied two goals on the goal-line. Neither side had scored for 10 minutes. But the only fact worth knowing was that Marcellin were four points ahead when the siren sounded. They were still alive in A-grade.

Supporters streamed on to the field. Dogs barked and one player wept. Glenn Cox accepted the slaps on the back with relief. Bernie Dinneen walked in circles with his hands to his face. "I can't believe it," he said. "I can't believe it." In the middle of the jubilation, Steve Thiesz hunched over and vomited. He walked a few steps then he vomited again, repeating the process until he managed to reach the dressing-rooms, where he slumped on his seat exhausted. The building work in Honiara had failed to maintain his fitness for relegation battles. Garry Connolly praised the players for a supreme effort. "You stood to a man," he said. The supporters clapped and cheered. Steve Thiesz smiled thinly. The color was beginning to return to his face.

In the Melbourne High rooms, players leaned against the wall and trained their eyes on the floor. Eventually, they scraped their bags across the concrete and sought their towels. The events of the match had to be washed away. In the medical room, the coaches stared at the statistics sheet. They mumbled about umpiring decisions before suggesting Cam Eabry and defender Richard Joseph as their best players. Coach Warren Fall was quietly fuming. "We let an opportunity slip to make ourselves safe," he said. It seemed prudent to leave the question about Catholics winning close matches for another time.

I eventually did ring Fall with the question and expected to be dismissed for being flippant. But he considered the question valid. The Melbourne High teacher had taken a step back after 20 years of coaching. In four years in the Amateurs, he learned that some sides were more difficult to beat than others. Most Catholic sides were in the difficult category. During 16 years of coaching in school football, he learned that some Catholic sides were never beaten. Assumption College was the worst. If the margin were less than a goal, the result would show that Assumption had won. "Some sides find something special when they have to," Fall said. "It's an intangible. I'm not sure where it comes from."

Melbourne High ensured they would remain in A-section by winning the next week. Marcellin won four of their last six games but, in the end, owed their place in A-section to a controversy that is covered in the next chapter. Mark Browne won the Marcellin best-and-fairest by one vote from centreman Glenn Cox, who won the A-section best-and-fairest. Captain Jayden Pertzel won the Unicorns' best-and-fairest, with Cam Eabry second. The Eagles sacked Garry Connolly as coach. Paul Herrick left Marcellin College to become principal of Newman College in Perth.

• • •

St Kevin's Old Boys v Old Melburnians
the Skobbers and the Redlegs

"It was without doubt the most depressing meeting
I've been to in my life."

Old Melburnians president Ric Pisarski

The next day I found out where the wind had gone during the last half at
Marcellin. It had camped behind the goals at Elsternwick Park, saving its
strength for an assault on another A-section match with a bearing on relegation. I arrived at Amateurs' headquarters, just off the Nepean Highway,
to find the wind howling down the ground as though a dam had broken.
The ball had a good chance of ending up in Bass Strait.

Yet the ground was receiving nothing like the buffeting that Old
Melburnians were taking. The Redlegs had ended the previous season as
runners-up. Victories in the first two games of the new season masked
problems that became apparent when results began going against them.
The decline was compelling. With each loss, a once-respected side unrav-
elled a little further. Opposition clubs looked on with ghoulish fascination.
Old Melburnians is the club for the old boys from Melbourne Grammar,
one of Australia's most esteemed private schools. The history of Melbourne
Grammar includes the 1858 match against Scotch College, which is celebrated as the first hit-out in the game that was to become Australian rules.
Such a long and distinguished history invites the knockers and, in the
Amateurs competition, Old Melburnians often attract the knockers. The
fascination with their decline rests on their status as tall poppies, as well as
an appreciation of good drama. The first act in this drama ended when
coach Neil Ross resigned and the match committee walked out on a
Thursday night after training. Old Melburnians were hardly alone in their
upheaval. A-section rivals Old Ivanhoe also had their problems in this
regard, and clubs all around Australia suffer coaching problems every
season. At Old Melburnians, small issues grew into large issues, resulting in
dissent and, eventually, overhaul. In this cycle, football is like every other
human endeavor.

Ric Pisarski barely played football before leaving Beaumaris High School. In his first year out of school, a friend dragged him along for a season at suburban club Chelsea Heights. After the season, Pisarski was having a kick of the footy with a friend of a friend in a front garden in Torquay when his new acquaintance invited him along to Old Melburnians. Pisarski had never heard of Old Melburnians. He'd never heard of Melbourne Grammar. But he took up the invitation to join Old Melburnians. He spent the 1974 season with the Redlegs and hated it. The 19-year-old resolved to leave the club but, over the summer, he received a phone call from new coach Tony Anderson.

Anderson was a defender in Melbourne's 1964 premiership side. Pisarski barracked for Melbourne. Anderson persuaded Pisarski to train under him before he decided to leave Old Melburnians. Pisarski trained with the Redlegs and developed a strong rapport with the coach. Anderson was so impressed with Pisarski that he told him he was good enough to play state footy. "What's state footy?" Pisarski asked. The key defender went on to play in the Victorian Amateurs' side for seven years. He also represented the All-Australian Amateurs in division two of the national carnival against Queensland, the Northern Territory and the ACT. Division one consisted of the Victorian Football League and its equivalents from South Australia, Western Australia and Tasmania. Back at Old Melburnians, Pisarski played in four premierships. In 1992, he became the Redlegs' president.

One of his first pledges as president was to bring in outsiders. Paradoxically for a club in which briefcases compete for floor space with footy bags, Pisarski believed Old Melburnians had the mindset of losers. He appointed Paul O'Brien as coach because the midfielder was from De La Salle, a club Pisarski regarded as winners because they were regular premiers during his playing career. The next year O'Brien invited another outsider, his long-time friend Roger Ellingworth, to be assistant coach. Old Melburnians won the 1993 B-section premiership under O'Brien and Ellingworth but the pair reversed roles for the next season, with Ellingworth becoming coach. In their first few games under him, the Redlegs defeated Collegians, the reigning premiers, in a match that Pisarski sensed was a turning point for the club. After defeating Collegians, Old Melburnians believed they belonged in A-section. They went on to become one of the few clubs to win the B- and A-section premierships in successive years.

Pisarski left Old Melburnians after the 1995 season to join the Amateurs executive. Three years later, he returned to the Redlegs and was elected president. One of his first moves was to appoint Neil Ross as coach. Ross was another outsider.

An injury had put Ross on the path to coaching at an early age. At 18, the recruit from Jordanville, a housing commission area in Melbourne's south-east suburbs, made his senior debut for Richmond. He and full-forward Michael Roach sat on the bench for the first half of a night match against West Australian club Swan Districts. Both came on at half-time and made their mark, with Roach booting 10 goals and Ross picking up a swag of kicks. The next weekend Ross broke his leg in a car accident that kept him out of football for two years. He tried out at Essendon and played at Port Melbourne but leg problems got the better of him. At 23 years of age, he left his disappointment behind and went to the Gold Coast, where he coached Coolangatta to a flag. His career led back to Port Melbourne, where he coached the club to two finals series before he was forced to make way for Darren Crocker. Ross said Port Melbourne had handled his sacking well. "I don't expect loyalty in football but I do expect honesty."

He took the job at Old Melburnians because he wanted to get his career back on track. In his better days at Port Melbourne, he was considered in the last two for the job as Jeff Gieschen's assistant at Richmond. He figured that, if he could turn Old Melburnians into a strong, consistent club, he might be able to head back up the coaching ladder. "I wasn't there for a holiday," he said. But the culture of holidays is strong in the Amateurs. Every year, clubs must deal with the loss of players to the travel bug. The players finish their university degree or apprenticeship, strap on their backpacks and leave footy behind. Old Melburnians, with their high proportion of graduates, have more trouble than most. Ross said he found the exodus frustrating. Part of him struggled with the question of why anybody would want to travel overseas when football success was around the corner at home. But he was forced to accept it as part of life in the Amateurs.

Ambitious outsiders often become frustrated in the Amateurs. Players put professional careers ahead of football and the absence of payments leaves coaches without the leverage to make demands. Some coaches find they're unable to make any demands at all. The education of many players means they fail to accept authority unless they feel that respect has been earned. Many Old Melburnians have tertiary educations; most have known a measure of success throughout their lives. But Ross said he never felt the need to prove himself. He said he was welcomed with genuine warmth, and the club was distinguished by its lack of cliques. He was mixing with doctors, lawyers and stockbrokers for the first time in his life and he was thriving.

He said the club was full of "quality people", which eased his worries as coach. Just as most players were disciplined in their professional lives, they carried that discipline into their football careers. If they were unable to train with the club, they completed a program from the fitness advisor in their own time. Tests were held every month, not to check whether anyone had been slack, but to see which areas might be improved. Ross said his only stipulation was that players had to tell him if they were unavailable for training. His end of the deal was to learn to be flexible.

This regime worked without a hitch in his first season. Old Melburnians were minor premiers. On the eve of the grand final, Ric Pisarski sent the members of the coaching staff a letter congratulating them on their season. Whatever happened in the grand final, Pisarski believed the club was in good hands. The Redlegs lost to the experienced Old Xaverians.

The trouble began after the grand final, when three of the top four players in the vote count announced they were leaving. Two were going overseas and Cam Eabry was going to Melbourne High. To top it off, best-and-fairest winner Michael Hazell would be out with a stomach hernia. Lack of numbers at pre-season training was also a worry, but the biggest blow was the death of Ross's sister-in-law from cancer at 36 years of age. Ross admitted he was distracted for a good part of the pre-season. For most of this time, he gave the reins to his offsiders. "I leaned on those guys pretty heavily," he said. "That's why you have assistant coaches."

The two opening victories were followed by two sound defeats. In the fifth round, Melbourne High won by a goal, with Cam Eabry best afield. The narrow loss unsettled Ric Pisarski. "It was abundantly clear that we were in a lot of trouble," he said. "To others it wasn't, but to me it was."

He believed the lack of intensity at training was reflected during matches. There was no cohesion and positional moves were confusing players. He tried to stick to his policy of leaving training and tactics to the match committee but, given his playing record, it was hardly surprising that he would have an opinion on football matters. Sometimes he would attempt to talk informally to Ross about football, but the coach would have none of it. "Butt out," was the message.

In round 11, lowly Old Ivanhoe defeated the Redlegs by 12 goals and Pisarski could sit by no longer. "I wasn't prepared to simply let us be relegated," he said. He undertook a review of every operation in the club. Two committeemen reviewed his position as president. He offered to step aside if it would provide a catalyst for change, but the reviewers advised against it. On the Monday, he called a meeting with the match committee. Two members of the club committee were also present. The meeting was an unwitting turning point. Pisarski's version of events is that he asked the coaches for suggestions on what could be done to arrest the slide. He said the lack of input stunned him. Chairman of selectors Doug Searl was convinced that injuries and departures had doomed the club to relegation and the assistant coaches had little to say. Even the coach was at a loss. "It was without doubt the most depressing meeting I've been to in my life," Pisarski said.

Ross believed that the underlying theme of the meeting was panic. His upbringing on the housing commission estate at Jordanville had taught him that the only way to survive hard times was to stick together. But he sensed that others at the meeting had a different view. Ross wanted more effort from committeemen. The previous year he'd been under siege from back-slappers but, with the club in strife, he felt that committeemen had become scarce. Ross failed to understand why some of them took holidays in Queensland or at the snow during football season, then expected the players to make sacrifices every week. He believed that nobody worked harder for the club than Pisarski, but few others pulled their weight. At the end of the meeting, he said he would struggle to continue in such an environment. He was implying that he wanted the club to be more professional, with the right people in the top jobs. His intention was to nudge unproductive committeemen into stepping down, but he failed to make himself clear.

Pisarski believed Ross was flagging his resignation. "I thought, 'I wonder if he's tossing in the towel'." The next morning, the president rang Roger Ellingworth. In the previous few seasons, Ellingworth had watched half a dozen Old Melburnians games a year, simply as a spectator. Neil Ross then asked him to return to the club on the coaching staff. His role was to be a mentor for four young players and to sit on the bench on match days. Ellingworth had been unable to attend the review meeting, so Pisarski rang to inform him of its contents. At the end of an hour-long conversation, Pisarski asked Ellingworth whether he would take over as coach if Ross resigned. Ellingworth was reluctant to commit beyond his role on the match committee – his wife was almost due with their second child. But he agreed to become caretaker coach if necessary. Pisarski reported his conversation with Ellingworth at the next review meeting on the Wednesday night. During the review of Ross's performance, one committeeman moved a motion to sack him. The motion was defeated 10-1, with Pisarski among the majority. "It wasn't an option to sack Neil," he said. "We'd made a commitment to him."

The next night at training, Ross was in the general manager's office when he came across the minutes of the review meeting. He began reading and discovered that his position had been subject to a vote. He also discovered that Ellingworth had been approached to succeed him.

The coach returned to the training session and informed his assistants of his discovery. "I was really upset that all this stuff had been done behind my back. Ric should have said, 'He's got a three-year agreement. There's no vote'." He told his assistants that the club had lost his trust and he saw no point in continuing.

His final task was to gain confirmation from Roger Ellingworth that Pisarski had approached him. When Ellingworth turned up for training on June 15, Ross asked him whether Pisarski had made an approach about taking over as coach. Ellingworth said yes.

After training, Ross led the players into the grandstand overlooking the ground on which St Kilda had blundered through decades. Behind them, Collegians were winding up training at their ground in Albert Park. Before them, cars were emerging from Dandenong Road into Queens Way. Ross told the players he was quitting. He said that, for the sake of his credibility, he had no choice. The chairman of selectors and two assistant coaches said they would go with him. They went to Pisarski as one. Ross asked the president whether he'd approached someone else to coach. Pisarski said no. Ross said he was lying. "Neil walked out," Pisarski said. "I've got no animosity towards him."

Pisarski was strictly correct in denying that he approached someone to coach. Ellingworth had been lined up to succeed Ross only in the event that the coach resigned. Ross accepts that his statement after the match committee meeting – that he was reluctant to work in unprofessional conditions – had been misread. In the end, it must be said that Ross and Pisarski both failed to make themselves clear. Months later, however, both men claimed respect for the other. There was regret but no rancor. Pisarski said it was wrong to introduce reviews when it became apparent that the club was in crisis. He believed he should have been holding reviews of all operations every six weeks or three months. "We didn't do that and it was a mistake." Ross was happy that he'd gained from mixing with good people from all walks of life, an experience normally denied those raised in a housing commission area. The spirit and dedication of Amateur footballers had impressed him. The only drawback was their propensity to travel.

The stunned footballers were left to deal with the fallout. Several were close friends with Ross and some were agitated by the upheaval. Andrew Topakas, a key forward known as Turbo, urged the players to take action. He and Pisarski had fallen out the previous season. He and Ross had enjoyed a voluble relationship, trading curses and threats, but gaining each other's respect. Topakas said the president should leave, not the coach, but teammates backed away from his call for a strike. Captain Ian McMullin had played in his first Old Melburnians premiership at 17 years of age. At 35, he'd been around long enough to know there are two sides to every story. Topakas was unconvinced. His displeasure would lead to more upheaval.

The level head of Roger Ellingworth was just what was needed in a crisis. Ellingworth began his senior playing career with Paul O'Brien at Melbourne under Ron Barassi. Then he went to Hawthorn, where he injured his knee. He had a reconstruction but the nerve ends failed to mend and he was forced to retire at 24. Coaches Allan Jeans and Alan Joyce kept him with the Hawks by employing him as a forward scout during the premiership years. "They taught me a lot in a short time," Ellingworth said. The Hawthorn connection was maintained when former ruckman Michael Byrne invited him on to the Sydney support staff in Melbourne. He then joined Old Melburnians.

His return to the Redlegs after a few years out of the game was bitter-sweet. The 37-year-old said he enjoyed his role as a mentor but his role with the match committee had become more difficult as the season progressed. "The atmosphere was getting darker and darker." He said there was no expectation on him to quit with the other members of the coaching staff. They had come as a bloc, with Port Melbourne the link. Ellingworth had returned with no ambition other than to make a contribution. His return as coach was simply to help the club through a difficult time.

As tradition dictates, the replacement of one coach with another sparked a sense of urgency. The Redlegs took a deep breath and finished within two points of Old Trinity. They lost the next game to Old Scotch by 12 goals before rebounding to defeat Melbourne High. Ellingworth's plan was to encourage his players to enjoy their football. If the enjoyment returned, the results would come. Many coaches claim enjoyment as a priority but their words are hollow; it's their own ambition that is paramount. From Ellingworth, the enjoyment mantra rings true. He had no pretensions about taking A-section by storm. He also had no idea what lay around the corner.

The fallout over Ross had prompted Andrew Topakas to decide that he was through with Old Melburnians. "If the club wanted to keep him, they could have," Topakas said. Two days before clearances were due to close, he told Ric Pisarski that he wanted to leave. He said he'd received the offer of a loan from an Old Brighton supporter that would help him clear his debts. Pisarski was unimpressed. He told him that loans were no different to payments in Amateur football. He believed that Old Melburnians deserved his loyalty in a crisis and he refused to clear him. Topakas left. Fellow forward Scott Oram, who was doing his apprenticeship under Topakas, left with him. Rumors had abounded that eight or 10 players would leave, but these two were the only departures. Pisarski sat on his conversation with Topakas for almost a fortnight before deciding to heed his principles. In the interest of Amateur football, he reported the conversation.

He told the Amateurs executive that an Old Brighton supporter had offered Topakas a loan of $6000 but the forward had pledged to stay at the Junction Oval if the club would lend him half that amount. Topakas said later that he never mentioned a figure and he never mentioned staying at the club. He admitted that he made up the story about the loan to convince Pisarski that he should be cleared, but the plan backfired. He felt he'd given the club enough. He'd helped it into a grand final and he'd employed three Redlegs in his building business. He also said he was unaware that loans were unacceptable. He had come to the Amateurs as an outsider.

The day after the alleged loan offer had been reported to the Amateurs, Marcellin thrashed Old Melburnians. On the Monday, I outlined the bare bones of the loan offer in *The Age*, and 3AW made thinly veiled claims about Old Melburnians in its *Rumor File* segment. The rumor was that an official from a troubled Amateurs club had taped a conversation with a player. Ric Pisarski is a private detective. It didn't take genius to recognise that the rumor was about him.

Amid the whirl off the field, the Redlegs were still fighting to avoid relegation. Their match against St Kevin's, like much of their season, was horrible but absorbing. In their anxiety to reverse their fortunes, they were trying too hard. They blazed away with the headstrong wind but the quarter-time score of 2.7 (19) indicated a side that was down on its luck. St Kevin's failed to score.

Roger Ellingworth was calm at the break. In his RM Williams boots and with his collar turned up, he had the look of rural distinction that is favored at clubs based on boarding schools. His jaw was strong and his hair neatly parted. In his trustworthy way, Ellingworth exhorted the Redlegs to kick a goal on the opening minute of the quarter. To the surprise of every-one, they did. The goal sparked celebrations that were exuberant for such an early stage of the game, but understandable given the wind and the Redlegs' plight. Then St Kevin's kicked into gear. Matt Lucas set his side in motion when he took a mark on the boundary line. The 19-year-old had been a rookie at the Whitten Oval before returning to the Amateurs because he was unwilling to sacrifice everything for morning and after-noon training sessions. For this shot at goal, he began his approach next to the fence. The ball curled through the goals and no one was surprised.

Lucas was renowned for his mercurial gifts. He wheeled through the forward line with his arm raised. Old Melburnians stared at the ground. The goal had confirmed their wretched season.

After the break, Lucas kicked St Kevin's only goal against the wind when he snapped from a pack in the goalsquare. The Redlegs battled fiercely but were only nine points up at the final break. Then Sam Lowerson and Robin Bowles took soaring marks and kicked goals to break the Redlegs' resistance. St Kevin's went on to win by 24 points, with Lucas kicking five goals in a performance that separated the sides. His partnership with Robin Bowles, whose dreadlocks and booming goals caught the eye, revealed strength in mid-sized forwards. Marcus Dollman and Nick Fraser, a dual best-and-fairest since leaving De La Salle and honoring his word to join St Kevin's if the club reached A-section, emphasised the work ethic in the midfield.

Old Melburnians' best were rover Toby Roberts, the son of St Kilda Brownlow Medallist Neil Roberts, and Michael Hazell, who overcame his stomach hernia to win his share of kicks out of the centre. Hazell's performance in even pulling on the boots was a symbolic boost for the Redlegs. A month earlier, the former E-section midfielder had been linked with the rumors suggesting an exodus from the club. His willingness to play with pain for his adopted club highlighted the folly of barroom gossip. It was also an example of success with outsiders.

After the match, Roger Ellingworth was reassuring. He compared the loss favorably to the debacle against Marcellin the week before. "There was some good stuff out there today." He noted that the club had the talent to turn around and avoid relegation. "If it comes down to the last minute of the last quarter of the last match, so be it."

The end of the address sparked the usual shuffle as one or two supporters sought a quick word with a player. Most Redlegs received a consoling pat on the shoulder as they unlaced their boots in silence; Ian McMullin received a stream of questions from his sons, Lachie, 10, and Josh, 7. McMullin offered patient answers under his breath, mindful that another loss had sucked all noise out of the room. On a seat outside the bar, his two sons continued to throw in the odd question as McMullin gave a short interview. The canny forward had played good football during an interrupted career at Collingwood and Essendon, but his original club had a special place in his heart. He admitted that relegation would knock the Redlegs around. "It'd be terrible," he said.

Little was he to know that the relegation saga would take more twists than the Great Ocean Road.

Neil Ross went on to coach a Collingwood rookie squad before selections were made in December. In the new year, he became a member of the Collingwood recruiting staff and a development coach at the Sandringham Dragons in the TAC Cup. Of his fellow Redlegs match committee members, Doug Searl took his first break from football since 1964, Mark Sarau returned to the helm at C-section club Ajax and Brett Mason became assistant coach at St Kilda City in the Southern league. Old Melburnians' season continues in the next chapter. St Kevin's season continues in chapter 21.

Nicky Winmar, forced to start on the bench after missing training, absorbs the game at Warburton. *Photo: Wayne Hawkins/Courtesy of The Age*

Fitzroy Reds and University Blacks salute the spirit of former Fitzroy ruckman Butch
Gale at the Brunswick Street oval. *Photo: Mark Daffey*

Reds' midfielder Patrick Jackson prepares to give the celebrations for the homecoming
of the Fitzroy guernsey a kickalong. *Photo: Mark Daffey*

Former Hawthorn and Brisbane utility Andrew Gowers, left, laps up his first premiership with Old Xaverians. *Photo: Mark Daffey*

Best-on-ground Adam Jones, left, takes in the celebrations after Xavs' sixth consecutive grand final victory. *Photo: Mark Daffey*

Youth worker Paul McKessy, in the cap, and former AFL ruckman Justin Charles seek broader horizons for North Footscray. *Photo: Mark Daffey*

Central Altona forward Tahal El-Hassan outpoints North Footscray opponent Jano Matar at the gritty Hansen Reserve. *Photo: Mark Daffey*

Young spectators take in the theatre at the Currie oval on King Island, where competition is keen despite the tally of three clubs. *Photo: Mark Daffey*

Currie ruckman Duncan Clemons marks strongly before Antarctic weather rules out any more high-flying. *Photo: Mark Daffey*

Long-haul midfielder Mick Jennings arrives in Melbourne after flying down from
Queensland. *Photo: Dominic O'Brien/Courtesy of The Age*

Former Essendon midfielder Chris Daniher takes a spell during a best-afield
performance for his hometown club, Ungarie. *Photo: Paul Daffey*

The Daniher brothers - Terry, Neale, Anthony and Chris - come from wide open
country in the Northern Riverina. *Photo: Paul Daffey*

Ungarie supporters keep score early in the match against outclassed neighbor
Girral-West Wyalong. *Photo: Paul Daffey*

Tom Wills grew up outside Moyston, near the Grampians, where he gained the
inspiration for "a game of our own". *Photo: Mark Daffey*

18

ORDER AND THE COURT

St Bernard's Old Collegians v Old Melburnians
the Bernards and the Redlegs

"The president has to be accountable for success and failure."

Old Melburnians president Ric Pisarski

Shane Zantuck played junior football in the tough northern suburb of Coolaroo. He went on to play at three league clubs but established his reputation as a fiery defender at Melbourne, the ultimate establishment club. He also became a wealthy businessman, with sportswear company Sportsco a nationwide success under his guidance. As a football coach, he used his awareness of class distinctions at St Bernard's in the Amateurs. The West Essendon club had always depicted the Yarra River as the great social divide but Zantuck took the issue further. During his term as coach in the mid-'90s, he contrived an edge by claiming that St Bernard's were from the western suburbs and that their rivals lived on Easy Street. Most St Bernard's players are from Essendon, which has more in common with Malvern than Sunshine, but Zantuck achieved his aim when opposition supporters derided St Bernard's as "western suburbs scum". The apogee of his campaign was ordering the team to dress down before a match against Old Melburnians, who were on top of the ladder. The next instruction was to meet at the South Melbourne pier. On a wet and freezing Saturday morning in July, the players took off their Blundstone boots and flannelette shirts and jumped into the icy bay. Afterwards, they marched into the Junction Oval looking tattered and feeling united. Old Melburnians looked on in disbelief. The tactic worked, with St Bernard's teaching the toffs from south of the Yarra a lesson in pride, unity and earthy attire. The clubs have enjoyed a spirited rivalry ever since.

Old Melburnians midfielder Simon Theodore has thrived on the rivalry. Theodore played in the Melbourne reserves when Zantuck was on the Demons' coaching staff. When they became opponents in the Amateurs, Zantuck renewed their acquaintance by giving colorful advice. Theodore absorbed it and gave it back. The sparring came to an end when Zantuck moved on from St Bernard's, but Theodore continued to thrive on the needling between the clubs. In their first match of the 2000 season, the 29-year-old shirtfronted a St Bernard's teenager and emotions bubbled over, culminating in a brawl in the crowd. An investigation into the brawl was held and St Bernard's were fined $500. Feelings would normally have run high for the return match, but this was no ordinary season. For a start, St Bernard's were on top of the ladder and Old Melburnians were near the bottom. Since the brawl in the crowd, Old Melburnians had been hit by the walkout of their match committee on a Thursday night after training. And on the eve of the match at St Bernard's, the Redlegs were docked the points for three victories. The decision consigned the club to relegation. The brawl was small beer.

The saga over the points for the three victories began on Thursday, July 27, at the hearing into the claim that key forward Andrew Topakas had been offered a loan to switch clubs. Old Melburnians produced the transcript of a taped conversation between Topakas and Ric Pisarski. Such transcripts can be accepted as evidence only when the defendant gives permission. Topakas withheld permission. The special investigation committee asked Topakas about his playing record and it emerged that the key forward had played for St Kilda seconds and thirds. The investigators checked his permit to play Amateur football. The permit stated that he'd played at Oakleigh and two Southern league clubs but there was no mention of St Kilda. Eyebrows were raised. Topakas told the hearing that Old Melburnians had advised him to leave the Saints off his permit application because, under the rules at the time, his years at Moorabbin would have denied him a permit.

In a phone interview, Topakas told me he'd thought nothing of leaving St Kilda off his application. He'd arrived at Old Melburnians knowing little about the stringencies of Amateur football after following a friend from Oakleigh when the VFL club folded. His aim was to play a decent level of footy with his mate. Topakas was asked to fill out a permit application during training one night. He said it was no secret that he'd played at St Kilda. Soon after he began kicking goals for Old Melburnians, it was reported in newspapers that he had a background at Moorabbin. "It's all a bit of a joke," he said.

Nobody was laughing at the hearing. The implication was clear. Topakas had played for Old Melburnians for almost three seasons with a permit gained through false means. The news was especially galling to Ric Pisarski. The president had reported the alleged loan offer from Old Brighton, believing he was doing the right thing by Amateur football, and it had blown up in his face. In the previous season, St Kevin's had reported Old Xaverians for an alleged player payment. The matter was investigated and Old Xaverians were cleared. In this instance, Old Brighton were cleared of offering a loan and, by peculiar circumstance, Old Melburnians were placed in the dock. Within a week they would face three charges of conduct unbecoming.

The Redlegs sought an adjournment. Ric Pisarski said five days wasn't enough to prepare the case. The Amateurs executive was worried that an adjournment would prevent the ladder from being finalised after the home-and-away season. A decision to take points from Old Melburnians and give the points to teams that had been defeated by the Redlegs would force the ladder to be recast. The possibility that the ladder would be recast would force the postponement of the finals.

The day after the hearing into Topakas's permit was announced, Old Melburnians lost the second last game of the season to Old Xaverians. The margin of four goals indicated improvement.

On August 2, the Wednesday before the last game, Old Melburnians arrived at Amateurs' headquarters with John Clements, a founding partner of Clements Hutchins and Co., the law firm that sponsors the club, and Terry Forrest, a Queen's Counsel. The investigating committee considered the charges and dropped two, as they were covered by the third charge. The third charge was that the club knowingly and deliberately withheld information that should have been on the permit application.

The investigators and Old Melburnians then questioned Topakas. Former Redlegs coach Neil Ross and chairman of selectors Doug Searl gave character evidence for the key forward. Written evidence was received from Kangaroos coach Denis Pagan and former St Kilda football manager Gary Colling. The Amateurs produced a list detailing the full playing record of Topakas, showing that he played with the St Kilda under-19s and reserves for three years and he played with Oakleigh for two years, not one, as shown on his permit application. Topakas said St Kilda paid him $30 a match for 60 under-19 games and $100 to $150 a match for four reserves games. He said he signed a contract to play three years at Oakleigh for $400 to $500 a game but the club folded without paying him. The investigation committee, which was chaired by Paul Lacava, considered the evidence and recommended that Topakas's permit be revoked. The permit committee would consider the recommendation the following night.

The hearing then turned to the charge against Old Melburnians. After talks between the investigators and Terry Forrest, it was agreed that the charge would be amended. The word "negligently" would replace "knowingly and deliberately". The charge now was that the club negligently withheld information on the permit application. Old Melburnians pleaded guilty and were fined $5000.

The Redlegs' greater concern was the recommendation to revoke the permit. Rule 37 in the Amateurs' regulations states that a permit can be cancelled without an explanation being given. The player is barred from playing Amateur football, but his club suffers no penalty. Rule 38 states that, if a player has infringed his Amateur status, his permit can be cancelled retrospectively to the beginning of the season. If the player has played in any victories, the points are lost and the club slips down the ladder. Topakas had played in nine games for the season. Three of those games were victories. The loss of points for those victories would send Old Melburnians from eighth place to 10th, which is the bottom of the ladder. With one game to go, there would be no chance of returning to eighth. The club would be relegated.

On August 3, a statement notified the media of the fine and declared that Old Melburnians had lost their points for three victories. Halfway through the statement, the assertion was amended. The statement said the permit committee was expected to ratify the recommendation to cancel the permit. The club would then lose the points for three victories. Old Melburnians were angry at the statement. It gave the impression that the recommendation would be rubber-stamped. Barrister James Nixon had poured too much of his life into the Old Melburnians Football Club to accept such a presumption. On the morning of August 3, he began exploring whether the Redlegs could avoid relegation.

Nixon pored through the Amateurs' permit and reinstatement guidelines in his Bourke Street office. The Old Melburnians life member had no argument that Topakas's permit application had been incomplete. But he concluded that it would be wrong to rule that the permit application had broken rule 38. He believed the key issue was whether Topakas had infringed his Amateur status. Under the 1998 guidelines, players were able to gain an Amateur permit if their earnings from football were less than $5000 over three years or $2000 over one year. These earnings were deemed travel expenses; the player was eligible for a permit. Going on the figures that Topakas revealed to the investigation, St Kilda had paid him an upper figure of $2400, clearly less than $5000. Under the guidelines, St Kilda had paid Topakas travel money. Oakleigh hadn't paid him, and Old Melburnians had certainly never paid him. Nixon believed that the key forward had never infringed his Amateur status. If full details had been given on his permit application, he would have been granted a permit.

Nixon rang Queen's Counsel Chris Dane, who is a friend and an Old Melburnians supporter. Dane read through the guidelines and agreed that Topakas had never infringed his Amateur status. Nixon wanted to turn up at Amateurs' headquarters and make a submission to the permit committee. He wanted to tell the committee that it would be wrong to subtract points after ruling that Topakas had infringed his Amateur status.

Nixon believed Amateurs officials knew him too well to listen to him. He believed the permit committee would be more likely to listen to someone they didn't know, especially when the newcomer was a Queen's Counsel. Nixon and Dane turned up unannounced at Elsternwick Park.

Amateurs officials were surprised at their arrival. Permit committee meetings are normally uninterrupted by submissions. Besides, it was felt that Old Melburnians had received natural justice when Terry Forrest spoke at the investigation hearing the previous night. Nixon and Dane were told they would receive a hearing but, in the meantime, they would have to wait outside. About 15 minutes after the meeting was due to start, they were invited upstairs. Nixon introduced Dane to the members of the permit committee. Richard Evans, the permit committee chairman, invited Dane to speak.

Dane began listing arguments against revoking the permit but Evans cut him off. Evans believed Dane should have been addressing the omissions from the permit, rather than presenting legal arguments questioning the power of his committee to take points from Old Melburnians. VAFA officials believe that the permit to signify Amateur status is the bedrock of the competition. Every February, Evans addresses the secretaries from all clubs and warns them that permit applications must be filled out correctly or the club risks losing points. Every year, as many as 25 clubs lose points for permit indiscretions. Evans believed the mere fact that Topakas had submitted an incomplete permit application, then signed an affidavit to say that all information was correct, left the permit committee with no choice but to revoke the permit. "By his omission, deliberate or otherwise, Topakas didn't give the permit committee the opportunity to make a valued judgment on whether he qualified to receive a permit," he said later. Then there was the fact that Topakas had earned money from St Kilda. He'd also played in the VFL and the Southern league, which Amateurs officials describe as professional competitions. The permit would have to be cancelled retrospectively to the start of the season.

Dane and Nixon protested when Dane's submission was cut off. They were then told that Topakas's permit had been revoked and the club had lost its points. The decision had been made before Dane and Nixon entered the room. Dane put his hand on Nixon's shoulder. He said they would describe the events of the night in an affidavit. Old Melburnians' miserable season had reached its nadir.

The next day – August 4, the day before the final match – Clements Hutchins and Co. sent a list of grievances to the Amateurs. The main complaint was that the permit committee had denied Dane the chance to speak and that, with the fine and the loss of points, the club had been punished twice for the single offence of submitting an incomplete permit.

"Your lawyers will inform you of the doctrine of double jeopardy," the law firm said. The club warned the Amateurs of Supreme Court action. If the Redlegs defeated St Bernard's, the court action would go ahead. If they lost, the action would be dropped, because the club wouldn't be able to avoid relegation even with the return of the points for the three victories.

Also on August 4, Paul Lacava submitted in writing the findings from the investigation committee hearing that was held on August 2. Lacava noted that John Clements didn't remain silent, as would be expected of an instructor to a Queen's Counsel, but raised many points with the investigators. Lacava said the investigators allowed Clements to speak because the investigation was considered informal. The investigators were impressed by the character evidence on behalf of Topakas. The Amateurs wouldn't stand in the way of him playing in another competition.

On the morning of Saturday, August 5, Old Melburnians players met at the Junction Oval and threw their weight behind the court action. The decision of the Amateurs had galvanised them. The return of key players from injury and the return of Lincoln Reynolds and Luke Holcombe from the Richmond VFL side would enable the club to field its best side of the season. The mood was at a season high. The bus pulled out for the journey across town to West Essendon. Most of the journey was taken up with watching a video of the final quarter of the Bulldogs and Essendon match at Colonial Stadium the previous week. The Bulldogs had won that match against the odds. The Redlegs were aiming to do the same.

The arrival of opponents spurred by court action was enough to make St Bernard's groan. Just when they were preparing for a rare finish on top of the ladder, along came a reminder of the low point in the club's history. In 1988, St Bernard's were charged with offering a Fawkner forward $2000 to transfer. The club claimed that a supporter had acted without consent but it was fined $5000 and suspended for the rest of the season. St Bernard's took the matter to the Supreme Court but their case was dismissed. The club was doomed to B-section.

This all happened in the year that I celebrated the end of my university years by wandering through northern Australia. From afar, I heard that Fawkner forward Terry Young had been the object of St Bernard's alleged affections. Young had shanks of curly hair, wild eyes and a torso like a tank.

He was easily the best, and most frightening, opponent I played on in the Amateurs, with one collision resulting in shaken bones and the air being forced from my body. But Amateur football in Victoria seemed so distant when I was in the tropics. I took little notice of the hubbub at St Bernard's. The only information I received was a newspaper clipping from my mother about the club auction that raised $30,000 to cover court costs. It was years before I returned to the club and, in my experience, the incident was rarely talked about. I sensed animosity towards the Amateurs executive, but it never clicked that this was anything more than the natural mindset of the club. It was only when I began reporting on Amateur football that I realised the degree to which St Bernard's felt scarred. If "1988" or "the court case" were mentioned, it was in mumbles and the conversation was steered elsewhere. For this reason, I believed I would be unpopular for making a return to the club on the day that it was to be reminded of its low point.

My fears proved unfounded. On a cloudless winter day in which the sun nipped at the skin, officials welcomed me back without reservation and I had a great time catching up with people I see too rarely. The court case was mentioned, but nobody seemed too bothered. President Andrew Vinecombe dismissed my question about feelings on the case with a wave of the hand. Vinecombe had assumed the presidency at 29 years of age. Three years later he was uninterested in an incident that had occurred when he was barely out of his teens. "There's no one from that generation left," he said.

On that count he was right and wrong. Several members of the committee were around his vintage, but many supporters had remained from the days of the court case. St Bernard's have a good record of retaining support, especially among those who were central to the glory years in the '70s. Players and supporters from that era set the tone of the club for two decades. Their passion was unstinting, but the club was ready for a new era when Vinecombe stepped in. A few years later, the change in mood was clear. The grimness that accompanied the relegation battles of the recent past was gone and the air was no longer thick with conspiracy canards. The prospect of success had created a lightness around the place. Everybody was looking forward to the finals. The club's most recent appearance in an A-grade grand final was in 1976, when North Old Boys triumphed. No rival of St Bernard's will ever create as much heat as North Old Boys. The two clubs share similar geography and history and they both kick with the left foot – that is, they're Catholic. The rivalry with Old Melburnians was fierce after the warm-up in the bay and, in most circumstances, the brawl in the crowd would have produced an edge for the return match. But the finals aspirations of St Bernard's had taken the edge away. The sight of the Redlegs' bus making its way down the hill to the ground was more a distraction than a signal for emotion.

St Bernard's began the game looking every inch like premiership contenders having their last hitout on the eve of the finals. The first 10 minutes were the smoothest I'd seen from a side in blue, black and gold. Slick hands shared the ball and the passing was crisp. In my time, St Bernard's sides were short; it always seemed that university teams and the clubs from south of the Yarra had the tall, gliding wingmen. But this St Bernard's side had a rare, almost garish, mix of height and athleticism. The problem was its failure to make its dominance pay. Both sides flipped the ball around as if it were a practice match. St Bernard's kicked seven goals for the quarter and the visitors kicked five. Old Melburnians captain Ian McMullin hit the mark with his summary at quarter-time. "They're thinking about next week," he said.

In the first minute of the new quarter, McMullin threw out his boot as the ball fell from a pack, kicking a goal without laying a hand on the ball. It was a small act of genius in a match that needed it. The clamor that surrounds most games at the bottom of the hill was missing. The umpires could be heard as though they were standing in the crowd, and St Bernard's defenders had lost their tongues. Defenders from the '70s would have been horrified. No self-respecting St Bernard's backman fails to give his opponent a bit of lip at the clubrooms end, but on this day there was silence. The gentle sun was lolling spectators towards sleep. Distraction came easy.

The ovals at St Bernard's are in a valley that runs off the Maribyrnong River. To one side is the hill on which the college stands. The main oval is cut into this hill. On the other side is another hill and a wire fence that separates the ovals from Rose Creek, a rank little waterway with a nice name but little else to recommend it. I spent a lot of time scrabbling around Rose Creek as a child. It was smelly and overgrown with thistles and nobody but innocents from on top of the hill went near it. We sailed our bikes over dirt humps or grabbed a stick and trawled along the creek in a practice we called "Harry Butlering", in honor of the host of a television wildlife series. When St Bernard's played at home, we crossed the creek and watched the match. Afterwards, we raced sticks along the creek before scrambling up the hill and heading home, with a footy under one arm and an eye on the dog.

Playing in the creek and scrambling up the hill would appear to be a thing of the past. The thistles have been cleared and the valley has been subdivided. Houses dot the hillside, but the empty blocks between the multi-storey brick monuments suggest that the spirit of the thistles lives on. It was an observation that heartened me. I've seldom returned to East Keilor since moving away but I'm sentimental about the smelly creek. It was a place where early teenagers and their imaginations were free to roam. On this day I was impelled to study the hill and wonder what became of Harry Butler because the match lacked an edge. Old Melburnians were battling away but their memories of victory were barely more recent than my memories of the creek. St Bernard's were intent on preservation.

Old Melburnians grew in confidence as the quarter wore on. A new belief was emerging. Ian McMullin sharked the ball from packs and tried to spin his way out of trouble. His groin injury prevented him stretching out but his compact strength was enabling him to get his boot to the ball, usually to advantage. As much as the 35-year-old was restricted to bustling in tight spots, Lincoln Reynolds galloped around the forward line like a horse on the plains. The grandson of Essendon legend Dick Reynolds was revelling in his return from the Richmond VFL side.

In the St Bernard's attack, Steve McKeon was struggling after spending a week in hospital with an infected hand. The archetypal mobile forward, he led well but swiped at the ball when going for his marks. It was hard not to feel for him as he tried in vain to complete a formerly routine task. Late in the quarter he was shifted to defence in the hope that he would find confidence.

In previous years, this might have been the cue for Luke Gollant to take a rest at full-forward. Gollant was one out of the box from the moment he left school and began with the old boys. The next year he went to North

Melbourne, where he kicked four goals in the first half of an under-19s grand final. Denis Pagan coached the side, which included Mick Martyn, Wayne Schwass and half a dozen others who went on to have long senior careers. Gollant kicked two goals on Martyn in his first game for the Essendon reserves but, around that time, he began a plumbing apprenticeship and found it was hard to impress when his hands were covered in blisters. St Bernard's eventually got him back. Gollant spent the next few years swapping between the goalsquare and the midfield, notably with Luke Vassallo, another player of moderate height and towering ability. The centre half-forward was Gollant's brother, Jason. When St Bernard's finally gained reasonable height in attack, Luke Gollant remained in the midfield, where he won an A-section best-and-fairest. Against Old Melburnians, he tried to motivate his side but his efforts were in vain. In truth, he was struggling as much as anyone. St Bernard's had more intensity in the canteen than in the centre square.

The Old Melburnians midfielders were having a great time. After every mark or free kick, Simon Theodore, the ruck-roving lawyer, showed the ball to the posse of St Bernard's supporters near the scoreboard. One or two of these supporters were defenders in the '70s and they knew their obligations. Whenever Theodore gathered the ball, they questioned his manhood and asked how much money he'd make if Old Melburnians went to court. Theodore thrived on the taunts and at one point gave the hecklers something to hoot about by kicking the ball into them. "They got quite excited," he said later. His teammates became excited when Nick Pirouet kicked a goal from a tight angle early in the last quarter. Court action looked imminent.

St Bernard's midfielder Daniel Byrne then went on a light-footed rescue mission, dancing around opponents and finding Nick Mitchell, who was playing a lone hand in attack, but the Redlegs had the game in hand. Memories of victory came flooding back and, after Ian McMullin had received a handball in the goalsquare, the celebrations were unrestrained. Lincoln Reynolds continued running wild and the dominance of string-bean ruckman David Holme was rude. "Let's go for percentage, boys," said one Redlegs supporter, to huge laughs from his friends. Midfielder Michael Hazell made the final statement with a clever clearance from a centre bounce. Rover Stuart Boyd finished off the good work with a running goal. "Is this the top side?" the supporter asked. "Let's come back here next week."

After several months in which nothing had gone right for the Redlegs, a spot of irony was in order. The frivolity continued when the siren signalled a 32-point victory. I hoped the mood would allow a comment from the supporters on the court action, but my effect couldn't have been greater if I'd tossed a stink bomb at their feet. The dispersal was hurried and efficient. A few supporters kept their eyes to the ground and scampered away, while those with a sense of the absurd allowed themselves a wry grin. One supporter claimed he knew nothing about the court action, which was like saying he had no idea that decimal currency had been introduced, and others offered the classic "no comment", words heard more often on the steps of parliament than the hill at St Bernard's. It was all quite funny.

My last hope was former St Kilda defender Neil Roberts, whose son Toby had again played a handy game on the ball. Neil Roberts has been a member of the media for decades. I was hoping he would furnish a colleague with some background, but the 1958 Brownlow Medallist was unwilling to help. A friend took on the role of escort and led him away by the elbow. "He doesn't want to talk," he said.

I told the escort I was speaking to Neil. The former Saint, who I later discovered was stricken with a hip complaint, eventually answered for himself: "I've got no comment. It's too political." He waved his arms and hobbled away.

The excitement on the hill was reflected in the dressing-rooms, where the Redlegs hollered like newly crowned premiers. James Nixon stood before the players and gave an impassioned speech. Roger Ellingworth, as modest in victory as he was composed in defeat, was glad to end the season with a win. Ric Pisarski said the club would seek an injunction on the Monday. Until then, the celebrations would be hearty.

In the social rooms, St Bernard's supporters were unimpressed by their side's insipid performance, but genuine in their praise for Old Melburnians. Some scratched their heads at the talent in the opposition. The Redlegs were surely the best side to be relegated for years. But, then, nobody knew whether they would be relegated.

I had a fine day at my old stamping ground but, while snaking up the hill to leave the ground, the feeling grew that the Old Melburnians saga was far from over.

Court action was dropped the next week when the Amateurs offered an appeal before the executive. Old Melburnians were careful to note the use of the word "appeal".

The hearing was held before the executive on September 11 at Elsternwick Park. Old Melburnians were represented by Queen's Counsel Graeme Uren. The club sought the services of Uren because he had no affiliation with Old Melburnians. He could be trusted to advise without being burdened by emotion. He is also one of Victoria's top few practitioners in administrative law. Uren outlined the club's argument. He said Old Melburnians had agreed to an appeal – not a rehearing. An appeal would be limited to the decision of the permit committee. A rehearing would reopen the case to all evidence relating to Topakas's permit. Uren noted that the findings from the investigation hearing on August 2 had been submitted in writing on August 4. The permit committee had met on August 3. Strictly, Uren argued, the permit committee had been unable to consider the evidence from the investigation hearing on August 2, which detailed Topakas's payments at St Kilda, because the evidence was yet to be submitted in writing. Without any such evidence, the permit committee had no right to cancel Topakas's permit.

Uren could have taken the tack explored by James Nixon. Old Melburnians believed that Topakas's earnings from St Kilda fell within the definition of travel expenses, as depicted in the Amateurs' guidelines for the 1998 season. They believed the permit committee was wrong to cancel Topakas's permit even after considering his earnings. But by leaving this view aside, and taking the approach that the permit committee had based its decision on evidence that was yet to be submitted in writing, they believed their case was watertight.

When Uren finished outlining Old Melburnians' argument, Bruce McTaggart called an adjournment. After the adjournment, Uren responded to questioning from the executive by reiterating that Old Melburnians wanted the appeal to be limited to the decision of the permit committee. McTaggart called an end to the appeal. Old Melburnians later claimed that McTaggart's final words were that the executive would reserve its decision. The club would be informed of the decision in writing within a few days.

On September 14, the Amateurs executive sent Old Melburnians a letter stating that the appeal was "de novo", a Latin term meaning "from the beginning". Another hearing was necessary to hear all evidence relating to Topakas's permit. Most appeals before sporting bodies, and many appeals before the courts, are open to all evidence relating to a case. In sport, this enables clubs or individuals to bring fresh evidence in support of their bid to overturn a decision. In this instance, the Amateurs executive wanted to address Topakas's playing history. The executive was inviting Old Melburnians to do the same. The aim was to ascertain whether the key forward should have been granted a permit before the 1998 season.

Old Melburnians believed they would have won such a hearing, but they resented the shift from an appeal to a rehearing. The Redlegs refused the invitation to submit written evidence to support their case. Then they refused to attend the rehearing. On September 25, by which time the Olympics had relegated the last round of the home-and-away season to a distant blur, the Amateurs executive dismissed the appeal. Old Melburnians would play in B-section.

Old Melburnians took the matter to the Supreme Court. They were prepared to wait until the new year for the case to be heard. In the meantime, there was a changing of the guard. Supporters rounded on Ric Pisarski at the annual general meeting, blaming him for the tumult that had shaken the club. Pisarski offered to stay in a lesser role, to help the club through difficult times that had begun under his leadership, but the offer was declined. "So be it," he said. He believed it was the way it should be. In pinning the blame on him and consigning him to the past, the club could begin anew. "The president has to be accountable for success and failure. The club now has the opportunity to move on."

For all that, Pisarski remains proud of his record. Under his leadership, the club won an A-section premiership, the first for four decades, and was a regular finalist. He believed his policy of bringing in outsiders had improved the club, but the disloyalty of some outsiders had proved unsettling. He would have saved the Redlegs from a sorry mess if he'd kept his conversation with Andrew Topakas to himself but, without knowing about the permit application, he believed he was right to heed his conscience. "It would have been wrong to let it slide." His final conviction was that Old Melburians were right to take their quest to avoid relegation as far as possible. "I thought the club had been treated very shabbily by the VAFA."

On October 27, the Amateurs were sent a summons to appear in the Supreme Court. Old Melburnians submitted in their evidence to the court a letter from Amateurs chief executive officer Phil Stevens, dated October 19. Stevens's letter outlines the reasons for the dismissal of Old Melburnians' appeal. He addresses the appeal hearing on September 11. "Having heard the arguments put forward by Old Melburnians, the hearing adjourned briefly to enable some discussion between executive members … A tentative view was reached that the hearing by the executive was a hearing de novo."

Bruce McTaggart swore an affidavit on December 5. He said he declared at the beginning of the appeal hearing on September 11 that it was a hearing de novo. John Clements swore an affidavit on February 14 disagreeing with McTaggart.

The hearing began in the Supreme Court on February 15 and lasted a day and half. No witnesses were called. Graeme Uren, for Old Melburnians, said the Amateurs executive had no right to cancel Topakas's permit retrospectively. He said the money that Topakas had earned from St Kilda fell within the 1998 guidelines of travel expenses.

Justice David Byrne asked before the lunch break on the first day whether the permit committee had used the wrong rule to cancel the permit. The Amateurs executive had said in correspondence to Old Melburnians that the permit was cancelled using rule 37. This rule requires no explanation, but it gives no scope for retrospective cancellation.

After lunch, Richard Tracey, Queen's Counsel for the Amateurs, and also one of Victoria's top few practitioners of administrative law, said that rule 38 had been used. Tracey, a former leading umpire in the Amateurs competition, said the VAFA defines an amateur player as "one who has not participated at any time in Australian football for gain". He said rule 38 was valid if any footballer had received money for playing football. Tracey said that Topakas had infringed his Amateurs status at St Kilda. He also signed a contract with Oakleigh for three years at $400 or $500 a game. Whether Topakas was paid was unimportant. He could pursue legal avenues to get that money if he wished.

A week later, officials and supporters gathered in court 13 for the judgment. Old Melburnians players and supporters gathered along one wall while barristers wearing black gowns and horsehair wigs reclined in their chairs, with legal tomes arranged before them. The lush maroon carpet and relentless wooden panels suggested a land locked in European winters. The sense of gravitas was at odds with the informality of football clubs – and most football hearings. The tipstaff asked that all rise for the judge. He then opened the court and asked God to save the Queen. Justice David Byrne seated himself at the bench. "I have determined that the position of the executive is good," he said. Old Melburnians' appeal was dismissed. After more than six months of wrangling, the ruling was delivered in 30 seconds.

In his judgment, Justice Byrne noted that the executive said it would restrict oral submissions to 20 minutes at the appeal hearing on September 11. This suggests that neither the Amateurs nor Old Melburnians considered a full rehearing.

Justice Byrne also noted that:
• No one thought it necessary to have Andrew Topakas at the appeal hearing.
• "Nothing turns" on whether the Amateurs declared an appeal de novo before or after the appeal hearing.
• The permit committee and executive committee said that, if Topakas's payments had been disclosed in 1998, he wouldn't have been granted a permit. "It must be accepted that the members of these committees are familiar with the permit rules." Justice Byrne bore in mind the 1997 case between the AFL and Carlton, in which the Blues tried to overturn Greg Williams's nine-match suspension for pushing an umpire. Justice Clive Tadgell ruled in that case that the decision of the AFL had not been "so aberrant that it cannot be classed as rational". Justice Byrne referred to the decision of the Amateurs executive in this regard.
• The executive signalled to Old Melburnians that it had material supporting its claim that Topakas wouldn't have been granted a permit if all relevant information had been provided on the permit application in 1998. "It may be significant that Old Melburnians Football Club did not seek to argue to the contrary when given the opportunity to do so." Justice Byrne was referring to the appeal rehearing on September 25.

- The permit committee used rule 38 to cancel the permit retrospectively. The money Topakas was entitled to receive from Oakleigh had no bearing on the decision.
- Old Melburnians were wrong to claim that a club must knowingly supply a flawed permit application before it could be considered in breach of regulations. Clubs must take responsibility for all information on permit applications.

After the ruling, Old Melburnians players and officials composed themselves on the William Street footpath. They had come to court expecting to win. Ric Pisarksi said it was not up to him to comment. His successor, Charles White, tersely informed me that he would have to look over the judgment before making a comment. The Redlegs party straggled towards the café on the corner. Some held briefcases or files; the rest had their hands jammed deep into their pockets. All heads were bowed.

White was helpful when I rang that afternoon. With the shock over, he seemed relieved to be able to get on with the new season. "We had a responsibility to our players and our members to take the case on," he said. "We believed we were right. We've been shown that we're not. We'll move on."

Others disagreed. James Nixon took two days off work to recover from the disappointment of losing the case. He was one of three lawyers who'd worked many unpaid hours on the case over many months. The others were John Clements and midfielder Michael Hazell. The trio believed the matter should go to the Victorian Court of Appeal. The club agreed that their arguments should be put to the committee but, in the meantime, the club delegate was obliged to attend a meeting for all clubs at Amateurs' headquarters.

At the meeting, Tony Orchard, the delegate for Melbourne High School Old Boys for 28 years, said Old Melburnians had gone far enough in their pursuit of justice. Orchard believed the club was undermining the good will of the competition and he objected to the bill that his club and every club in the competition would face if the Redlegs were to overturn the dismissal. If Old Melburnians won the appeal in the courts, the Amateurs executive would charge each club $1700 to cover legal costs. The Old Melburnians delegate waited until the conclusion of the

meeting before approaching members of the Amateurs executive. He told
executive members that the Redlegs were sure to drop their appeal.

Pressure was mounting not only from Melbourne High School Old
Boys. Straight after the St Bernard's match, several players had announced
they would leave Old Melburnians. By the time of the new season, two
dozen had gone. Others felt the saga was tarnishing the name of
Melbourne Grammar School. Finally, 10 days before first round of the new
season, Old Melburnians and the Amateurs executive released a joint statement announcing that a settlement had been reached. The terms were
confidential, but the club would take its place in B-section. Charles White
acknowledged in an interview that Old Melburnians had been in danger
of disintegration if they continued down the legal path. "The club has
suffered enough," he said.

The Age ran my story announcing the Redlegs' backdown on the day
that the Amateurs competition was to hold its annual pre-season dinner.
After months of updates on the saga, one or two sub-editors who'd tired
of the story were almost as happy with the announcement as the Amateurs
executive. Charles White was unable to attend the dinner at the Crown
Casino because he was interstate with work. Other Old Melburnians
officials believed they had spent too much time on football to attend yet
another function. No Redlegs officials turned up at the dinner, sparking
nudges and winks and rumors of a boycott. White said there was no
boycott; officials were simply exhausted after the wrangling of the off-
season. Now they had a new season to face. The club planned to gain its
revenge by winning the B-section premiership.

*Before the off-season commotion, ruckman David Holme won Old Melburnians'
best-and-fairest. For the new season, Ian McMullin stepped down as captain but
agreed to play on. Simon Theodore was appointed captain, with Michael Hazell
among his deputies. Roger Ellingworth returned to being an assistant coach. Andrew
Topakas joined Chelsea in the Mornington Peninsula Nepean league and Scott
Oram joined VFL club Sandringham. Stuart Boyd went to Phillip Island. Others
went to rivals in the Amateurs, with Lincoln Reynolds and Nick Pirouet joining
A-section club Old Trinity. Tony Orchard stepped down as the member for
Melbourne High School Old Boys. A-section finals are covered in subsequent
chapters.*

19

THE LONG-DISTANCE RUCK-ROVER

Wickcliffe-Lake Bolac v Dunkeld
the Magpies and the Roos

"I reckon he's crazy. I can't believe it."

Bill Simmons, stepfather of Mick Jennings

Throughout the season, it was rare to go a weekend without hearing a good footy yarn. At Echuca, I heard about former rugged defenders Ron Andrews and Jim Jess getting a kick for Balranald on Saturdays and going pig-shooting on Sundays. Outside Wangaratta, the story was told of Michael Long's brothers taking Tarrawingee from the wooden spoon to the premiership. At Lavington, a prospective recruit arrived for his interview in a Tiger Moth aeroplane. At Moyston, a committeeman mentioned in passing that a rival club was flying a midfielder from Queensland every week. I nearly dropped my beer.

Later that month, I was at Melbourne Airport to meet Mick Jennings, who emerged through the arrival gate looking tousled and tanned, with not an ounce of fat on his wiry frame, wearing denim shorts and a T-shirt with the caption "Football is life, nothing else matters". He had a small bag bearing a rugby top that listed the premierships of his football club and the boots I'd requested as a photo prop. The flash of the camera prompted a teenager to ask Jennings for his autograph, just in case he was famous. Jennings blushed, bringing contrast to his dark stubble. Then he pleased those shivering around him by slipping on the rugby top. In the depths of the Victorian winter, the 31-year-old had developed the habit of travelling from the Sunshine Coast to play in the Mininera district league in western Victoria. It had to be asked whether he knew anyone else in the world who travelled across a continent to play local sport. "I haven't heard of anyone," he said. "There's got to be a first time for everything."

Jennings said that Wickcliffe-Lake Bolac had paid him well when he was coach and this was his way of putting something back. The club some-times slipped him a few dollars to help him out, but it was the success of his landscaping business in Queensland that made the arrangement pos-sible. The interest in his journeys had him scratching his head. He believed my calls had been a hoax. On arrival at the airport, he expected a bunch of mates to jump from nowhere and stir him up for believing that *The Sunday Age* would be interested in a bush footballer with more frequent flyer points than sense. But there was only one mate at the airport, Rick Tassell. He and Jennings grew up in Ararat, playing football and cricket and learning how to box. Tassell once diverted from their regular routine and reached the semi-finals of the Stawell Gift. In his last football match, Tassell tore his hamstring early in the first quarter and collected a premiership medal after the siren. Jennings also collected a medal after the siren. The pair share a life of sporting memories. Now Tassell and his pregnant wife Maureen had driven from Geelong to create another one. Tassell laughed as the camera clicked away. The combination of Mick Jennings and a touch of glamor tickled his sense of the absurd. Jennings shrugged. His journeys were giving new meaning to local sport in a big country but he failed to see what the fuss was about. "I think everyone makes too much of it," he said.

The trip to Ararat was scarcely more believable than flying across two states to play football. I turned on the radio to learn of a dust-up in the Essendon and Bulldogs match at Colonial Stadium. The road between Taylors Lakes and Melton had never been so fraught with commotion. The excitement continued until Beaufort, at which point in the broadcast Chris Grant ran in from the boundary line and screwed the ball on his left foot to give the Dogs a famous victory. At the Ararat Hotel, Mick Jennings failed to share in the excitement. The midfielder said he rarely received AFL news in Queensland; for this reason, he had little knowledge of Essendon's phenomenal season. He still loved playing footy but he had less interest in following the game. It had to be remembered that, while Jennings was standing in the Ararat Hotel, he was living on the Sunshine Coast. As we spoke, one or two old acquaintances shook his hand and stopped for a chat. One well-wisher presumed he was still living down the road. Jennings leaned on the wall, tired and disoriented. He'd set out from Noosa Heads at 3pm and arrived in his home town at 11pm. Now he just wanted to say hello to his mother.

On his first footy trip back to Victoria, Jennings walked into his mother's house and gave her the shock of her life. "What are you doing here?" she said. On the second weekend he surprised her again. By the third week she was forced to accept his explanation that he was returning every weekend to play football. She said he was mad. On this night, mother and son caught up on local news while Jennings unwound. He'd done a day's work before travelling for eight hours. His cup of tea was well-deserved. We turned in about 1am.

Jennings was up early the next morning to visit his brother Dave. The pair had played together over many years, at Ararat and at smaller clubs south of their home town. Usually they came as a package: Dave as coach and Mick as assistant coach. Mick stepped up into the top job at Wickcliffe-Lake Bolac when Dave headed back into Ararat to coach the Rats. Mick said it was the making of him. In one year he tied with a team-mate for best-and-fairest in the competition but their side was bundled out of the finals. The next year he injured his knee and coached on the side-lines before taking drastic action in the run-up to the finals. Unable to watch any longer, he took off his knee brace and played on a half-back flank. After each match, he put the brace back on. The apparatus stretched from his calf to his upper thigh. "I looked like Robocop," Jennings said. The sight of him removing the brace to run on to the ground inspired his teammates. The Magpies sneaked into the finals before brushing aside favored opponents to win the flag.

Not long afterwards, a broken engagement persuaded him that he needed a break. He'd been a welder in an Ararat factory for 10 years and the time seemed right to explore beyond Victoria. So he packed his car and headed for Cairns, where he found another world. He worked in bars and met European backpackers. He went on fishing trips in Cape York. "It really broadened my horizons, I can tell you that," he said. Jennings had every intention of returning to coach Wickcliffe-Lake Bolac but found himself seduced by his new life. The prospect of staying in the tropics appealed more than returning to a factory at home. Magpies president Dave Watson had counselled him to go away and enjoy himself. Watson was less enthusiastic when Jennings informed him that he wanted to stay away and enjoy himself, but the Magpies' president said the club would back whatever decision Jennings made. The midfielder promised that one day he would pay him back. Around this time, 10 committeemen from the Port Douglas Crocodiles filed into Jennings's loungeroom and asked him to coach their club in the Australian rules competition in Cairns. Such a powerful posse was hard to knock back. It was clear that the midfielder would be in Queensland for a while.

His attitude amid the palms and the mangroves reflected his attitude during grisly winters in Victoria. He was captain of the representative side, finished second in the competition best-and-fairest award and took the Crocs to the grand final. "It was the time of my life – just what I needed," he said. But it failed to stop him moving on. When his Dutch girlfriend scored a job in Noosa Heads, he went with her.

One of his first moves in his new home was to check out the football ground. A phone number was listed next to the gate. He rang the number and introduced himself. The Noosa Tigers asked him to coach but he resisted because he was setting up his gardening business. So the Tigers appointed a 23-year-old as coach and Jennings became assistant, to help him out. The coach was a brilliant footballer; the Tigers won the first nine games with him firing at full-forward. But he was too young and wayward to be a leader. He was forever falling out with the committee. "They couldn't see eye to eye on any issue – from what footies to use, to what meals to serve on Thursday night," Jennings said. The committee wanted to sack the coach and replace him with his assistant, but Jennings stood by the young spearhead. In the end, they were both sacked. "The players were devastated by the whole thing and lost the next two games," Jennings said. Several Tigers were about to quit the club when Jennings called a meeting at his house and persuaded them to keep playing. He was later proud that the Tigers resumed their winning ways.

In the meantime, he began training with a rugby union club. He was about to indulge his curiosity and make his debut when a former team-mate rang from the Western District. Jennings told him about the upheaval at Noosa Tigers and his plan to try his hand at rugby. Wickcliffe-Lake Bolac were on the phone before he could say "scrum". An agreement was struck. Jennings would forsake weekends in the sand and sun to play footy under moody skies with old mates. "I said I'd come down and play a few games and see how it goes," he said.

He slotted straight into the Magpies' midfield and never looked back. The travelling tired him but he saw no reason to complain. His only worry was whether the distances were taking the sting out of his performance. Every Friday he was driving 130 kilometres from Noosa to Brisbane, fly-ing to Melbourne and catching a lift to Ararat. All up, the journey was more than 2000 kilometres, the same as the distance from London to Sicily or London to Kiev, but his teammates assured him that his form was fine. The greatest test came on the weekend that he was unable to get on a flight out of Brisbane until 9.30pm. At midnight he hired a car at Melbourne Airport and drove 220 kilometres to Ararat, where he fell into bed feeling like he'd travelled halfway across the country, which he had. The next afternoon he finished among the Magpies' best.

That experience persuaded him that he must book in advance to gain reasonable departure times. He found that, if he booked two weeks ahead, a return flight from Melbourne to Brisbane cost $280. "I've become a really good flight consultant," he said. His total weekend travelling costs, with petrol and airport parking fees thrown in, came to $350. The cost of hiring a car at Melbourne Airport was a one-off. Every other weekend, a teammate was at the airport to meet him. Fellow midfielder Matt Hanrahan sometimes picked him up on the way through from Melbourne. Defender Roger Flanner, the teammate who'd rung him in Noosa, once made a special trip from the Western District to bring him home. "His attitude is, if you're flying that far, I can drive that far," Jennings said.

All this was relayed during a conversation over a breakfast of steak of eggs. Jennings looked quizzical at my reference to dietary trends. He'd eaten steak and eggs every match day since he could remember. After three league best-and-fairests and several placings, it was hard to argue with the results. The dishes were left to Jennings's stepfather, Bill Simmons, who listened in while finishing off the pots and pans. Simmons had travelled around Australia and loved every minute. He failed to see why anyone would travel overseas. He also failed to see why anyone would travel from Queensland to Victoria to play football. "I reckon he's crazy. I can't believe it."

Jennings sipped his cup of tea. He'd heard it all before. "This is probably my last year. I couldn't think of a better way to finish – with a club that's meant so much to me." His final task before leaving was to surprise his mother once again. This time it was a birthday present. Nola accepted her decorative plate with bashful relish and gave her son a kiss. As the car edged away, she stood on the verandah wiping tears from her eyes. Jennings waved, and paused. He said she did the same every weekend. I felt privileged to witness the tender scene. Jennings had offered me a bed as soon as I suggested meeting him at the airport. I was grateful for being welcomed into the family home, but Jennings thought it was no big deal. "We're an open family," he said. He pointed out the modest, brick home of Richmond defender Scott Turner as we drove through town to pick up Rick Tassell.

The two friends reminisced as we passed Alexandra Oval, the home ground of the Rats. On the road out of town, we passed the Maroona Hotel and Jennings described a bet with the publican, Jim Moriarty. One summer Moriarty offered free beer if Jennings could run from the town to the pub. On Friday nights, Jennings would run the 19.5 kilometres, drink beers on the house and score a lift back home at the end of the night. The dedication to fitness and time with friends seemed a neat summary of his life. Another part of his character was revealed when he fidgeted and fudged the conversation for the rest of the journey to Lake Bolac. I thought he might have been sick of having a journalist in his ear since breakfast, but the midfielder said later that his mind had drifted to the match. He'd always put pressure on himself to perform but his Queensland trips increased the stakes. There was no point travelling more than 2000 kilometres to play a dud game.

The sight of James Fitzpatrick at the entrance to the ground settled him. The ruckman with the gentle manner sold us a program and had a short chat to Jennings before we edged around behind the cars with their grills to the fence. The sky was dull and the ground was wide and damp. Low-roofed, solid clubrooms backed off from the wing. Tassell and Jennings bounced out of the car. Tassell was seeing former teammates for the first time for the year but Jennings was more excited because he hadn't seen the Magpies for a week. His reaction was in keeping with the reaction of many footballers who train away from their club. By match day, they're ready for the reunion. Several Magpies were in the same position as Jennings. Midfielder Trent Aldous was among those who lived in Melbourne and colorful forward Troy Richardson returned every week from Port Fairy. The lure of home underpinned the Magpies' line-up.

The club's heart and soul, however, continued to live a few paddocks from the ground. Centre half-forward Stuart Knight had won four league best-and-fairests. In one of them, he tied with Jennings. President Dave Watson said they were also tied for the title of the Magpies' favorite son. "They're equal favorite sons. We'd better not differentiate." Watson, a wiry farmer with a thoughtful way about him, was avuncular towards Jennings. He admitted the club had been worried when it recruited him and his brother Dave. Ararat was a tough town that bred tough men and Mick had the reputation of a brawler. Watson said he learned that it was the loyalty of Mick Jennings that landed him in trouble. He believed that Jennings was unable to stand by while his brother or his friends were under threat. "He was backing up his mates." It was this loyalty that had ingrained Jennings in the hearts of people around Wickcliffe-Lake Bolac. Watson said there were few more respected players in the competition. Persistent finishes in the top three in the league medal support his claim.

Besides his loyalty, Jennings is renowned for his toughness. Nobody who passed comment on the midfielder failed to mention his disregard for safety. His father, Bruce, had watched his son all his life and remained in awe of his toughness. The first comment Rick Tassell had made at the airport was that Mick was tough. Any clubman I spoke to cocked his head and expelled a small breath before mentioning his ruggedness and durability. One or two also described him as ruthless in his pursuit of the ball. I could see that he was all skin and muscle, and I gained the impression that he could handle himself in a stoush, but to me his main traits were kindness and generosity. It would be interesting to watch him play.

The trait he displayed most in the first quarter against Dunkeld was industry. He often battled through tangles of arms and legs to fire out 15-metre handballs, low and direct and guaranteed to bring teammates into the game. I thought he was too unselfish. Sometimes he should have dropped the ball on to his boot, especially in the forward line. Dave Watson recalled a first quarter in which he had 19 handballs and no kicks. "He sees that's his go," Watson said.

Jennings provided many opportunities but his teammates often wasted them. Troy Richardson, the bald forward with a flair for theatre, led and marked with confidence but sprayed his kicks like a rotary sprinkler, not that it worried him. He knew the ball would return in his direction before long. The Magpies had won a single game the previous season – in the last round – but the return of many local heroes and strong local pride had enabled them to rise to the top of the ladder.

Dunkeld hit them with tractors and sheds in the second quarter. It was a classic case of two sides trying to sort each other out before the finals – the last of the winter rites – and it was as bruising as anything I was to see for the year. While watching Jennings, I wondered whether matches in Queensland would feature the same reckless abandon. Somehow I couldn't see it. In Queensland, the sun always shines and football is a sporting option. In the towns of Victoria, football is a cultural imperative. Lake Bolac has had a club for 125 years. In the early days, the team would drive horse and cart beyond Hamilton and camp overnight, just to get a game. Such stories seep through the generations, helping to give meaning to the absurdity of risking pain on a grim afternoon. Not everybody in football knows their club's history, but few would make sacrifices unless they felt a sense of history in their bones. In all the crunching of bones against Dunkeld, Jennings injured his hip. The siren went and the players trudged from the ground to boisterous applause.

After the break, the Magpies established a pattern of dominance. James Fitzpatrick earned the tap-out and his side peppered the goals. Mick Jennings battled away and Trent Aldous kicked with equal neatness on either foot. Pat Hoey, the eccentric forward who cuts his socks off at the ankles, jumped high and often and, in defence, the steadiness of Brian McGuinness confirmed that this was the best country team I'd seen outside the major leagues for years. McGuinness was a Fitzroy draft choice; to play him at full-back seemed an outrageous luxury. Fellow key defender Damien McMaster was also in control but he was forced to check himself after being hit in the head with an elbow. At three-quarter time, McMaster poured out his frustration with a plea to his side to avoid reports going into the finals. In wearing his heart on his long sleeves, the coach earned a few unintentional laughs but nobody could mistake his depth of feeling. The Magpies returned to their positions and scooted to a 74-point victory, ensuring top spot after the home and away rounds.

Mick Jennings greeted the siren by shaking the hand of every teammate and every Dunkeld player before completing his mission by shaking hands with the entire Roos' coaching staff, a sensitive warrior to the end. In a fortnight, he'd be back for another finals campaign but, before then, he planned to spend a weekend fishing in Queensland. He said he looked forward to a rest. The thought of him throwing in a line off the warm coast brought to mind a statement from Rick Tassell early in the match. Tassell glanced up at the dull sky as the players squelched through the mud. "It's hard to imagine Mick will be back in the sun at Noosa this time tomorrow," he said.

Wickcliffe-Lake Bolac won their two finals with ease, completing their rise from last to first with a comfortable victory over Streatham-Mininera-Westmere Rovers in the grand final. Dunkeld lost the first semi-final; Brad Mawson won their best-and-fairest. Midfielder Trent Aldous won the Wickcliffe-Lake Bolac best-and-fairest and finished second in the league award after being trumped in the last round. Mick Jennings farewelled the Magpies with a heartfelt speech at the presentation night after receiving a plaque that commemorated his career.

20

PORTRAIT OF NICKY WINMAR

Warburton-Millgrove v Upwey-Tecoma
the Kookaburras and the Tigers

"He rang me and said, 'Hey Cuz, you can have your car back'."

Warburton-Millgrove president Paul Kercher

Nicky Winmar looked overwhelmed, like a reluctant hero trying to figure out the unfamiliar admirers who seemed to know so much about him. A dozen St Kilda fans formed a ring around the former Saint before the senior match at Warburton. They smiled and nodded and let him know that, two years after his departure from Moorabbin, they still adored him. He would never be forgotten.

The fans wore St Kilda jumpers and scarves. Some wore Nicky Winmar badges; others toted swap cards. Michael Skilney said he had 18 plastic figurines of his hero on a shelf at home. "I cornered the market," he said. The Glenhuntly artist, a 52-year-old with thinning, sandy hair and a romantic's gaze, had led his friends from the south-east suburbs through the misty valleys beyond Melbourne to present Winmar with his portrait of the Saint hoisting his guernsey and pointing to his skin at Victoria Park in 1993.

Skilney likened Winmar's gesture to the Black Panther salute at the

1968 Olympics. He believed that Winmar emulated Tommie Smith and Johnny Carlos, the sprinters who protested against racism in America by raising black-gloved fists on the medal dais after the 200 metres. "It was a great moment in AFL history," Skilney said. His friends nodded, wide-eyed, waiting for a response. "That was a day to remember." Winmar held the artwork in front of him and cocked his head. The yellow sun of the Aboriginal flag shrouded his defiant figure. He looked up shyly. "I'm honored," he said. "It's a great picture."

The Saints fans crowded next to Winmar as one camera after another was summoned to record the moment. The 34-year-old smiled at the centre of the group, holding the artwork to his chest. He seemed flattered that anyone would drive into the cold, blue hills to show him their hearts, but the fuss had thrown him. He'd been linked with the Americans who raised their fists to the sky, but his response was more in keeping with Peter Norman, the Australian silver medallist who stood bemused as the Americans challenged *The Star-Spangled Banner*. On a grey day in a sleepy town, Winmar felt caught in the spotlight. He responded to the gentle barrage of questions with one or two stilted replies before the inquiries trailed off and he excused himself. The Saints fans nodded and smiled.

I buttonholed Winmar short of the pavilion. Clutching his bag with all his footy gear, he told me about his arrival in Warburton and his appreciation of the mountain view. But his shyness receded and the sun burst through only when he talked about football. It was evident that he still cared about his performance. The previous month, he'd kicked 5.5 against Woori Yallock. "Should have kicked 10," he said. Questions about a two-match suspension for striking made him awkward. His response was to say that he preferred staying out of the centre square. "There's too many head-hunters." He shuffled as he said he liked the club and he liked the coach. His bag continued to dangle at his side. It was half an hour since he'd parked his car and he hadn't yet made it to the rooms. He was waiting for the word. I thanked him for his time and he proceeded on to the verandah of the pavilion. The chunky heels of his elastic-sided boots sounded on the floorboards and he entered the old room with the crackling fire. Finally, he could put down his bag.

The fire is at the heart of a pavilion that is among the wonders of

Victorian country football. Nobody seems to know its age but the club celebrates its centenary in five years and the pavilion might as well be 100 years old. Behind the pavilion, the beginnings of the Yarra River bubble and swirl, and lone chimneys send tendrils of smoke drifting towards the peak of Mount Victoria. Nicky Winmar emerged from the rooms after 10 minutes and took a spot towards the end of the pavilion. He drew on a cigarette as he drew in the peace. In an hour, he would feel at home in the noisy crush of the match, but in the meantime his teammates knew to leave him alone. He looked across the reserves match with a faraway frown. Forests teemed up the hillside. The air was crisp and the leaves were damp. It was just as he might have imagined Victoria when he was a young footballer with a dream.

Winmar grew up in Pingelly, a town in the wheatfields south of Perth, where golden stalks sway on the brown earth. Whenever it rained, he grabbed his football and practised his skills until it was dry. Then he watered the backyard and practised again. He knew from watching the football replays that, to make it in Victoria, you have to be good in the wet. He also knew you had to be fierce in the clinches. Sometimes, when his father took him on shearing trips, he used the time by practising his tackling on the sheep. His efforts were rewarded when he began shining for South Fremantle. In one match, he kicked seven goals in a quarter. St Kilda offered him the chance to realise his Victorian dream.

The Saints had to fly Winmar to Victoria to sign a contract. To keep him away from the scouts from the newly formed West Coast, they kept him in a motel room for three days, put a pair of sunglasses on him and whisked him out of Perth on a midnight flight. "It was like going from Russia to America," Winmar said later. In Melbourne, he went through his own cold war. He battled homesickness for several years. It failed to stop him igniting the competition with his skill and daring, but it contributed to his erratic behavior. Sometimes, when the glare of AFL football became too much, Winmar fled to the country. St Kilda coaches were dispatched to track him down and bring him back. After his AFL career had ended, he fled to the country again. This time there were no coaches to persuade him to return.

The mystery was why he went to Warburton. During his AFL career, he normally went to places outside Ballarat, his wife's home town.

Warburton-Millgrove supporters were telling me that Winmar was in their part of the country because of his friend Tony Elbourne. "Here he comes now," one said. "You can ask him yourself." Elbourne cut a solitary figure as he wandered down the hill towards the entrance gate. Standing in front of the old pavilion, he explained his part in Winmar's choice with a shrug and a chuckle. The improbability of Nicky Winmar lobbing on his doorstep had taught him that wonders never cease. Winmar had taken his son's under-12 team for training during the final weeks of his career, when he was with the Western Bulldogs. The session was part of Winmar's promotional duties but Elbourne promised the Bulldog forward a favor in return. Winmar remembered the promise. He liked the hills and the peace. After the season, he returned and asked Elbourne whether he could stay and go fishing for a few days. "He stayed a week," Elbourne said. "Actually, he never left. Three weeks later the club fixed him up with a house and a car and he was away."

Warburton-Millgrove were stunned. A player fresh out of an AFL career of 251 games had wandered into their arms. Once the shock was over, the action was swift. The coach, Brendan Woods, gave Winmar the keys to his house and moved back in with his parents. The club bought him a V8 Commodore for $2000 and gave him money to get through the pre-season. He was promised match payments in line with those of star players at leading country clubs and it was arranged to pay his bills and provide food. In return, the club gained the best recruiting tool in its history. President Paul Kercher said training was like a circus. Players returned from everywhere, with star onballer Jason De Graaf breaking his coaching contract in northern Victoria because he wanted to play with Winmar. "I was putting in clearance after clearance," Kercher said. "Everyone just wanted to play." About 60 players regularly attended training, more than anyone could recall. Crowds at training were bigger than attendances at home games the previous season, when the Kookaburras finished second-last. For the final practice match, the club held two fund-raisers and took $20,000. "That's unheard of," Kercher said.

It was obvious from the first match that the Kookaburras would be powerful. De Graaf was unpopular in Kerang, where his contract had been tossed in the bin, but he put the wrangles behind him and found dashing form. Winmar gained his share of kicks without dominating. He was more of a burst player, with a big mark or a booming goal to keep the Burras ticking over. Numbers at training continued to be high, even if Winmar's attendance was spasmodic. The midfield star often went to Melbourne to see friends or work in Aboriginal affairs. Once he phoned from interstate to ask for money in his account so that he could get home. Before the Olympics, he flew to the Northern Territory to carry the torch. Sometimes he told Brendan Woods that he would be unable to train; other times he had no excuse, so he let it slip. He turned up every Saturday without fail but, if he hadn't phoned to explain his absence from training, he started on the bench. Woods said this happened six or seven times. "We didn't make any allowances." The coach also took a tough line with money. If he felt that Winmar was out of line in asking for cash, he ordered that no money be paid. Officials worried that Winmar would leave but Woods held his ground. Through their trials, Winmar developed great respect for his coach. He even asked him to be his best man. Woods said it was an honor to be asked.

Winmar respected the strength of character in Woods but, more so, he respected the 28-year-old's return after a brain aneurism. "I think he admired that," Woods said. The pair traded compliments. Woods told Winmar he was a legend through his achievements at St Kilda. Winmar shook his head. "Nah, Cuz," he said. He believed Woods was the legend after returning from a life-threatening condition. Woods believed that Winmar had little concept of his impact in 12 years at St Kilda and one year at the Bulldogs. Confirmation came when a Saints fan in town lent Winmar a videotape. The dual best-and-fairest was astonished. "Cuz, was I that good?" he said. Woods told him he was. He continued to tell him throughout the season. Winmar, who once was considered a Brownlow Medal prospect, needed propping up like anyone at Warburton-Millgrove. Woods boosted his confidence with regular feedback. In return, Winmar played hard for as long his faltering fitness would allow.

On this day, Woods stepped back before the match to allow Terry Wheeler to address the players. As a child, Wheeler went to every match and every training session at the Warburton ground. It was his duty to fish the footballs out of the river. When his father was in committee meetings, he grabbed the car keys and went for a drive. "We were involved in this club from the bassinet," he said. Wheeler left the Kookaburras after winning the best-and-fairest at 17. He played his first senior game for Footscray as a rover. His second game was in the back pocket, where he remained for the next decade.

Back at Warburton, supporters craned their necks to see the charismatic former Bulldog. The St Kilda fans were excited after receiving a special invitation to join them. The floorboards sighed under the weight of the gallery as Wheeler spoke about the two most important days in his career: his premiership with the Kookaburras' under-16s and his premiership as playing coach at Williamstown. They were his only two flags. Wheeler had the room in thrall as he asked the Kookaburras whether they were prepared to pay the price to win a premiership. He assured them it would be the most magical moment of their careers. Michael Skilney emerged from the rooms tingling with the power of premiership oratory. "It sent a shiver down my spine," he said. His expedition to see Nicky Winmar was delivering all sorts of treats.

Winmar wheeled through the warm-ups with the familiar No.7 on his back. In the royal blue, black and white panels, he looked at home in a guernsey with the St Kilda strip at heart. "Come on, Nicky," the Saints fans yelled as the Kookaburras completed a run-through near the goalsquare. Winmar squinted at the cars under the fir trees behind the goals, trying to work out the source of the cries. He raised his hand with a half-wave before his teammates wheeled around and began a run-through back to the centre square, pulling Winmar along with them. The Saints fans handed around mugs of soup and sandwiches. Then they sipped tea and ate slices of cake. Michael Skilney leaned on the bonnet of his car and sucked in the air. "I just love the atmosphere," he said. His wife, Lesley, smiled as she poured more tea.

The start of the match was as bright as the sky was steely. Warburton-Millgrove were unable to be knocked off top spot but they were eager to impress the legends on the sidelines. The legends had been at a lunch announcing the best ever Warburton-Millgrove team, in which Terry Wheeler was named ruck-rover. Five players from the 2000 side were in the team, including Rohan Hubbard and Jason De Graaf, who were creating plenty of run from the half-back line. Brendan Woods, another legend, began the day with a strong mark. The main topic on the sidelines was whether the team on the paddock was the best in the club's history.

The only side that bore comparison was the 1995 team. Half a dozen players from the premiership side had returned to the club since the coup in signing Nicky Winmar. The disappointment was that Winmar was on the bench. He'd told me that he was to be eased into the match because suspension and injury had limited him to one match in the previous month. Brendan Woods said later that Winmar had failed to advise him that he would miss training. Winmar was brought on 20 minutes into the opening quarter. By then, I was cooped up in a storeroom writing a story about the day for *The Sunday Age*.

I emerged just after half-time to find Upwey-Tecoma clawing to preserve their slim chance of making the finals. Dogged ruckman Tim Hedge kicked three goals through sheer force of will but the home side had too much run. Jason De Graaf, leaning forward, like a racehorse with its ears pinned back, sprinted from defence into the forward line, kicking three goals as the Kookaburras attacked in waves. I asked spectators about Winmar's performance and gained curiously varied responses. Some said he was quiet; others said he was a solid contributor. The bench reported figures of six kicks and seven handballs in the second quarter, which seemed a fair return. My immediate thought was that people expect too much of former AFL players. Some spectators want eight screamers and nine goals before they begin to be impressed. But in half a quarter I began to see why some believed that Winmar had done little. Every time he got the ball, he was swamped. The sight was hard to reconcile with my memories of the free-wheeling midfielder from Moorabbin, but I didn't have to think far back to put his match in perspective. Old Melburnians forward Ian McMullin was often caught but never pinned and he always managed to get a kick away to advantage. At 35, McMullin remained dangerous because he was good in close. Winmar was about the same age and confined to the same style of game. His appetite for the ball was undiminished. He grew frustrated at the logjams that must arise in the depths of a Victorian winter, but he kept putting his head down. Once or twice, he emerged from a pack and unleashed a long and graceful torpedo. Spectators reacted like they were watching fireworks melt in the sky. This was what many had come to see. Nicky Winmar was letting his spirit soar.

Terry Wheeler enjoyed the torpedoes, almost despite himself. "They were good to see," he said. As the head of football at the Australian Institute of Sport, he is firmly in the modern school of coaching, the school that regards torpedoes with suspicion. His experience in coaching had honed his ability to spot a footballer's condition at a glance. It was an ability that eluded me. In his street clothes, I thought Winmar looked in good nick. "I'm looking after myself," he said. "I watch what I eat." His upper body still had a decent cut and, even if the sweep of his thighs suggested his days of frisking around the paddocks were over, I was prepared to accept his statement that he was at the weight at which he finished his AFL career. I told Wheeler of this exchange, which had been faithfully reported in the newspaper, and he laughed. Then, remembering he was talking to a reporter, he downgraded his reaction to a conciliatory frown and added words to the effect that Winmar might just be over his AFL weight. "Give him his due," Wheeler said. "He's run from one end of the ground to the other. He knows how to get the footy."

Wheeler was more inclined to reminisce on his teenage years, when he knew every inch of this ground. Leaning with both elbows on the fence, and with the trademark cheeky grin and twinkle in his eye, the 45-year-old was pleased to see the centre circle displaced towards the town end. "It's a pay-off," he said. "The ground slopes 11 feet from end to end." His greatest pleasure was in the grey skies and the utter stillness. He moved his gaze up Mount Victoria. "It's a typical Warburton day. You can't see the tops of the mountains for the clouds."

The Kookaburras soaked up the applause of the legends and shuffled into the old pavilion after victory by 60 points. Jason De Graaf had been best afield and Steven Cole had also performed well in defence. Nicky Winmar stood behind the crowd next to the fire, clutching a can of Coke and smiling beatifically. "I thought I played well," he said. He moved off to say hello to a group of Aboriginal friends. His satisfaction was plain. On the field, he felt at home. In the afterglow of the match, he received the pats on the back and knew in his heart that he was on this earth to play football. In the days between matches, he had a problem. Life's little details had a habit of slipping his grasp. It was impossible not to hope that everything would turn out all right for him.

Winmar went on to play in his first senior premiership. Soon afterwards, he left the handbrake off his car and it rolled out of his driveway into the river. President Paul Kercher laughed when recounting the story.

"He rang me and said, 'Hey Cuz, you can have your car back'." Kercher ordered a tow truck and sold the car for $1000. He believed the money spent on Winmar had been recouped by fundraising and recruiting windfalls and his attention to the juniors. He said Winmar took several Kookaburra teammates into the Melbourne rooms to see Jeff Farmer and he organised grand final tickets for himself and the vice-president. His point was that Winmar had good intentions. "I liked the bloke." Others were less sure. Some in the town tired of him ordering a beer and walking away from the bar, expecting someone else to pay. Once he had a haircut and strolled out the door. The town had agreed to pull behind him but his empty pockets and his inability to take care of his affairs wore thin. Many were relieved when he agreed to play with Yarra Junction. Then he announced he would play with Mitcham, then Scoresby. In court, he was found guilty of assaulting his wife, now estranged, and fined $3000. In the new year, he ended his days in Victoria and returned to Western Australia.

After the victory over Upwey-Tecoma, I was driving back through the pitch darkness of the Yarra Valley when a blackboard out of the front of the Launching Place Hotel announced a Patsy Cline tribute show. Cline was an American country singer with a voice like a bell. She sang for the dreamers and the soaring hearts, for the wandering souls prone to losing their way. I decided that, if Patsy Cline had met Nicky Winmar, she might have sung a song about him.

Warburton-Millgrove defeated Wandin by eight points in a wet grand final. In a rare event, Upwey-Tecoma finished fifth and missed the finals. Jason De Graaf won the best-and-fairest at Warburton-Millgrove and the best-and-fairest in the competition. Nicky Winmar finished eighth in the club award. Onballer Geordie Atkins won the Upwey-Tecoma best-and-fairest.

Now or Next Year

21
TOUGH ORDER AT ELSTERNWICK PARK

Mazenod Old Collegians v North Old Boys
the Nodders and the Griffins

"The team is very well-prepared."

Mazenod president Peter Hanley

In 1984, my first year in the Amateurs, I learned that the B-section preliminary final is the toughest game in the competition. Nobody with a faint heart was given any hope of coming out alive. "It's the last chance to reach A-grade," explained St Bernard's coach Paul Daffey, my father's cousin. I was an 18-year-old in my first season in senior football. Every week was like a trip to the moon. It was only after the victory over Old Paradians by three points prompted normally undemonstrative men to jump into each other's arms and fall on to the ground and that I realised the coach had a point. This really was a big occasion. It turned out to be the most emotional experience of my football life. The victory over Ivanhoe in the grand final the next week was considered a bonus. Pity all this was wasted on a teenager.

Perhaps in an attempt to relive a moment that had passed in a youthful blur, I ventured to Amateurs' headquarters to see Mazenod play North Old Boys. It was my first B-section preliminary final since that glorious day and it never stood a chance. The first problem was the venue. The St Bernard's preliminary final was at the Harry Trott Oval, where spectators could reach over the fence and twist the players' ears after the ball was taken over the boundary. The old Harry Trott has since made way for the grand prix track, which is a shame, as it was a popular oval. Elsternwick Park, by contrast, can be the enemy of atmosphere. The Amateurs association took over its showpiece in 1966, an era when even vegetable gardens were expansive. Facilities were improved greatly in 1983, and the wings have been brought in, but the openness of the ground continues to diffuse the shouts of spectators and leave players feeling lost. It takes a close final to bring the crowd to life.

The first quarter of this preliminary final was an eyesore. The ball eluded players like a pet rabbit on the hop. No one seemed able to score. There were no physical contests and neither side could establish any rhythm. Finally, NOBs scored a goal after 17 minutes. They went into quarter-time with a narrow lead. Then Mazenod clicked into gear and the match picked up. NOBs battled away but they were relying on too few. For many years the Griffins had boasted depth that was the envy of the Amateurs competition. Now they were forced to watch as a club that mirrored their fortunes took control of the game.

North Old Boys entered the Amateurs association at the end of the Depression but were expelled a few years later for fielding an unregistered player. In 1963, they re-entered the competition and went through the grades unchecked. Marcellin and Mazenod are among those to proceed through the grades with a stumble of one year, but NOBs remain the only club not to miss a beat. It's significant that these three clubs drew from areas with many young families. Influx of players enabled them to gain momentum. NOBs spent most of the three decades until the early '90s based opposite the zoo in Royal Park. There are more lions and tigers than young families in Royal Park, but the area is central for former students of St Joseph's College.

The college is a forbidding, brick building in Queensberry Street, around the corner from the Victoria Market. Its students come from Brunswick through to the red-brick houses in Pascoe Vale in the north, and Footscray through to the market gardens at Werribee in the west, descending on the concrete enclave in North Melbourne for their final two years of schooling. For three decades, the school was a phenomenal feeder for North Old Boys. During that time, NOBs were a power in A-section. In the '70s, the club played in four consecutive grand finals; in the next decade, they played in more. The distinctive purple jumper with white bands was last seen in an A-section grand final in 1991. A few years later they were relegated. The next year they were relegated again. The school continued to command its corner of the inner city. For the football club, the forbidding red bricks had come crashing down.

NOBs began to decline when St Joseph's junior school in Pascoe Vale and the senior school severed links. No longer was it automatic that students would proceed from the northern suburbs into North Melbourne. By extension, no longer was it automatic that footballers would proceed to North Old Boys. The effect was heightened by the change in demographics at the senior school. Many students from the inner suburbs were the sons of immigrants from Asia and Africa, with few having an interest in Australian rules. Beyond the inner city, the sons of European parents inherited a passion for soccer. In the suburbs of the red-brick houses, the flight of young couples to new estates left a population of pensioners. The number of keen, young footballers proceeding from the school to the old boys slowed to a trickle. The rise of Therry-Penola Old Boys, based in Oak Park, exacerbated the problem.

Revival began when the Griffins appointed Essendon premiership player Frank Dunell as coach for the 1997 season. Dunell had coached traditional rival St Bernard's. He was an outsider, untainted by decline, and his arrival heralded a new era. Supporters for whom the decline was unpalatable began returning. In an attempt to improve their playing stocks, the club had to look beyond the school. The search was fruitful at Newman College, the traditional home for Catholic country students at campuses in the inner city. One or two players came along and they soon invited their friends. During the late '90s, North Old Boys became a home away from home for country footballers.

NOBs' move from their ground next to the zoo to the Gillon Oval, the ground of former VFA club Brunswick, also redefined the club. Former prime minister John Curtin played at centre half-forward for Brunswick early last century, when the area was solidly working class and its inhabitants were of British and Irish stock. By the time the NOBs moved into

Brunswick, the suburb was one of the cultural melting pots of Australia. Immigrants from around the Mediterranean had moved into the terrace houses on narrow streets. First it was the Italians and Greeks. Then it was the Lebanese and the Turks. Just as falafels and hommus have come to feature in Brunswick restaurants, footballers from these communities have started popping up on NOBs' team sheets. Joe Saad walked in off the street with a few friends. By 19, he was a key forward with the Griffins' fortunes in his hands. At the Amateurs' 2000 vote count, a ballroom of guests from every club watched highlights from the season on a large screen. The clips featured high marks and inspiring goals. In one highlight, Joe Saad marked the ball inside the centre square. With his back to the play, he sauntered to his mark. Elsternwick Park is a massive ground, but Saad had the confidence of a man on his patch. The ballroom broke out in gasps as his drop punt sailed through the goals at post height. If NOBs were to challenge Mazenod, they needed Saad to kick goals. If he wanted to bomb them from inside the centre square, no one was about to complain.

Mazenod are like the NOBs of one or two decades ago. Most Mazenod players grew up around Glen Waverley, in a heartland of suburbs for young families. The production line of recruits from Mazenod College to the old boys' club ensured premiership momentum. The Nodders skipped through the grades after joining the eastern suburban churches competition in 1979. A decade later they joined the Amateurs and did the same. With their fleet of talented runners, they thrashed all-comers on their postage stamp near Waverley Park. Their wingmen had surfie haircuts and their defenders ran forward in waves. It came as little surprise when they reached A-section.

In A-section, the Nodders stumbled. As often happens, momentum had masked a club structure that was unprepared for lean times. The Nodders were demoted after one season and resolved to learn from their mistakes. Slowly, they improved their depth and structure, but for the first time they realised that the production line of recruits from the college wouldn't last forever. The population in the heart of the eastern suburbs was ageing, with young families now heading to the suburban fringe, and the school sports curriculum was more diverse. Club officials were shocked to learn that tall students had drifted from football because Mazenod College was ranked second in the nation in volleyball.

The club took a forward step by appointing Dave Murray as coach. Murray played in the VFA before racking up 150 games for Mazenod. Throughout his playing career, he was also a fitness coach in the AFL. He prepared Collingwood under Leigh Matthews and Carlton under David Parkin. At Hawthorn, he became an assistant coach. For two years, he guided players and plotted tactics as part of the Hawks' coaching team, but he needed to know whether he could fly solo. At Mazenod, he quickly sized up his talent and concluded he had a team of runners: lean and largely medium height. He designed a philosophy around attacking in numbers and doubling back in defence. "It's about running both ways," he said. Lack of height would be overcome by isolating forwards on slower opponents. He adapted training drills from his AFL days and, working around his job as a sportsmaster at St Kevin's College, he watched league clubs train to try to pick up more. The purpose of every drill was explained. Mazenod president Peter Hanley spent the pre-season watching in wonder. "His training methods are magnificent. It's go, go, go all the time."

During the season, Murray had every match filmed. It helped him learn the traits of every opposition player and provide feedback for his own players. After every match he made a 10-minute package of highlights. Every Tuesday after training, the players ate their soup as he played the highlights. "Visual feedback is so important," he said. Such preparation is standard at higher levels but, in the Amateurs, it set Mazenod apart. Murray's attention to detail paid dividends in the preliminary final against NOBs.

One of the reasons that the Nodders were finding scoring so difficult early in the match was the placement of Chris Harrison on the bench. Harrison had kicked more than 50 goals but Murray held him back to ensure the right match-up. He wanted to him to play on Nick Vogels, who was the Victorian Amateur under-19 captain when he played at University Blues. The Blues believed Vogels was too slow for senior football, so he transferred to NOBs. Murray thought his pace could be exposed. "No disrespect to Nick; he's a great bloke," Murray said. "But we wanted him isolated in the goalsquare." In the second quarter, Murray took off Vogels' opponent and brought on Harrison with instructions to drag the defender to the teeth of goal. Funnily enough, NOBs had always planned to play Vogels on Harrison. The two would have lined up on each other at the first bounce if Mazenod had played their regular cards.

Harrison is slight and fair-haired, quick of mind and feet. Vogels is low to the ground and robust, with black hair and a bullish attack on the ball. It was Harrison's qualities that shone through. He kicked three goals before the NOBs coaches cottoned on to the mismatch. Vogels was moved into the midfield, a tactic that had been used to great effect during the season. In the five minutes before half-time, the computer science student from the Western District gave his side a shake-up, bustling through packs, scattering opposition midfielders in all directions, and driving the ball forward. His performance dragged NOBs back into contention. The margin at half-time was Harrison's three goals.

The third quarter was a stalemate. Mazenod remained systematic but failed to kick goals. NOBs kicked poorly, blazing away on the run, with their key forwards starved of quick supply. Joe Barker, the brother of Hawthorn forward John, had missed the previous match because his wife had given birth. A loyal servant of the club, he was desperate to play in a winning final. Barker tried to play himself into the game but his fellow target in attack seemed distracted. Joe Saad has charisma. He is shorter than most marking forwards, but his torso is sculpted from stone. He walked in circles, chest out, chewing gum, with his dark fringe flopping into his eyes. The previous month, Muslim custom had required him to accompany his teenage sister to Italy on her tour with a Victorian soccer side. The break had halted his momentum. During the first semi-final, his most notable feat was kicking a goal and breaking a window. But Mazenod feared his ability to cut loose. For all the Nodders' method, they would have no answer to magic. Their plan was to cut the supply to Saad from the midfield. It was working but Mazenod president Peter Hanley refused to relax. Hanley had been in charge for eight years. The aim of returning to A-section was consuming him. He sat on the slope by the far wing, furiously knitting his brow as a friend sat beside him in silence. The third quarter of the toughest game in the Amateurs didn't strike him as the ideal time for a chat. "I get very nervous," he said. The siren sounded and we hopped the fence. Hanley did offer something as we strode towards the huddle. "The team is very well-prepared," he said. In his agitation, it was like a declaration of victory.

As much as the president was nervous, the coach was clear and concise. Dave Murray, a compact 34-year-old, coiled and ready to spring, bent low and made each point in sequence, chopping the air with one hand. He raised his voice step by step until reaching the desired peak. There was energy in the huddle but nobody was getting too excited. "Keep your hat on," was the motto of the season.

Early in the last quarter, Joe Saad lined up for goal from half-forward. If he kicked a booming goal, anything could happen. Saad tried to pass short, missed his target and NOBs lost all belief. The underdogs peppered the goals, but there was no conviction. Mazenod held their nerve. Their depth and unity, the product of growing up in young families in adjacent suburbs, came to the fore and the match turned their way. Captain Andrew Pickering paddled the ball in front of him for minutes. To Peter Hanley, it must have seemed like weeks. The ball eventually bounced into his hands and he passed to the leading Chris Harrison, who kicked his fifth goal. Mazenod teammates swarmed on Pickering as he returned to the centre square, a big grin creasing his face.

The attacks became irresistible waves. Momentum is difficult to stop in any match; in a knockout final, it's impossible. Half-back Mark Murray kept chugging downfield as the Nodders luxuriated in victory despite themselves. The siren blew and they put their hats back on. Not even victory by 24 points in the toughest game in the Amateurs was enough to inspire a few hugs and leaps. They gathered inside the boundary line, patting each other on the back and reminding each other of the job still to be done. NOBs players trudged from the field in silence. Their parents faced long drives back to the country. The Mazenod people began filtering back to the eastern suburbs as their players walked from the field unfurling the tape from their wrists. Only when every player was in the rooms would they break into song.

It was a long way from the excessive '80s.

Mazenod defeated Old Brighton, considered the most talented B-section side for several years, by seven points in the grand final, with Andrew Pickering best afield. Midfielder Nick Meehan and half-back Steve Polan shared the Mazenod best-and-fairest. Chris Harrison was the leading goalkicker, with 58. Midfielder and captain Brett Collison won the NOBs best-and-fairest.

Old Xaverians v St Kevin's Old Boys
the Xavs and the Skobbers

"Xavs teams can dig deep."

Old Xaverians coach Tim O'Shaughnessy

The A-section preliminary final the next day was the best match I was to see for the year. The only game to come close was the relegation battle at Marcellin the previous month. The match at Marcellin had drama born of desperation to survive. This match at Elsternwick Park had drama born of desperation to excel. Xavs were trying to remain on track to equal the record of six consecutive A-section flags. They looked wobbly in the second semi-final but their record of beating the odds was beyond question. The previous year, they finished four games behind Old Melburnians, only to defeat them convincingly in both finals. St Kevin's were striving to reach their first A-section grand final. Injury had derailed their attempt the previous year. Now, there were no injuries.

The two clubs went into the match sharing a keen rivalry that owes little to the Amateurs competition. Until 1998, the two clubs had barely played each other in the Amateurs. The nub of their rivalry is the public schools competition, in which they're the only Catholics. Xavier College traditionally dominates the public schools' competition; St Kevin's College is simply the other Catholic team. In recent years, the football teams from St Kevin's College have improved. In the Amateurs, the fortunes of St Kevin's Old Boys have also improved. The club was formed in 1947 and dawdled for almost 50 years. The change came when coach Tim Hart and president Tim Corrigan resolved to shake the club out of its lethargy. The under-19s were strengthened and an effort was made to accommodate recruits from the country. Under Hart and Corrigan, St Kevin's Old Boys became contenders. In 1997, they earned promotion to A-section for the first time in their history.

Ruckman Michael Blood went to school at St Kevin's College. In the late 1980s, he played in the Hawthorn reserves. After leaving Glenferrie

Oval, he joined Old Melburnians in B-section. In 1993, he joined Old Xaverians in A-section. He settled in at Old Xaverians, helping the club rise to prominence. After a few years he was named captain; he wore the No.1 guernsey with pride. Before the 1998 season, he received a parcel. It was a St Kevin's guernsey with No.1 on the back. The club was appealing to him to honor his promise to join St Kevin's if the club reached A-section. Blood declined. After five years at Xavs, he was settled at his adopted club. His decision fuelled the rivalry from the public schools' competition. That rivalry would now spill into the Amateurs.

If St Kevin's Old Boys dawdled through the decades, Old Xaverians were little better. They usually dawdled in a higher grade than St Kevin's, but they dawdled all the same. Their one period of distinction began with the D-section flag in 1976. Five years later, they won the A-section flag. By the mid-'90s, this remained their only triumph in the top grade.

The path to continuous glory began after the club had been knocked out of the A-section finals in straight sets in 1993 and '94. Captain Matt Hannabery led a meeting of senior players that included Michael Blood, key forwards Matt Bourke and Dan Richardson, and midfielder Anthony McDonald. The players wanted to turn the club around. Their resolution was to work harder. Over summer, they gathered at dawn for long runs or weights session. Before the season, midfielder Anthony Leoncelli joined them. In September they won the premiership. The next summer, they gathered for more long runs and weights sessions. Before the season, Anthony McDonald's brother James joined them. They won another premiership. Leoncelli and the McDonald brothers went on to become midfielders at Melbourne, but the Xavs continued to recruit and they continued to run and do weights over summer. Five years after the meeting of the senior players, the club had won five flags. Less than a fortnight after winning their fifth flag, the football staff met to consider the next season. Nobody at Xavs is afraid of hard work.

Part of the work is overcoming a high turnover of players. While most players remain products of Xavier College and the under-19s, the club is able to maintain its reserves of talent through its AFL network. Full-forward Dan Richardson is a player manager with Elite Sports Properties, a company with 90 AFL players on his books. Coach Tim O'Shaughnessy was on the football staff at Collingwood. Former coach Barry Richardson has been on match committees at four AFL clubs. Several Xavs premiership players and coaches have moved from Toorak Park to AFL clubs. Through contacts, Xavs know what's going on with footballers moving in and out of the highest competitions. They know when a player leaves an AFL club or a VFL club and is looking for a home in local footy. They also know when talented teenagers just out of school want to start careers at a leading Amateurs club. They offer good facilities and strong support. The recruits keep coming in.

Xavs' vaunted depth was to be tested in the preliminary final. Injuries had forced the club to include three players who'd been in the reserves all season, with Ned Ireland to play a key role in the forward line in his first senior game. The concern of Xavs supporters was overshadowed when St Kevin's pulled the biggest selection surprise of the season. An excited murmur rippled through the crowd when Marcus Olive, big and bold, with a crop of bleached hair, ran on to the field with a winning grin. Olive had won club and competition best-and-fairests before a knee injury sidelined him. The civil engineer then went to work in London. He returned on the eve of the 2000 finals and played in the last reserves match. The result was a strained hamstring. After a fitness test on the eve of the preliminary final, it was decided to call him up for his first senior match in almost two seasons. He was worth the risk because he made his teammates walk tall. Even running on to the ground, he had an air about him. It seemed like something was about to happen.

Olive began the match in the ruck and in the forward line. He was as rusty as an old door. Xavs supporters jeered as he dropped marks and missed the run of the ball. Halfway through the second quarter he collided with an opponent after the Xavs player had marked. Olive was reported for charging and sent off for 15 minutes. He hauled his long frame towards the boundary line as the Xavs player staggered to his feet.

Xavs took advantage of their extra man. Ned Ireland weighed in with two goals as Xavs reined in the lead through their marking forwards. St Kevin's needed more height and bulk in defence, but they fought on before veteran Rob Gross, a Victorian Amateurs representative as a key forward and a key defender, lumbered in for a vital goal. Gross careened around the forward line as the siren sounded with Xavs a point up.

By the time that Olive was allowed to return to the field early in the third quarter, Xavs supporters weren't fussed. They saw him as a carnival act whose touch had deserted him. A minute after jogging on to the field, Olive had an opportunity to mark. He took a few tentative steps then launched himself into the flight of the ball on the wing. A minute later he took another mark in the same spot. After another mark, the crowd sensed a dangerous awakening. He took another mark and the crowd reached a new pitch. Olive was no longer a carnival act. When mercurial teammate Matt Lucas jogged from the ground nursing his wrist, Olive became the main show. He was moved from the ruck to full-forward, where he marked and kicked a goal on the siren. St Kevin's had a two-point lead.

There was unease in the Xavs huddle. It was an uncustomary feeling. They had more depth and more talent but a grinning giant with sideshow hair was threatening to upset the better order. Tim O'Shaughnessy did a manful job of maintaining calm. He didn't mention Olive; instead, he stressed that the opposition had no chance of covering four marking forwards. He jabbed at the key match-up on his whiteboard. The plan was to have most forwards upfield, leaving teenage bull Alistair Parton isolated with Ben Dollman. Parton was at least 15 kilograms heavier than Dollman. Xavs were banking on their young forward's marking strength. O'Shaughnessy reminded his players of their history of great escapes. It was a matter of belief. "Xavs teams can dig deep," he said.

In the St Kevin's huddle, coach Mike McArthur-Allen was giving the performance of a lifetime. There was none of the crouching of younger coaches who seek intimacy with their players; McArthur-Allen stood tall and projected his voice over Elsternwick. His message was to play the last quarter as if it were the last quarter of their lives. A crowd of hundreds was silent, transfixed, before erupting with a burst of energy at the finale. "Just makes you want to get out there," said a supporter, breaking into a jog. Excitement bubbled away as a sea of middle-aged men in corduroys and brogues danced towards the fence. For one moment in this era of planning and process, emotion was king.

Marcus Olive continued to captivate. With his size and charisma, teammates became obsessed with looking for him. Sometimes other scoring chances were missed as midfielders kicked to the blond talisman. Midway through the quarter, Olive reached up to take yet another strong mark and boot his fourth goal. Xavs seemed to have no answer. Their only option was to outscore him. In stepped Al Parton, who fulfilled the match plan by taking two marks against his lighter opponent. Parton kicked two goals. Xavs moved nine points clear in time-on but St Kevin's refused to concede. Midfielder Jordan Grigg continued to put his body in the line of avalanches. Fellow midfielder Marcus Kempton kicked a goal but it was too late. In the end, four marking forwards had the edge on Marcus Olive: Xavs' depth had won the day.

St Kevin's players sprawled across the room, devastated by the four-point loss. It was their second successive loss in the madness and fury of a preliminary final. "Your courage has been nothing short of miraculous," said McArthur-Allen, pledging that the club would reach the next grand final by winning the second semi-final. Marcus Olive grinned as friends filed in to greet him. There was no guarantee he would be around for the next finals campaign. "I might go back to London," he said.

Half-back Mick Kavanagh won the best-and-fairest for St Kevin's. Matt Lucas was left to nurse a broken wrist. Marcus Olive was found not guilty of charging. He then returned to London. Xavs' grand final is in the next chapter.

22
LAST RITES UNDER
WAVERLEY LIGHTS

Boronia v Blackburn
the Hawks and the Panthers

Vermont v East Burwood
the Eagles and the Rams

"Are they in the same league that Vermont's in?"
Electrical wholesaler, curious about East Burwood

As a means of farewelling Waverley Park, the Eastern Football League and the Victorian Football League decided to hold their grand finals at the superseded stadium over one weekend, describing it as a festival of local footy. The Eastern league would hold its under-18 grand finals on Friday night and its division one and two grand finals on Saturday, beginning in the early afternoon and stretching through the evening. The VFL would hold its grand finals on the Sunday.

For the Eastern league, the idea had merit. Anger at the closure of Waverley Park as an AFL venue had helped to swell crowds during the home-and-away rounds, with regular attendances of 2500 for big games in division one. Officials were hoping to shore up this support and attract new fans. It was hoped that nostalgia for Waverley, the novelty of the first night grand finals in Victoria, maybe even Australia, and a parade of juniors would boost the attendance beyond the tally for the previous grand finals. In 1999, about 11,000 reportedly attended the grand final in division one and 7000 went to the decider in division two. Officials were hoping that 30,000 would attend the double bill at Waverley Park. It seemed more likely that Roy Cazaly would make a comeback before the crowd would reach this figure, but there was no harm in talking things up.

I rolled up at 4pm to find a meagre crowd. On the field, the players from both teams looked like juniors as they lined up in parallel rows before the old members' area. The national anthem drifted through the clear afternoon as sunlight bathed the empty seats. To be fair, it was early in the program. To be fair again, if others were feeling like me, it was a wonder anyone was there at all.

It felt strange and unsettling to turn up to a match at 4pm. Since scampering on to the field as the mascot for Riddells Creek at four years of age, I've been turning up to the football at lunchtime, never at afternoon tea. Here, my rhythm was thrown, but never mind. I settled in for the division-two grand final. Both sides fiddled around before Boronia broke the deadlock after 11 minutes. Lanky Boronia centre half-forward Lucas Appleby then defied his height with two running goals. The Hawks had been beaten in the previous two grand finals. This might be their year for promotion.

Boronia continued to make the running as cries of support became lost in the vastness of the stadium. Most spectators seemed too intimidated by all the space to make a noise. Some became emboldened as the crowd grew, but for long stretches of the first half the ball moved up and down the field in a weird hush. The peeling paint of the empty seats and the quaint scoreboards contributed to the feeling that we were on the set of a low-budget film, maybe about hard times in an industrial town. Not so long ago, the scoreboards at Waverley Park were considered the height of modernity; now they looked as if they were dipped in sepia. The sparseness of the crowd magnified the perception of decline, but it has to be said that the old stadium had seen better days.

The best things going for the ground were the surface, which was flawless, and the press box, which was large. Most weeks I did my round-ups for *The Sunday Age* in musty storerooms or in the passenger seat of my car, with the laptop on my knee. Behind the glass at Waverley, I had a dozen phones to choose from and a desk that stretched the length of the half-forward flank. I nipped up to the press box at half-time and made the phone calls while keeping one eye on the game, which drifted into tedium. Lucas Appleby kicked four goals and was best afield as Boronia skipped to an 82-point win. Defender Dion Festini was among the best for Blackburn.

The main reason for heading to Waverley, besides the novelty of local footy under lights, was the grand final in division one. The Eastern league offers arguably the highest standard in local football and Vermont and East Burwood are the league's greatest rivals. In the 37 years before this match, the clubs had shared 25 flags. East Burwood were dominant in the early going before Vermont motored past them in the '80s, on their way to becoming the most successful club in Australia. In the past 15 years, Vermont had missed only two grand finals. This was their eighth in a row. East Burwood went through a lean patch in the '90s before reaching the grand final in 1999. After triumphing with ease, coach Alan Richardson was asked what it was like to defeat Vermont in a grand final. He said it felt fantastic. "But it wouldn't have been as good if it wasn't Vermont." Respect for the Eagles heightened his reward.

Richardson was born into an East Burwood family. His father played in six flags with the Rams in the '60s. Alan Richardson played in his first flag with the Rams in 1985, when he was a teenager. The bullocking defender went on to North Melbourne, where he played reserves, and Collingwood, where his greatest disappointment was breaking his collarbone during the 1990 finals and missing out on the historic flag. After a decade with the Magpies, he found his way back to East Burwood.

Throughout his football career, Richardson continued working as an electrician. Part of being an electrician is buying equipment from electrical wholesalers. Part of going to the wholesalers is talking about football. When Richardson took on the job of coaching East Burwood, the wholesalers were unsure whether they knew the Rams. "Are they in the same league that Vermont's in?" Richardson would confirm that they were, then provide a short history lesson. The wholesalers didn't want to know. As far as they were concerned, Vermont were the famous ones. After the triumph over Vermont in the 1999 grand final, Richardson went to every electrical wholesaler in the eastern suburbs and stocked up on new equipment. He made sure the wholesalers knew that East Burwood had defeated Vermont.

East Burwood had an easy run into the 2000 finals, winning the last four games by large margins. In the final game, they welcomed back their three players from the RichmondVFL side:Travis Edwards, Paul Arthurson and Cameron Dean, the son of former Collingwood and Richmond player Robert Dean.The trio had filled in for injured players at Punt Road for most of the season. Alan Richardson took himself out of the East Burwood side for the second semi-final in an attempt to lessen any unease in his club over the Richmond players' return. The Richmond players struggled to adjust to the tempo in the Eastern league. East Burwood led at half-time in the second semi-final before Vermont made some astute tactical moves and ran away with the game.

Richardson was wondering whether to return for the preliminary final when the illness of one of his players paved the way for his inclusion.The 34-year-old had several goals kicked on him. "I had a shocker," he said. But his side kicked two late goals to defeat Bayswater and earn another grand final against Vermont.

The decision to hold the grand final at Waverley Park offered Richardson and the returned players from Richmond the chance for redemption. Richardson was reluctant to coach from the stands at Waverley; he believed the coaches' box was too far from the play. If he was on the ground, he could call in teammates for marks and ensure the shape of the backline. The Richmond trio, meanwhile, would offer valuable experience on Waverley after playing several matches under lights during the VFL season. Vermont had two players who'd been regulars in the Richmond VFL line-up: Matt Edwards and Adrian Burgiel. Edwards would play in the midfield but Burgiel was injured.

The two sides ran on to the ground as the junior parade began winding up. Children from clubs throughout the Eastern league, wearing jumpers in all colors of the rainbow, hopped and skipped out of the still air and made their way into the warm belly of the member' grandstand.The two sides went about their final preparations before pockets of fans scattered behind the goals at both ends and on the far wing. Most spectators in the disappointing crowd of 11,000 were huddled in the seats beneath the coaches' boxes on the members' wing, rubbing their hands and wrapping scarves tightly around their necks. The solid black guernseys of East Burwood had a dull sheen under the glaring lights. The purple guernseys of Vermont, with the golden eagle glistening on each chest, looked almost summery in the crisp darkness of late August.

The players took their positions just before the 7pm start. Vermont wanted to atone after a tepid performance in the previous grand final. Their intentions in this match were clear: they would be more physical. Opponents elbowed and jostled at all points on the enormous ground before the ball was bounced into the brilliant night. Players crashed and bashed before Vermont captain Andrew Lamprill, the former Melbourne utility, received a shuddering hip and shoulder after 90 seconds. The tone was set for the match. Spot fires broke out all over the ground, with opponents grappling and shoving and wrestling each other to the turf. Tension crackled, which was some achievement in the desolate stadium. It was a tribute to the rivalry between two great clubs that there was any crackle at all.

Supporters barracked in the clear air as play proceeded in fits and starts. Both sides employed midfield tags and sophisticated rotations. The match was dour, with both clubs struggling to take the step from small grounds in suburban pockets to one of the biggest grounds in Australia. They were also struggling in the dewy conditions. The ball squirted from pack to pack and end to end. East Burwood broke free to kick two goals in the first quarter and Vermont kicked one. Players snarled at their opponents as they jogged to their huddles.

The spite reached another level in the second quarter when an East Burwood player was hit heavily in the ear shortly after running on to the ground. East Burwood ruckman Adam Slater ventured in to support his teammate and was sent off. Alan Richardson later described Slater as "an emotional ruckman". He admitted that Slater was often embroiled in spats with opposition players or the crowd. Slater's brother, Lucas, the Rams' centre half-back, is in the same mould. The two brothers sometimes direct their emotion into protecting each other, which strikes many as a waste of resources. Sheer size ensures they can stick up for themselves. "They didn't need to protect each other," Richardson said.

Adam Slater began shuffling his 113 kilograms from the field to a cacophony of abuse from Vermont fans. He replied by giving the fist to the crowd and smiling smugly, which enraged Vermont fans into further abuse. Spectators rose from their tattered seats and roused the former national stadium with suburban passion. Tempers continued to flare on the field, not that Rams defender Travis Edwards took any notice. There was never a player so jolly in such a tense match. Before the season, Edwards gave up his job at De Bortoli Wines in the Yarra Valley and returned to the family trucking business so that he could tailor his days around Richmond training. Now he was back at East Burwood and smiling like a Cheshire cat. The sight of his bald head gleaming in the lights was a regular feature as he scythed through the Vermont attack. Vermont rover Brad Cullen was one of the few winners for his side. East Burwood went into half-time with a four-goal lead.

On the members' wing, I conducted a straw poll on the decision to hold the grand final at Waverley. Spectators were lukewarm about its appeal for local football – the ground was too big and the stands so empty – but they were adamant that it should be retained for the AFL. Their reason was that they were from the eastern suburbs and they wanted league games in their region. I'm not from the eastern suburbs and I think league games should be played more centrally. This reasoning failed to impress the Eastern league supporters.

In the third quarter, fierce Vermont defender Todd Power attempted to bend the match to his will, hitting packs and clearing paths for his smaller teammates, while veteran Andrew Dwyer was lively after being switched into attack. But the Eagles' reward for a quarter in which they tried everything to wrest the advantage was three behinds. The Rams kicked one goal. Scoring on the big ground was rare.

The last quarter continued grudgingly until full-forward Stuart Wynd kicked his fourth goal and the celebrations began. East Burwood players gave each other high fives and pats on the back while several clubs held their vote counts and one or two completed pre-seasons. At least it seemed that long. The night was cold and the match was over. A sparsely populated Waverley Park in such conditions was miserable.

Vermont offered respite at the 10-minute mark when they kicked their first goal since late in the second quarter. Eagles supporters gave a muted cheer and headed for the exits. Their night was summed up when Todd Power lined up an opponent and knocked out a teammate. The game was delayed for five minutes before Eagles wingman Chris Henderson was carried off on a stretcher. The lack of action on the field drew attention to the rowdy fans with hours of drinking under their belts. Some had arrived early in the afternoon for the reserves grand finals. Three or four games later, they embodied the pitfalls of a long day's night at the football.

At the 22-minute mark, a spectator lightened the mood by surging from the damp seats wearing only white socks, football boots and a smile. Hopping the fence, he sprinted through an imaginary slalom course before setting his set sights on the outer wing. His pale skin drew the light as he almost impaled himself on the fence. Then he dashed up the aisle and disappeared into a huddle of security workers. The siren mercifully rang two minutes later to signal victory to East Burwood by 54 points. The Rams leapt into each other's arms after their second successive grand-final triumph over the old foe. Alan Richardson was due to buy more electrical equipment.

In front of the grandstand, a couple of Vermont players became incensed at an East Burwood supporter. Vermont officials dragged the players back towards their despondent teammates while blood streamed from a cut above the supporter's eye. The supporter later rang Vermont officials to apologise for taking a swing at a Vermont defender after the siren. He said he had no explanation for what he did. East Burwood centreman Derek Coghlan introduced some perspective when he stepped on to the podium to accept the award for best afield with modesty and grace. He then did his duty as captain by accepting the premiership cup. While standing next to the celebrating East Burwood players, I was struck by their size. The view from the distant stands had failed to do them justice. All were powerfully built – incredibly so, for a local footy side – and few lacked the height to take their turn in a key position. The happiest hero was mid-fielder Matt Dobell. "Mate, I'm rapt," he said, bouncing around like a jack-in-the-box. A few days later he would be in hospital for microsurgery on the ear that was hit in the second quarter, but in the meantime he was celebrating his first flag after playing in three losing grand finals with Golden Square. He bounded off to join his teammates on a victory lap around the empty stadium as workers began dismantling the podium. I looked up at the lights that shone like fluorescent saucers in the black night. Then I took a last look at the rows of seats and the retro scoreboards.

The rain began falling as I walked to my car.

Adam Slater won the East Burwood best-and-fairest. Todd Power won the Vermont best-and-fairest by one vote from Brad Cullen. Alan Richardson stepped up to become the coach of the Coburg Tigers in the VFL. Vermont coach Michael Kennedy resigned to take a teaching post near Ballarat. Of the second-division clubs, Boronia wingman David Van Hoorn won the club and competition best-and-fairests and half-back Steve Cochrane won the Blackburn best-and-fairest. A heritage order has imposed restrictions on development at Waverley Park. At the time of publication, the AFL was considering expressions of interest for development of the ground.

St Bernard's Old Collegians v Old Xaverians
the Bernards and the Xavs

"Don't worry. We'll be right today."

Xavs wingman John Bowen

The next day I was at Elsternwick Park for the A-section grand final in the Victorian Amateur Football Association. Old Xaverians, aiming for their sixth consecutive flag, went into the match with the chance to create history; St Bernard's had the chance to move on from history. The West Essendon club had won one A-section flag, in 1975, with a team of hardness and daring. For years afterwards, the players were wheeled out whenever it was felt that St Bernard's needed motivation. The trouble was that none of the subsequent teams came close to matching their deeds. In time, the distant A-section flag cast a shadow over the club. This grand final offered St Bernard's the perfect chance to emerge from the shadow and move on to another era. After 25 years, it was about time.

The club deserved its shot at success. St Bernard's changed in the late '90s, when a young committee finally took the baton from the '70s warriors and Garry Foulds was appointed coach. Foulds played for Essendon for 16 seasons in 300 unassuming games. Simon Madden once said that Essendon forwards had been spoilt with Foulds in the side because the wingman and defender was the perfect kick to a lead. Foulds brought this efficiency to St Bernard's, but his calmness and reason weren't for everyone. Some believed the club lost its impassioned soul, and a handful of players left. What remained was a core of players with commitment to success. The club built on this core, attracting new players and supporters. St Bernard's still had a feisty soul; the culture would always reflect the swashbuckling era of the '70s. But now they also had talent and athleticism to trump their opposition. After being the best side during the season and winning the second semi-final in a canter, the odds were short on a St Bernard's win in the grand final.

Xavs rebounded from the second semi-final to score a breathless victory over St Kevin's in the preliminary final. Then they cast the match from their minds. Within minutes of the siren, they jogged on to the oval behind Elsternwick Park and did their warm-down away from the hullabaloo – just 21 players and the coach, doing stretches and some rudimentary drills to focus their minds on the week ahead. During the week, the club was rocked when the teenage sister of a midfielder was murdered at Doncaster Shoppingtown. Old Xaverians rallied around the midfielder but many were unsure quite what to do. A priest from Xavier College addressed the club after training on Thursday. He asked players and coaches to keep the grieving family in their thoughts and prayers, but he assured everyone it was all right to continue with their regular routine.

The club received a boost at selection when full-forward Dan Richardson was cleared to return from a dislocated shoulder and Andy Gowers, the Hawthorn premiership wingman, confirmed he would play with a broken hand. Supporters were nervous and the Amateurs world at large wrote them off. Many considered that the club had played its grand final against St Kevin's, but the players had other ideas. Before running on to the ground, dependable wingman John Bowen turned to president Andrew McLean. "Don't worry," he said. "We'll be right today." McLean instantly felt calm. He gave his club every chance of overcoming the odds yet again.

Bowen was one of four players striving to play in his sixth consecutive flag. Such experience proved valuable in the opening quarter, when Xavs proved more settled. St Bernard's frittered away the early use of the breeze before surging with trademark lightning handball through the centre. But on the occasions when St Bernard's threatened to break clear, Xavs reeled them in like patient shepherds. Xavs' captain Michael Blood was winning in the ruck. Xavs' centre half-forward Adam Jones separated the sides when he booted two goals from outside 50 metres. The underdogs led by 10 points at half-time.

After the break, St Bernard's rover Daniel Byrne took the match and ran with it. The 21-year-old is renowned for the twinkle-toed footwork that has come through boxing training. Twice he took the ball from the centre and danced into attack to kick the goals that put the favorites in front. For one goal, he defied the laws of physics by controlling his kick as he was pushed to the ground. His rare balance and composure had netted five goals by early in the third quarter. It should have been enough to inspire his side to victory, but his teammates proved less able to rise to the occasion. St Bernard's continued to stream through the centre but their delivery up forward was wayward. At the other end, Xavs refused to panic and kicked three late goals against the wind. St Bernard's led by two goals at the last change. It wasn't enough. A lack of confidence corroded the huddle.

Xavs hit the front six minutes into the last quarter when Andy Gowers streamed down from full-back to kick a running goal. St Bernard's would barely touch the ball again. With their inexperience in big games so painfully obvious, they froze. Xavs ran riot, kicking goal after goal. Dan Richardson started the celebrations by twice running into open goals. His team managed a 10-goal turnaround in the last quarter to win by 45 points. Xavs had again defied the odds; their reward was matching University Blacks' record of six consecutive A-section flags. Adam Jones was named best afield after kicking three inspirational goals.

St Bernard's supporters were shocked; the meltdown was embarrassing. The reasons for their capitulation began to sink in during the presentation of medals. One by one, Xavs players stepped on to the podium to receive their medals as the sweat glistened on rippling muscles. They were so much bigger than their opponents. The summer gym sessions had enabled them to stand their ground. Their finals experience had enabled them to keep their cool. In the end, they shrugged off St Bernard's with ease.

Richmond premiership forward Barry Richardson pointed out the strength of the Xavs players. He also allowed himself a rueful smile. The father of Dan coached Xavs to the premiership in 1995 before returning to the AFL and becoming the chairman of selectors at Melbourne. He then went on to Carlton and Geelong. All these Xavs premierships later, he was reviewing his decision to leave the Amateurs club. "I should have stayed," he said. "I could have been a legend."

Back at the St Bernard's rooms, I was impressed by the way they were taking the loss. No more did the club hide behind a shield of bravado. More than one supporter believed that the better club, not just the better team, had won the day. The lesson was digested and the aim was to keep improving. Over the previous two decades, St Bernard's typically followed a season in the finals with a season on the brink of relegation. This time there was change in the air.

Ruckman Michael Blood won the Old Xaverians' best-and-fairest. The quartet that has played in the six flags – Michael Blood, John Bowen, Dan Richardson and Andrew Dillon – won the Victorian Amateurs' award for the personality of the year, an award normally handed to one person for special achievement. It is the most prestigious award in the competition. Barry Richardson remained the chairman of selectors at Geelong. Forward Nick Mitchell won the St Bernard's best-and-fairest. President Andrew Vinecombe left to work in administration and marketing at VFL club Sandringham.

23
Tyranny of distance

Pakenham v Warragul
the Lions and the Gulls

"Who the hell do these guys think they are, these faceless
men down there?"

*West Gippsland league president Bob Utber on
Victorian country football directors*

Half-time functions at local football matches are normally agreeable affairs.
Officials from both clubs gather loosely around a table laid out with plates
of sandwiches and jugs of beer, with the urn and a box of teabags placed
at one end of the table or over by the sink. Many of the officials have
played against one another before the arthritis set in and their waistlines
began to expand. They stand around and compare notes on the torpedo
after the siren that won the flag or the problems of rounding up enough
teenagers to play in the thirds, feeling good about their place in the wider
football family. The only topics to stir disagreement are the gherkin spread
that continues to find its way on to the cheese sandwiches and the state of
the head on the beer.

But at half-time in the preliminary final of the West Gippsland league,
the air was thick with murmurs and indignation. Two days before,
directors of the ruling body in country football voted unanimously to
move three clubs – Beaconsfield, Pakenham and Warragul – from the

West Gippsland league into a new competition that would stretch from Beaconsfield on the suburban fringe, through the Latrobe Valley, to Sale in East Gippsland. The proposed league was nicknamed the highway league, because it would link clubs on the Princes Highway. The three clubs from West Gippsland wanted no part in the highway league. They said they would lose players and sponsors. Distances up to 200 kilometres are too large and there is no cultural link between clubs on the urban fringe and opponents in East Gippsland. The only connections are the Princes Highway and the word "Gippsland". The new league would be the death of them.

West Gippsland league president Bob Utber was angry at the decision to shunt the three clubs from his league into the new competition. Utber was president of Pakenham before he was president of the West Gippsland league. The Lions won a premiership under his leadership. But he was quick to add that his playing career was spent at two smaller clubs in the West Gippsland league. Both those clubs wanted to leave West Gippsland and move into a competition in which they would play smaller clubs. The West Gippsland league let them go. Utber said it was the way it should be – clubs should be allowed to choose their own fates.

In his capacity as West Gippsland president, Utber began speaking to everyone from old boot-studders to young defenders at Pakenham, Beaconsfield and Warragul when it was first proposed that these clubs would be forced into a new competition. His survey led him to conclude that such an order would kill the three clubs. The issue was working him up like nothing else in almost five decades of serving the league. At 14 years of age, he began writing for *The Barracker*, the weekly program for West Gippsland matches. Now the Victorian Country Football League directors who gathered in a plush building in Melbourne wanted to change the competition to which he'd devoted his life. He stepped on to a table during the half-time function and launched into a tirade against the VCFL directors. "Who the hell do these guys think they are, these faceless men down there?" His face reddened as he blasted the directors for five minutes. West Gippsland club officials stood frowning. Utber was breaking half-time protocol. He clenched his first and tapped his heart. "It's coming from here," he said. "There will be a war."

Utber stepped down from his table as an uneasy silence fell on the room. Later, he said his tirade was out of character. "I never raise my voice at anything, really, but the league has been my life. My passion came out." The businessmen and tradesmen from Beaconsfield and Pakenham muttered approval at Utber's broadside. Officials from Warragul were despondent at the order to shift from a competition they'd only just joined. But the farmers from the small clubs felt like the directors had thrown them a lifeline. All they wanted was the chance to be competitive. It would never happen while the clubs from the big towns with skateboard ramps and shopping strips played against the clubs based around struggling dairy farms.

The officials from the small clubs gathered by the sandwiches. Photos depicting the limited glory of the Nar Nar Goon Football Club dappled the walls. The last premiership photo had been taken in 1980. The officials were wary of going on the record but one of them said the restructure was the best thing since sliced bread. "It's an attempt to get the small teams playing small teams and the big teams playing big teams." Another official described a season in which every team from his club, from firsts to fourths, suffered regular defeats by 20 goals. He said it was hardly surprising that teenagers were turning away from football. The West Gippsland league had attempted to help out the small clubs by introducing a seeded draw but the new scheme failed to produce any change. "At the end of the day, the same teams made the five." The conclusion of the small clubs was clear: they wanted the big clubs out. The vote to shift them into the highway league was a godsend.

Beaconsfield president John Airdrie understood that the small clubs were battle-weary. But he failed to see why his club should travel through the catchment area of three leagues and three shires because it was successful. "Expecting Beaconsfield, which is basically a metro club, to travel to Sale and Maffra is too much," he said.

Airdrie explained that most of his players work or study in Melbourne and return home for training and matches. The extra travel for matches in the Latrobe Valley and East Gippsland would prompt them to join suburban clubs. Airdrie stressed that he would relish playing the big clubs in the highway league. "We're not frightened of the competition; we would welcome it." But the overriding issue was travel. Convoys would have to leave before dawn to reach Sale in time for the thirds. Even shorter trips to play clubs in the Latrobe Valley were out of the question. "What have we got in common with them?" a supporter asked.

The half-time function finished in a low, rumbling stalemate. Officials shuffled out of the room to watch the match, leaving the ladies to finish the cleaning-up. With the last of the leftovers stored away, the ladies sat beneath the sepia photos and enjoyed a refreshing cup of tea. One of them leaned her head against the brick wall and relaxed after a job well done. Her smile gave no hint of the discord that had crackled through the room.

The discord began to rise in the '90s, when the gulf in population between towns on the urban fringe and the farming towns widened. Beaconsfield and Pakenham are among the fastest-growing towns in Australia. Their football clubs could only grow stronger. Neither club dominated in the '90s. In fact, neither won a premiership until the end of the decade. But they were among a group of clubs that ruled the top half of the ladder. These clubs revolved through the finals, while the clubs below them sank into the mire. Lang Lang and Koo Wee Rup struggled to notch one victory a season and left the competition. Nar Nar Goon and Kilcunda-Bass thought about joining them. The clubs on the urban fringe saw that the small clubs were struggling, but there was nothing they could do about it. The big clubs enjoyed life at the top and they claimed that every club had as much right to be in the competition as the next. Pakenham was a founding member of the West Gippsland league. If the Lions went to another competition, it would be like chopping off an arm. But the league was founded in 1927, when the town of Pakenham was like any other town in West Gippsland. In recent years, Pakenham has become a template for studies on urban sprawl. The dairy farmers from Nar Nar Goon claim that Pakenham has simply outgrown them.

In the heart of Gippsland, directors from the old Latrobe Valley league looked at the events on the urban fringe with interest. The Latrobe Valley league is traditionally the strongest competition east of Melbourne. But in the '90s the might of Traralgon scared the rivals from smaller towns. Clubs such as Churchill drifted away to more compatible competitions, leaving the Latrobe Valley league with less than 10 clubs. In 1995, South Gippsland club Wonthaggi joined the Latrobe Valley league and the competition changed its name to the Gippsland Latrobe league, in an attempt to reflect that it had embraced the region. The change failed to staunch the departure of clubs. In 1998, Bairnsdale tired of driving hours into the Latrobe Valley to get walloped and dropped back to a more local competition. The number of clubs was down to eight. During the 1998 season, Warragul struggled to win a game. At the end of the season, Warragul officials applied to move their club from the Latrobe Valley league into the West Gippsland league. Officials in the Latrobe Valley were horrified. A competition with seven clubs is no competition at all. The issue would take months to solve.

Warragul's problems began when the State Electricity Commission was privatised under the Kennett Government and an estimated 10,000 jobs were lost. Without work at the SEC, no one in Warragul had reason to head into the Latrobe Valley. It became a problem for the football club when supporters began to feel cut off from the teams against which the Gulls played. Without work, there were no football chats during smokos, no analysis of kicks and marks over the photocopying machine. No ribbing the Moe and Morwell supporters when the Gulls beat them; no getting ribbed when it was the other way around. The supporters missed these chats. They missed their link with a culture. Without the smokos and the office banter, their interest drifted. Matches against Traralgon and Moe and Morwell lost their meaning.

Around the same time, Hawthorn were trying to attract members for home games at Waverley Park. Warragul was a fruitful recruiting zone for Hawthorn, with Gary Ayres among the favorite sons. Many in the town felt a link with Hawthorn and, with Waverley Park only an hour away, it made sense to watch the Hawks rather than a local club that was losing its appeal. The Warragul Football Club also lost its appeal for players. Many saw no point in driving east into the Latrobe Valley and joined old school friends and cricket mates who played in West Gippsland. Other players stopped returning from Melbourne each weekend and joined suburban clubs. Warragul cleared an average of 20 players a season in the late '90s.

The club was in danger of going under when president Tony Flack decided to act. A maths teacher at the secondary college, he called a meeting before the 1999 season, placed a blackboard at the front of the room and demanded 35 names by the end of the night or the club would fold. Veterans filed forward to scrawl their names; they would come out of retirement to save the club. It was the first step in a long battle.

Every Thursday night during the season, reserves coach Chris Ayres, the brother of Gary, was among the clubmen who made phone calls until their fingers were sore. Every week, they gathered together a reserves side that was like a ragbag of the old and the untalented. By the end of the season, 81 players had been used, including Barry Round, the Brownlow Medallist who returned to his home town to play one game at 49 years of age. The reserves failed to win a game for the year. The seniors scored one victory. At the end of the season, Tony Flack said enough was enough. The focus of the town had turned west, towards Melbourne and the urban fringe. The club must join the West Gippsland league if it were to survive. "It was a marketing decision," Flack said. "We had to market ourselves to the players."

Latrobe Valley officials fought to keep Warragul but their efforts were in vain. The Gulls won a 12-month permit to play in the West Gippsland league and the players began returning straight away. The response of the Latrobe Valley officials was to urge the ruling body in country football to get a wriggle on with its proposed restructure in Gippsland. The restructure would concentrate on creating a viable major league in the region. Recommendations were due to be handed down mid-season. For the Latrobe Valley officials, the restructure couldn't come soon enough.

Warragul took a couple of months to settle into the West Gippsland league. They were seeded in the top half of the draw and struggled against strong opposition. But even while they were struggling, they noticed that gate takings were double and triple those of previous seasons. In the derby match against Drouin, a club just a few kilometres down the road, spectators were jammed against the fence. About mid-season, the Gulls started to find form. Things were rolling along nicely. It had been the right decision to move into the West Gippsland league. As far as the Gulls were concerned, they were staying there.

Pakenham and Beaconsfield also wanted to stay where they were. They made no submissions about the restructure because they didn't see any need. They were staying in West Gippsland. Then the report was released recommending a new league comprising the top five clubs from West Gippsland and five clubs from the Latrobe Valley league. Sale and Maffra, the easternmost clubs in the Latrobe Valley league, were to be frozen out. The two East Gippsland clubs jumped and down until it was agreed that another report would be released. Again, Pakenham and Beaconsfield didn't make any submissions. Again, they didn't see any need. But when the recommendations of the next report were accepted, they raged about the lack of consultation.

The report recommended that Pakenham, Beaconsfield and Warragul join the seven clubs of the Latrobe Valley league to form the highway league. Pakenham president Peter Holland made 10 phone calls wanting to know why VCFL directors would jeopardise the life of his club. None of the calls were returned. Later that weekend, he spoke passionately about his club's 21 premierships, more than double the tally of the nearest rival. He claimed that smaller clubs such as Cora Lynn wanted Pakenham to remain in the West Gippsland league. "Cora Lynn has one shop and it's closed. They use Pakenham as a yardstick. They want us to stay."

Holland's claim was hopeful: most of the smaller clubs wanted the big three clubs to go. Holland ended up falling out with one of the smaller clubs, Rythdale-Officer-Cardinia, where he served as coach and then president before moving to Pakenham. Holland remains a life member at ROC, but his fight for Pakenham ruled out cordial relations with his former club.

The Mornington Peninsula Nepean league offered a logical solution when it invited Pakenham and Beaconsfield into their competition. The peninsula league is strong. It's also not far away. A move into the peninsula league would have lessened travel and provided worthy opponents, but the two clubs refused to go to a competition that didn't have netball. They said such competitions were unfriendly to families. I could see no reason why a netball competition couldn't be started. I also see no reason why football and netball can't be aligned with every league in the state, but my suggestion earned grunts.

During the preliminary final at Nar Nar Goon, I spoke to several netballers about the proposed highway league. Pakenham and Beaconsfield netballers realised the football competition was uneven but it wasn't their problem. When asked to suggest an alternative to the highway league, one netballer suggested splitting the West Gippsland league in two. In a competition with 11 clubs, that would be impractical. Warragul netball president Nicole Varty said the restructure amounted to the football officials "going off on a little tangent", but her impish humor was untypical.

Others said the decision was disturbing. "It stinks," said one. The country football directors were portrayed as villains.

Warragul football president Tony Flack cast his eye over the preliminary final and predicted an exodus from his club. "These boys would be snapped up by Drouin a minute later." Gulls committeeman Gavin Ough agreed. "It'll be the death of us," he said. "We couldn't go through it again."

The morbid response to the restructure cast a long shadow over the day. In any other circumstances, spectators would have been itching to see whether Warragul could continue their improbable surge. The Gulls gathered steam from midway through the season. With a month to go, they were an outside chance of making the finals if they won every game. In the last round, they needed to win by 20 goals. They won by 22 goals before breezing though their first two finals. Pakenham unexpectedly lost the second semi-final to Beaconsfield. With Warragul in barnstorming form, Pakenham seemed ripe for another upset. It was a preliminary final with tantalising possibilities.

But the match was as flat as a footy without a bladder. The two teams battled away but nobody took much notice. The first problem was the howling wind. The Nar Nar Goon oval is exposed, perched on a flat on the outskirts of town. Any cheering that did arise was swept up and blown across the paddocks. The next problem was the timing. It was strange to be watching a local footy match the day after the AFL grand final, which had been brought forward because of the Olympics. But the main problem was the decision to slot both these clubs into the highway league. Most supporters discussed the restructure instead of the match. The most interesting duel of the day was the stand-off between the big clubs and the little clubs at half-time. Those who watched the match felt hollow. They sensed they were witnessing a death march. It was a strange day at the footy.

Between many interviews on the restructure, it became apparent that Pakenham were holding sway through a midfield led by Michael Holland and an impassable force named Ashley Green. At 16, Green was drafted from Warragul to Essendon before playing senior football at Brisbane. He returned to Warragul for one season before becoming assistant coach at Pakenham, where a mid-season walkout by the coach left him in charge of an undefeated side. In the preliminary final, Green had a touch of the old-fashioned defender about him. His jumper was tucked in and his socks were up. In an era in which key position players are like elongated wing-men, he had thick arms and thick legs. He commanded centre half-back with stately calm, standing in the way of opposition attacks, blocking them and dispensing the ball to his runners. Not for him the modern penchant for dashing upfield.

Green led Pakenham to a forgettable victory by 25 points. Teenage wingman Leigh Baldry was the best player for the Gulls.

Warragul scored a victory after the season when country football directors recognised that the highway league would kill the Gulls and granted a reprieve. The club was to stay in the West Gippsland league.

Now Pakenham and Beaconsfield set to work. Instead of raging against an apparent injustice, they began to outline just why they were outraged. They revealed evidence that sponsors and players would be lost. They took legal action and demanded to see minutes of the meetings about the restructure. The greatest coup in their fight to save their clubs was winning two hearings from Sports Minister Justin Madden. The first meeting was in Madden's 12th-floor office at the top of Collins Street. The second was in his parliamentary chambers. About half a dozen representatives from Pakenham and Beaconsfield were seated around the minister's desk, drinking cups of tea and putting forward their points of view. Greg Trappett, the Victorian Country Football League general manager, was also present. Madden believed the two clubs had reasons to be disgruntled but he told them he was unable to interfere. Instead, he acted as a mediator. He asked Trappett to take the gripes of the clubs back to the VCFL directors. Trappett did as he was asked. The directors began to fidget.

The clubs continued to push their gripes on to directors by ringing them at home, sometimes three or four nights in a row, until the directors gave in and picked up the phone, hoping to listen once and the problem would go away. What they heard turned them around. These grievances had never been outlined before they'd taken a vote on the highway league. Another vote was held and the decision was turned around. Having made a unanimous decision on the eve of the preliminary final, the board now voted by a majority of one to scrap the restructure. Another attempt at a restructure would be made the next season. Only this time the clubs would direct the change. The ruling body would remain in the background.

Peter Holland said the fight exacted its toll. "It's taken five years off our lives. We were very, very relieved to win – at an expense." Pakenham and Beaconsfield were faced with raising $10,000 each to cover legal fees. They also had to remain true to their word that they would help to bring about change. The two clubs entered talks with clubs in several leagues about new competitions. Change would be achieved after all.

Greg Pullen, the chairman of the task force that proposed the highway league, said he expected resistance when he embarked on the restructure. He knew that no change is achieved in country football without considerable pain. He denied the claims that he failed to consult enough parties. "It just means we didn't consult until we came to their point of view," he said.

His biggest regret was the anonymous phone calls to his home at the height of the drama, with threats to his children such as: "Tell your father he's a dead man." Pullen said he could shoulder personal abuse, and he believed there was no substance in the threats, but it upset him when his children were afraid to answer the phone at night. He was also disappointed that the directors had voted unanimously in favor of his recommendation, then caved in to pressure. It wasn't the first time that VCFL directors had backed down on a decision.

Some friendships were ruined forever during the fallout from the proposed highway league. Given the inevitable restructures that must arise as families continue to move from the farms to the cities, it's likely that more friendships will crash and burn. If there is a positive amid such pain, it's the confirmation that country football still rouses the deepest passions – even at half-time over beer and sandwiches.

Pakenham defeated Beaconsfield by 43 points in the grand final at Cora Lynn. The score, 7.13 (55) to 2.0 (12), reflected the muddy ground. "It was a slopheap," said Pakenham president Peter Holland. His son, Michael, was best afield and also won the Pakenham best-and-fairest. Fellow midfielder Dan O'Loughlin won the league best-and-fairest. Leigh Baldry won the Warragul best-and-fairest after earning unanimous votes for best afield in the preliminary final. Fellow midfielder Ryan Flack, the son of Tony, finished second in both the league and club best-and-fairests. Ashley Green returned to Warragul as assistant coach. When all the fuss died down, Greg Pullen resigned from the board of the Victorian Country Football League.

24
COOKING THE GOOSE

Edithvale-Aspendale v Mornington
the Eagles and the Bulldogs

"If you win the mind games before the first bounce,
you're in for a good day."

Edithvale-Aspendale midfielder Troy Shannon

A measure of the depth at Edithvale-Aspendale was the decision to exclude the captain, Craig Phillips, from the side for the grand final because he lacked match fitness. Another six or seven players with regular senior experience would also have been worthy members of the side. Opposition clubs were jealous of the Eagles' talent. Most of them threw up their arms and grumbled about chequebook success. The Eagles admitted they'd recruited certain players for certain positions, but they preferred to talk up their junior program. Whatever the composition of the side, it was among the best to play on the Mornington Peninsula, possibly the very best. The only weakness anyone could see was jostling egos. During the season, the senior players had voted their full-forward out of the club, claiming he wasn't worth the trouble. The Eagles got over the hiccup and confirmed their strength with a crushing victory in the second semi-final. They were raging favorites for the flag.

Yet much of the attention in the lead-up to the grand final was on

Mornington. The Bulldogs had recovered from the second semi-final thrashing, but victory the next week had come at a cost. The centre half-forward, Tim Allen, strained his hamstring and the full-forward, Simon Goosey, was hobbling. In better fitness, these two were the leading choices for the key forward posts in the Victorian Country team.

Tim Allen played senior football at three AFL clubs before returning to Mornington and becoming the outstanding attacking target in country football. Tall and mobile, with a powerful build and a thumping left foot, he's like a character from the Greek classics come to rest on the wind-blown ovals by Port Phillip Bay. Allen tried retirement when work and family commitments got on top of him, but the urge to play was strong and, a month into the season, he returned. In the second semi-final, he kicked five goals in 15 minutes. Some said it was the best quarter of football they'd seen in the competition, but it wasn't enough to hold off the Eagles. Mornington needed Allen to perform more heroics if they were to have any chance in the grand final. The tweak in his hamstring was inconvenient but he said there was never a doubt that he would take the field. "Even if it was torn, I would have played."

As good as he is, the conjecture over Allen was relegated to second place behind the speculation over Simon Goosey. The Goose kicked nearly 100 goals for Richmond under-19s before moving to Mornington in 1988 after his wedding. One of his first moves was to head down to the local football club and ask for a game. Mornington officials asked where he'd spent the previous season. Goosey told them about Richmond. The officials thought he was pulling their legs. Goosey broke his leg in his first season on the peninsula but the next year he kicked more than 100 goals and Geelong drafted him. He spent a season at half-back at Kardinia Park before leaving in frustration, a decision that remains his only regret in football. "I suppose I got a bit impatient. I thought I'd done enough to show them what I was capable of, but they didn't put me in the seniors, so I came home."

He continued playing at half-back with Frankston. Dropping into the hole in front of the goalsquare, he took mark after mark and finished third in the Liston Trophy. The next year, he played in attack with the wind and in defence against the wind, one of the highest accolades in football. By 1996, Goosey had confined himself to the forward line and embarked on his coaching career. He took Mornington to the premiership in his first season. The Bulldogs lost the next grand final by three points before playing in the following two grand finals against Edithvale-Aspendale. A fierce rivalry developed.

In the first year in which the two clubs led the competition, Goosey kicked bags of 12 and 14 goals in the home-and-away rounds before booting 10 in the grand final. The next year, he booted another 10 in the grand final but the Bulldogs fell short. The Eagles celebrated by singing songs about beating Simon Goosey.

Before the 2000 season, the Eagles made sure they recruited a full-back to curb the Bulldogs' star. John Hynes had spent a couple of seasons at Carlton, where his bulk was against him – he was the player who accompanied Lance Whitnall to the fat farm in Queensland. Goosey had twice come within a bootlace of breaking the record of John Coleman, who kicked 160 goals for Hastings as a teenager, but Hynes was unperturbed. The 21-year-old had one willing battle with Goosey before the full-forward began suffering from an ankle injury. Goosey continued playing every weekend, with representative matches increasing his workload. In the Australian country carnival, the pain in his ankle prompted Goosey to pull out of the Victorian side before the grand final. The coach advised him that he was vice-captain and asked him to reconsider. Goosey decided to push himself. He kicked 11 goals and fulfilled an ambition by earning a place in the All-Australian side. Back at Mornington, he pushed himself through a spree, kicking 17 goals in one match to break his own league record and race to another century. By the preliminary final, the ankle was restricting him badly. He was unable to jump and every kick brought a shiver of pain. He kicked four goals but it was the goals he missed that stirred excitement. Late in the game, Goosey had a shot from 30 metres and barely kicked beyond the man on the mark. He denied there was any problem but few believed him. The peninsula strengthened its fixation on The Goose in the lead-up to the grand final.

The crowd was bubbling. Spectators squeezed in on the bank of grass between the social club and the scoreboard or spilled from the grandstand on the opposite wing. Families snaked through any gaps they could find, while teenagers in baggy jeans and baseball caps gathered in knots besides the pie stall. Behind the goals, spectators jostled six- and seven-deep, clearing their throats for the appearance of The Goose. This crowd had rattle and hum; it was liveliest I encountered for the year. The spectators were from the bayside suburbs and the small farms towards the coast. The northern border for the competition is the Mordialloc Creek, which is nowhere near the bush, but the competition has always taken its flavor from the pastures and brine of the peninsula. It began before the suburbs began to sprawl towards the sea, and it continues to regard itself as a country competition. For many years, the Mornington Peninsula league had only one division. In the late '80s, the Nepean league joined up. Later on, clubs from the near side of Gippsland swelled the numbers again. Any competition with three divisions should draw 10,000 to the main grand final, but few grounds are better suited for such a crowd than Frankston Park.

The old ground on the rise overlooking the bay is understated. Its grandstand is long and low and wooden. Unlike the exalted constructions on the goldfields, where windfall led to loftiness and decoration, the grandstand at Frankston leaves the footballers to reach for the sky. The church on the hill at the bayside end lends a touch of grandeur that off-sets the boxy, brick social club in the opposite corner of the ground. The practicality of the social club is matched only by its ugliness. The match can be watched from behind the glass in the social club but, on a day that draws a heaving crowd from miles around, the idea seems ludicrous. A crowd of 10,000 in Frankston Park is a perfect fit. The lazy sunshine of early spring inspired one or two tearaways to wear board shorts.

In the dressing-rooms beneath the teeming grandstand, Edithvale-Aspendale midfielder Troy Shannon urged his teammates to play to their potential. "This is our last chance to play four quarters of footy," he said. Edithvale-Aspendale had lost only one match, late in the season against Mornington. The Eagles rebounded to kick eight goals in the first quarter of the second semi-final before easing back. In almost every match, the Eagles had broken the resistance of the opposition before easing back. Shannon believed it was about time they won every quarter.

In 1989, at the age of 17, Shannon played on a wing in the Edithvale-Aspendale side that was reputed to have been the best in the history of the club. After playing in the Eagles' premiership side, he went to Melbourne, where he played for three years before spitting on an umpire after a tribunal hearing. The suspension for a season cost him a place on the senior list and pulled the shutters on his AFL career. Shannon sometimes looks back and wonders what might have been. He marvels that contemporaries such as David Neitz and David Schwarz went on to such long and distinguished careers. Then he thinks again. A self-confessed lair, he believes the AFL would have been a sporting straitjacket. "My personality wouldn't have allowed me play at that level."

Shannon spent a season at Frankston before embarking on a football odyssey. He followed David Glascott, his Frankston coach, to Perth, where he thrived on the big, dry grounds and missed out on the best-and-fairest at West Australian Football League club Perth by a vote. Then he returned home and spent a season travelling up and down the highway to North Albury before his work managing a building project took him to Alice Springs, where the football again was fast and attacking. Throughout his odyssey, the gregarious Shannon said he "got off" on meeting new people in all parts of the country. He also never lost contact with Edithvale-Aspendale, training now and then, or playing the odd season between ventures. The Eagles welcomed him home when Shannon finally settled back into the club.

He plays nominally as a wingman. Really, he runs where he likes. His whippet legs carry him deep into attack and deep into defence, with taggers always at his side. Shannon likes to sort out the tagger before the first bounce. His favorite trick is to give him a squirt with the water bottle. Almost every player is too stunned do to anything; the ones to watch are the few who react – chesting him, or grappling, or maybe slipping in a punch. Shannon knows then that he's in for a busy afternoon. "It's a mind game," he said. "If you win the mind games before the first bounce, you're in for a good day."

For this grand final, the Eagles decided to break Shannon's tag by playing him as a tagger. He was to pick up Mornington ruckman and key-position player Andrew Morrison. Shannon had finished second to Morrison in one of the local awards. Morrison lined up for the grand final on the half-forward line. The 24-year-old was tall, almost skinny, with bleached hair. Shannon was inches shorter, just as lean, and he also had peroxided hair. Shannon broke from the Eagles' warm-up and jogged towards Morrison. Eagles fans nudged one another and hooted. Shannon feigned a punch and danced, with a grin as wide as the wing. He feigned another punch and danced some more, taunting the Bulldog with his words and his feet, throwing his shoulder and threatening to jab. Morrison had no idea what was going on. He began the match like a stunned rabbit. So did his teammates. The Eagles took the ball from the first bounce as though it were a training drill. After a few early goals, Sam Anstey broke Bulldog hearts by racing down from his wing to shark the ball off a pack at full speed. Anstey had played some of the season in the Collingwood reserves. He followed his incisive roving by screwing the ball through the goals, leaving his opponents stranded. The Eagles then lost a key forward to a hamstring injury, but didn't skip a beat. Burly Wayne Langford slotted into the key post without a problem. The Eagles had a bottomless well of depth.

Langford provided a bustling target, taking front position and keeping defenders out with body strength. Every Eagle in the key positions had a strong body, with enormous, sweeping thighs like those of former Carlton colossus John Nicholls. Mornington opponents often were pushed aside. A feature of both teams was the predilection for dyed hair. Several players sported shades of blond. One Bulldog midfielder preferred burgundy and Eagles defender John Hynes was a coppertop. Frankston Park was awash with treated follicles. In all this brashness, trash talk filled the air. The Eagles strutted and crowed. They had no interest in shutting their mouths in case a few indiscreet words came back to haunt them. They were having a ball and they let Mornington know it. Troy Shannon set the tone, stepping into opponent's faces and yapping in their ears. He said later that he gives his mouth a good run because it motivates him. "It's a way of putting pressure on myself. People think, 'He'd want to get the ball if he's going to do that'." With Shannon, it's natural. His ebullience enables him to carry it off. Most of his teammates looked like they were trying too hard. Shannon was the coolest kid in the class and they were keen to win his favor.

Andrew Morrison emerged from the opening blitz and worked himself into the game. He began running to the rights spots and finding the ball, lending a glimpse of his loping athleticism. Then he was the target of a shocking handball towards the centre of the ground. The ball looped into the air and the match went into slow motion. Morrison stooped to gather the ball and two Eagles lowered their shoulders from either side. The ruckman crumpled in a tangle of arms and legs. Mornington fans grimaced and turned away, expelling the air from their lungs in sympathy. It was shaping as one of those days.

After 20 minutes, Simon Goosey tired of failing to see the ball in the forward line and began making his way to defence. The sight of him jogging through the centre square, tall and pale, slightly stooped with thin, fair hair, sparked a stream of abuse from Eagles fans. Goosey parked himself in the backline as abuse continued to rain down. His opening gambit was to grab the ball from the ruck and try to force a passage. It was the first decisive act by a Mornington player. Eagles fans strained forward and shouted until they were red in the face. Goosey tells himself that the tirades from opposition players and supporters are a compliment. "They don't do that to some bloke who's sitting on the bench," he said. But the vehemence of the abuse was startling. Most Eagles supporters wedged between the scoreboard and the social club or jostling behind the goals were intent on withering the Mornington coach.

In the dying minutes of the first quarter, the Bulldogs kicked their first goal. Inevitably, Edithvale-Aspendale replied within seconds. The Eagles, in a reprisal of their opening salvo in the second semi-final, led at the first change by almost eight goals.

In the Mornington huddle, Simon Goosey pleaded with his young side to run and run. Maybe, in the end, it would run into some luck. "You've got to create something," he said. In two years, the Bulldogs had lost 16 players from their premiership side. The only solution had been to fill the holes with juniors. Truth be told, the Bulldogs had surprised themselves by reaching two grand finals after the exodus. The coach was proud of his young side. He, like many in the competition, regarded Edithvale-Aspendale as a club that was flash with the cash. The Eagles denied the accusations but the fact remained that several players were from outside the club and few teenagers had managed to break into the side. Of the Bulldogs, only two players had come from elsewhere: Goosey and wing-man Matthew Sinnott, whose family formed a convoy from the Western District to watch him throughout the finals. The Goose implored his side to take the match up to the Eagles. Against all odds, the Bulldogs responded.

Tim Allen was the only Bulldog with the strength to match the Eagles. The big forward parked his frame in front of a pack before taking a mark and lining up from inside the centre square. He swung his left foot through a wide arc and sent a drop-punt sailing through the goals. His next move was a short pass to Goosey, who shaved the goalpost to the jeers of the crowd. Minutes later, Goosey led out again and took a strong mark with John Hynes on his hammer. The defender rode Goosey into the ground with every kilogram of his considerable bulk before arching over his opponent on the mark. Goosey was shaken as he hauled himself to his feet. Hynes greeted him by feigning a head-butt and loosing a grin. Goosey kicked a behind and set off another wave of ridicule. Eagles fans hurled abuse as Troy Shannon and another defender ran in to chest the key Bulldog. Goosey ignored the taunts and trudged to his mark, stooping.

In the next attack, Goosey juggled a mark as an Eagles defender took a swipe at him. The defender had natural hair. His swipe was half-hearted and his act was unconvincing. The umpire paid a free kick and Goosey kicked a behind. Another defender had a word in Goosey's battered ear as the spearhead replaced his glove. He stood on the mark with his hands barely above his head.

The ball was kicked in towards one of the defenders who'd been mouthing off at Goosey. Tim Allen chased the defender down and pinned him near the boundary line. The defender, who also had natural hair, got to his feet looking stupid. For a moment, the Eagles were silenced. Something in me reacted to the tackle. I believe that lairising has its place, especially if it's done with style. My father, on the other hand, believes that lairising has no place, especially if it's done within his time zone. It's an aversion I've always put down to the strictures of his generation, yet here I was yelling at a mouthy defender about getting what he deserved. Then I started waving my arms and brandishing my notebook at him. It's a strange old world when you realise you're becoming like your father. Tim Allen chipped to a midfielder as I tucked the notebook under my arm. The midfielder hit the post – just the Bulldogs' luck. From the kickout, Allen floated into a pack. He settled into his ride, sent two opponents sprawling, and took a mark of strength and grace. The defenders knew they looked second-rate. One emerged from the jumble clutching his elbow; the other, the mouthy defender who'd just been pinned, gave away a 50-metre penalty. Allen curved the ball through the goals. He was playing a quarter to rival his brilliant cameo in the second semi-final. He is a player worth travelling to see.

The Bulldogs then made a bad move by putting him on the backline.

No doubt they were trying to hold their ground before half-time, but the move backfired when Wayne Langford marked in the goalsquare. Aaron Martello, another Eagle with legs like Big Nick, also marked and kicked a goal. Tim Allen's heroics had come to nothing. The Eagles led by the same margin by which they'd led at the first change: 45 points.

The two goals in time-on provided the momentum for Edithvale-Aspendale to continue their spree after the break. I spent most of the quarter behind the bayside goals but the ball rarely came into the Mornington forward line. In their boredom, the fans around me warmed up with a few light insults for Simon Goosey. When the ball finally did arrive, they took their cue to let fly with a stream of witless putdowns. Goosey marked in front of John Hynes, who continued to gloat and grin despite his inability to keep up with an injured 32-year-old. Goosey missed from a tight angle, and more derision was launched. The main offenders tended to be fat and ruddy. My guess was that few of them had touched a footy since the schoolyard. It was easier to stand behind the fence and abuse those having a go.

By this time, Tim Allen was playing in the ruck, where he found a daunting opponent. Kane Batzloff continued to win the knocks and the Eagles continued to sweep the ball from the middle. Batzloff played at Essendon before deciding to travel around Australia. He was halfway across the Nullarbor when his car broke down. The cost of attending to his car ended his trip and he returned to the bayside suburbs of Melbourne, where the Eagles swooped for his signature. Batzloff towered over all opponents. His midfielders gobbled up his offerings with unrelenting hunger. Troy Shannon kicked a running goal from a tight angle and took a slalom course back to defence, giving high fives to his teammates along the way. Half-forward Richard Sampieri finished the quarter by slotting a goal from the boundary line. Edithvale-Aspendale could do no wrong. The scoreboard showed a lead of 100 points.

Even with such a lead, the Eagles began the last quarter with two defenders camped on Goosey's toes and spectators continuing to call for his head. Troy Shannon, a step ahead of everyone since running out of the race, said enough was enough and introduced a magnanimous countdown to victory. For the rest of the quarter, he offered The Goose a hand whenever the full-forward went to ground and gave him a pat on the back whenever possible. A showman to the last, he knew there was more style in compassion than overkill. His parting gesture was to turn the match into his own. The peroxided playmaker had the ball at his command and was a worthy winner of one of two medals for best afield. Kane Batzloff won the other. They were easily the two most influential players on the ground and, after winning the grand final by 99 points, their team had a compelling case to be regarded as the best in the history of the competition.

Simon Goosey accepted the defeat with grace. I found him leaning on the fence in bare feet, sipping a can of Coke and speaking gently to supporters wishing him well. "They were just too good," he said. He was reluctant to offer his ankle injury as an excuse for kicking 1.7, and neither did he moan about the abuse. I'd been given the word that The Goose brings attention on himself. He thrusts his fist into the air, high-fives his teammates, yells and hoots and plays up to the crowd. I saw no such exuberance, for the good reason that his side was getting flogged. But whatever his record over the years, the slander directed at him during the grand final seemed excessive. Goosey said later that it upsets him only when his two children hear it. "Occasionally it can get a bit personal but I suppose they pay the money, they say what they want."

In the winners' rooms, coach Brett Wright said a major reason for the victory was the closeness of the coaching panel. Wright played 340 senior games with the club and won seven best-and-fairests. His fellow coaches had been with him throughout his career. The panel stood behind him, absorbing their premierships in all three grades in silent modesty. A senior player was less modest, strutting around in a celebration of victory and prompting Wright to laugh. It seemed pertinent to ask the coach whether he encourages lairising. "We've got natural flair," he said. "I don't try and strangle it."

Kane Batzloff won the Edithvale-Aspendale best-and-fairest before fulfilling his travelling ambitions and going overseas. Troy Shannon took the assistant coaching job at Rye. John Hynes took a coaching job in Cairns and took a handful of players with him. Sam Anstey went to Port Melbourne. The Eagles lost a dozen players from their premiership side. Andrew Morrison won the Mornington best-and-fairest from midfielder Reece Singleton. Simon Goosey had an ankle operation straight after the season and pledged to play for another three years.

25
BEYOND THE BIG STICKS

Stanhope v Nagambie
the Lions and the Lakers

"He's just a lamb now."

Nagambie legend Tiny Finnigan on Shane Loveless

Sunshine bathed the Lancaster oval as spectators crowded in front of the social rooms and lounged on the bonnets of cars nudged against the fence. Thousands of spectators turned up to see whether Nagambie could win their third successive flag or Stanhope, a club that had struggled to survive, could complete their rise from easybeats to premiers. Thousands more had come to see a shootout between two of the greats of country football. Both spearheads had been wild and woolly in their youth. One settled into an AFL career; the other never settled at all. Gavin Exell followed his disorderly years by playing in attack and on the wing at Geelong. After returning to the country, he played upfield until, at 37 years of age, he allowed himself to drop back to the goalsquare. His reward was 100 goals for the first time in his career. In the second semi-final, Exell kicked nine goals. With him in form, Stanhope were favored to complete the fairytale.

Shane Loveless followed a few eventful years in the big league with many eventful years in the country, moving around forward lines in three states, living off his ability to put the ball through the big sticks. Clubs paid him good money and he repaid them with bags of goals. The arrangement usually lasted one or two seasons. At Ardmona, he created the suspicion that he was getting old by staying for three years. For the fourth year, he was named coach. His failure to attend training brought an end to his tenure and he moved down the road to Nagambie. He continued to kick goals, usually by the hundred, but the suspicion that he was getting old was confirmed when he lost interest in terrifying the opposition. Sometimes entire backlines emerged unscathed.

When Loveless did decide to give the game away, Nagambie were concerned at his timing. He stopped playing on the eve of the finals and went to Sydney, where, at 196 centimetres, and with the strength of Atlas, he was perfectly suited to Olympic duties as a bouncer. When Nagambie made the grand final, the Lakers wondered about luring him back. The lure would require money. The Nagambie rowing club had been enjoying prosperous times, with renovations to the lake and facilities in town attracting lucrative training camps and regattas. The least the rowers could do was help their cousins from the football club. Their offer of $100 a goal was relayed to Loveless and a committeeman from the football club was assigned the task of bringing him back. Nobody was sure whether the scheme would bear fruit. Just hours before the game, the coach had no idea whether the big spearhead would play. It looked as though The Loveless Show, an extravaganza that had riveted fans for 24 years, would wind up without a final act.

The Loveless Show began in Sale, where he was a potential ringmaster in cricket, boxing and cycling. He chose football, which offered the most applause of all. His first move was to Footscray under the zoning laws. He lasted 28 games for 72 goals, a healthy return for a young forward at a struggling club. In one game he kicked eight goals and put on a performance that excited fans across the nation. I remember watching footage of him on *World of Sport* holding out his opponent to take a mark before poking the ball in his opponent's face. After every goal, he puffed out his chest until it nudged the grandstand. He was the Tarzan of the goalsquare. In his third season, he shared in the club goalkicking award. Then all too soon he was gone.

The reasons for his departure remain unclear. He left around the time that Ian Hampshire replaced Royce Hart as coach, and both men had more on their minds than a problem forward. Speaking from his farm in Tasmania, Hart laughed at the rumor that he and Loveless had come to blows. He said disagreements were part of coaching and he had his share with Loveless, but there was no altercation. His main memory was of a considerable talent with more flamboyance than dedication. He chuckled when recalling a promise from Loveless to take the women in the office out to lunch. The party arrived at his car, only to find it jacked up and devoid of wheels. It had been repossessed, an incident in keeping with his short but colorful career with the Bulldogs. "He was a likeable ratbag," Hart said. Hampshire remembered watching in amazement when the girlfriend of Loveless carried his bag for him. He pointed out the practice to his wife, who warned the coach not to get any ideas.

Loveless moved from Footscray down to Glenorchy, where his introduction to Tasmania was a shirtfront in the opening minutes of his first game. It was the beginning of a wretched relationship. A suspension cost him the chance to build any momentum before the finals, just as his irregular training habits and erratic behavior cost him respect. On the eve of the grand final, his teammates voted to exclude him from the team. The regretful president, Barry Manson, drove him to the airport the next morning in the car that the Magpies had lent him. After dropping him off, Manson allowed himself a smile when he discovered a glovebox jammed with parking tickets. At the end of the day, the smile had been replaced. Manson said Loveless failed to produce during the season but, to this day, he believes that a born performer like him would have found something before 20,000 raucous spectators jammed around the small North Hobart oval. The New Norfolk coach had planned to play the Hunnibel brothers on Loveless. The coach couldn't believe his luck when Loveless's absence enabled the two brothers to play upfield. New Norfolk won a tight grand final. Loveless had made his mark even while he flew over Bass Strait.

His next destination was Tatura, in the heart of orchard country in the Goulburn Valley, where he struck up an enduring rapport with his coach, Brian "Tiny" Finnigan. Tiny Finnigan was one of the toughest men in the Goulburn Valley league, a quality that earned respect. During the week, Loveless was a laborer for Tiny Finnigan. On Saturdays, they played in the key forward slots. "I had to play near him to keep an eye on him," Finnigan said. Loveless created a storm in the Goulburn Valley. He fended off entire packs to take marks and made a mockery of the large grounds by booting goals from anywhere. In his excitement, he sometimes bared his bum to spectators and once or twice he turned around and gave the front view. "He was fiddling with his lad," said an official from another club. Horrified spectators screamed. Then they invited their friends to scream with them. Crowds mushroomed, with fans arriving from across northern Victoria to gape in awe at his talent and shout in fury at his antics. One day at Tongala, the abuse became too much and Loveless belted a spectator. Policeman marched him off the ground and up to the station, where he was held until club officials bailed him out after the match.

Off the ground, he was renowned for punting and lollies. One night he turned up at the house of a Tatura official clutching a bag filled with $10 worth of chocolate frogs. It was the age when video recorders had just entered Australian homes. Loveless sat and watched videos with the official's son. The four-year-old ate so many chocolate frogs that he threw up. Loveless left the official to clean up the mess and hopped into his car to drive home. The club had given him a Fiat, which was a handy runaround car, if small. Loveless was quite a sight driving from the passenger's seat while stretching his right leg over the driver's seat towards the accelerator.

He kicked almost 200 goals in two seasons before moving across to Kyabram, which had been impressed by his application to coach. Officials were less impressed when Loveless used a practice match to sort out which under-18s might survive the rigors of senior football, but the club quickly grew to like him. He was described as enthusiastic and intelligent. Loveless played himself at centre half-forward, where his athleticism had more room to shine. Gus Underwood, a leading former footballer and respected football writer in Kyabram for three decades, said Loveless reminded him of Tony Lockett. "He's as good as I've seen in the Goulburn Valley." Loveless kicked 87 goals in a side that failed to make the finals before being caught dipping into the funds for the players' trip at the end of the season. His explanation that he was taking an advance from the money that the club owed him fell on deaf ears. He was sacked. It was time to leave the Goulburn Valley.

He went home to Sale, where tallies of 110 and 142 goals left no time to misbehave. Sale officials reported that Loveless was a huge asset – no trouble at all. He then headed from the east of the state to the west, where his father had worked in the '50s and some relatives still lived. The Casterton ground is known as Island Park, because of the island that is left in the centre when the nearby river floods. Loveless had no problem kicking from the island. He also impressed rivals at South Gambier by booting goals from way out on the Blue Lake oval. Some claimed his goals were the longest seen in the competition. Loveless moved on to South Gambier and the next season was named coach. The appointment was a letdown. The full-forward failed to bring in the recruits he promised. He failed to do much at all. After a handful of games, club and coach agreed to part. South Gambier now claim it was the best thing to happen to the club. The shambles left by Loveless prompted the appointment of a disciplined local, Peters Sims. The club won six consecutive flags and Sims won the national coaching award.

Loveless then rang Apsley, which is just on the Victorian side of the border. Former treasurer Robert Munn believed that the big forward had studied the clubs in the Western District before making his choice. "It was as if he searched us out," Munn said. Apsley warned him that their cash reserves were modest. Loveless said he simply wanted to play in a successful side. The Magpies thought long and hard about the risk of upsetting a balanced team. They took him on but found reason to regret their decision when the first cheque he presented at the bar bounced. Clubmen scratched their heads and decided to let it ride. A successful union developed. Munn said the unexpected recruit was friendly, helpful towards the young players, and dynamic. "He was a big, big, solid man who could take a game apart."

In the first half of the grand final, Loveless kicked uncharacteristically poorly and Penola shot to a 10-goal lead. After the break, he went into the centre to take on John Mossop, the red-headed ruckman from Geelong. The pair went at each other like old bulls, crashing bodies and lashing out until their guernseys were destroyed. When his fitness gave out, Loveless returned to the goalsquare. Apsley hit the front in time-on before Penola fought back to win a memorable match. Loveless disappeared but the Magpies made sure they would keep his memory alive. They still have the cheque that bounced.

On the salty plains of northern Victoria, the big forward lasted only five games before Kerang Rovers sacked him for striking an opponent behind play. He spent the rest of the season further south at Colbinabbin, where he kicked 68 goals in 10 games and told officials he would make no move without telling them first. The next anyone heard he was at Ardmona, where he found his resting place in football, the Kyabram district league.

By now 35 years of age, he ignored his footballing twilight and found a new dawn. In one match against Nagambie, he kicked 22 goals. In another game, he tucked an opponent under one arm and put another in a merciless headlock. He frightened opponents and scandalised the crowds. He also kicked 152, 140 and 165 goals. Ardmona played in three grand finals for two flags before Loveless repeated an old pattern by presenting immaculately for the coaching job. Again, he made all the right noises about recruiting and training and dress codes for the players, but again he was a letdown. He turned up one night a week during the summer months; when the season began, he failed to turn up at all. He said his job required him to drive around Victoria picking up television satellite dishes. Ardmona secretary Michael Nethersole laughed at the memories and stressed that the full-forward did everything asked of him on the field. There were no hard feelings when, as a coach, Loveless again proved himself a brilliant forward. Five games into the season, there was another parting of the ways.

So Loveless was available for hire. Clubs, however, were wary. The spearhead was costly; he was also as big as a house. His taste for lollies and distaste for training had pushed his weight beyond 150 kilograms. By comparison, Tony Lockett had been 112 kilograms in his final year at Sydney. The one man who believed Loveless would be worth the investment was Tiny Finnigan. The legendary Finnigan had coached Nagambie to a premiership at 21 years of age. Twenty-one years later, the Lakers had failed to win another flag. The club was obliged to listen when Finnigan said it was only a good forward away from success, and here was the answer. The defender on whom Loveless had kicked 22 goals strongly supported the proposal. Others were not so keen. In the end, Finnigan convinced clubmen that Loveless wouldn't be their problem. "Don't worry," he said. "Leave him to me."

Without being unfriendly, Loveless had little to say. He'd arrive just before the match and leave after the siren, not to be seen for another week. But the players loved him. His presence enabled them to walk tall. It also enabled one half-back flanker to play without an opponent for a year, because the opposition would sacrifice a forward to play two men at full-back. Clubs were obsessed with Loveless, talking about him, designing strategies around him, trying to avoid getting caught in his path. Yet they could do nothing to stop him. Coach Rohan Aldous gave his side one basic instruction: go long to the big bloke. "We just used to kick it up and he'd catch it. That was our game plan." In the grand final, Nagambie were six goals behind when the full-forward took out two key players – one with a hip and shoulder, the other by falling on him. Nagambie won their overdue flag.

The next year, Loveless remained on target and the Lakers won every game. But off the field, he was tiring of dealing with ulcers and gout. He stopped eating lollies and drinking Coke, and he shunned all rich foods. He lost 34 kilograms in half a year, trimming down to 117 kilograms. His health improved and he continued kicking goals. Halfway through the 2000 season, his third season with the Lakers, he had an average of four goals a game when his job in security at the Royal Children's Hospital in Melbourne fell through. He moved back to Sale, which proved a long way from the Goulburn Valley. He tired of the six-hour journeys and applied for a clearance to his hometown club. But the clearance was held up and the cut-off date passed. Loveless was left with the Lakers.

In early July, soon after the clearances cut-off had passed, Nagambie president Tracy Lang called a meeting and informed the players that the money had run out. There would be no match payments for the rest of the season. Eyebrows were raised at the timing. "I know it sounds terrible but it wasn't planned that way," Lang said. She believed afterwards that the crisis pulled the club together. A lethargic season had received a shot in the arm.

The Lakers played to their ability but, off the field, several lost interest in the club. Some of them had planned to celebrate Loveless's 2000th goal in senior football, with former teammate Doug Hawkins lined up to pay tribute, but the function was cancelled. Not long afterwards, Loveless stopped turning up for games. His decision to work in Sydney suggested his career would end in anti-climax. The Lakers lost the second semi-final by 16 goals and looked set for an ignominious exit, when fate played into their hands. In the first semi-final, the score was level after two periods of overtime. Finally, Merrigum struggled to a famous victory over Lancaster in near darkness, but three periods of overtime took their toll. Nagambie rolled past their exhausted opponents in the preliminary final.

It was Pat McNamara, the former state National Party leader, who hatched the plan to lure Loveless back from Sydney. McNamara had been a rowing partner of Tiny Finnigan. Now retired at Nagambie, he was president of the rowing club and keen to help fellow sportsmen in need. In the hours before the grand final, it was unclear whether his offer of $100 a goal would be accepted. The Lakers went about their preparations as they had without Loveless for the previous finals. Then the door opened and an excited babble stirred the room. Shane Loveless strolled in with his bag slung over his shoulder. "Gidday boys," he said, chewing gum and grinning. It was if he'd just popped out to get a newspaper and returned a month later. The 41-year-old changed into his bike shorts and the frayed jumper that had been custom-made to cover his bulk. A showman all his life, there was no way he would miss the final act of the most compelling show in country football.

The sight of him ambling on to the wide oval earned gasps from the crowd. The big spearhead absorbed the attention before joining his teammates in a crooked line for the national anthem. He clasped his hands behind his back and tilted back his curly blond hair, angling his chin skywards. His tracksuit top ended halfway down his belly, leaving the frayed jumper to shamble towards his shorts, while the national anthem crackled through antiquated speakers. When the music stopped, he peeled off the token tracksuit top and tapped a few teammates on the bum. The teammates nodded and remained silent. They would never know what to say to him.

The ball was shared from flurry to flurry before Loveless conjured the first decisive moment of the match. He didn't so much lead as lumber. His size compensated for his inability to rise higher than the grass and he met the ball with three or four players crowding in from behind. Loveless cradled the ball in his huge hands as the pack forced him to earth. He ambled to his mark, soaking up the roars, before kicking a behind from 35 metres. A minute later, Nagambie took an early lead when Wes Shelton, the son of Essendon premiership defender Bluey Shelton, hauled in a big mark in the goalsquare.

The Lakers were superior in the air but they lacked zip on the ground. Injured midfielders were struggling to keep up with their fitter opponents. Stanhope midfielder Simon Harrison is small and light. His frame is more suited to a racetrack than a footy ground, but his courage and nip frustrated the Lakers until a brawl erupted on the wing. It began with two players disagreeing about the force of a tackle. Teammates piled in to parade their feathers, a few their fists, and the fight broke up almost as soon as it began. Everyone returned to their positions and awaited the bounce of the ball. Loveless had not moved from his goalsquare.

Gavin Exell returned his players' minds to the job by leading and marking. Then he made another lead and took another mark. Two goals were kicked with a minimum of fuss. In his youth, Exell had been more dynamic. He burst into country football in Bendigo before going to Carlton, where he resented being named among the emergencies before half a dozen games without making his debut. "I was probably a bit stupid when I was young," he said. "I didn't do myself justice. I took the easy way out and headed to Queensland."

He ended up at Geelong, where he kicked nine goals in the famous match in which Hawthorn rebounded from the dead at Princes Park. The next week he'd failed to kick a goal when St Kilda captain Danny Frawley was moved off him and on to a rampaging Gary Ablett. Exell went on to kick eight goals.

At 37, Exell was ready to retire when Stanhope persuaded him to join them as playing coach. He was impressed from the moment he walked in. "I've never seen a club like it." The Lions had risen from winless jokes to finalists with a bunch of young locals. The arrival of the coach and a student who came up from Melbourne with a Stanhope friend raised the tally of imports to two. The Lions settled into a pattern in which opposition clubs would come at them for a quarter before falling away. The two goals from Exell in the shadow of the quarter-time siren suggested the pattern was repeating itself.

For the second quarter, I watched from behind the goals while Nagambie kicked with the breeze. Unfortunately, most of the play was at the other end. Exell received two free kicks and kicked two goals. In the

Nagambie forward line, Loveless walked in wide circles with his chin cocked at the sky and his jaw working the gum. In years gone by, he might have made life difficult for his opponent, but Tiny Finnigan believed he'd mellowed with age. "He's just a lamb now," Finnigan said. "Well, maybe not that docile, but he's toned down his ways."

Every few laps of his wide circles, Loveless offered a few friendly words to his opponent, Michael Betson, a 32-year-old with bandy legs and an honest face. Betson had played with Loveless at Ardmona. In his opinion, the big man was overly aggressive. Betson watched the match with arms folded, determined not to drop his guard. He replied in passing to Loveless, but his eyes never left the play. Loveless walked on with an air of amused detachment. Sometimes he stopped to inspect the hand he'd been shaking since early in the first quarter. Mostly, he kept his chin high and gazed towards the gum trees and low plains that stretched across the valley. Soon he would leave all this behind.

On the outer wing, spectators leaned on cars or hunched over the fence, lapping up the warmth in surfing shorts and singlets while listening to the men's 1500 metres freestyle final in Sydney. The broadcast of the Australian quinella filled the balmy air as Nagambie scored a few late goals to stay in touch.

Early in the third quarter, Gavin Exell booted another effortless goal, his sixth. At the other end, Loveless made heavy work of keeping Betson away from the ball and taking a chest mark. The effort sent him crashing to the earth, which stoutly took the load. Loveless got up and made a speculative step, as if he were about to play on. A more unlikely idea was impossible. The crowd would have expected the reserves to bound on to the field and perform *Swan Lake* before they expected the big man to dash towards goal. Loveless smirked and trudged back to his mark accompanied by jeers. He lined up for a small eternity, deep in concentration, and the ball drifted through for a behind. The crowd jeered again. Loveless inspected his sore hand and resumed chewing gum.

Exell kicked his seventh goal like he was tying up his shoelace. By the end of the quarter he'd nine. His kicking was metronomic, with his left foot swinging sweetly and the ball sailing between the goalposts from every angle inside 50 metres. At the other end, Loveless grew frustrated. He threw his head back and screamed into the air after kicking another behind. The crowd jeered, but the jeers were muted. It was remarkable how one man could intimidate a crowd of thousands.

The final act in the Loveless melodrama began when he took a mark in the goalsquare and booted the ball through the goals with all his considerable force. The goal was disallowed. He'd been penalised for pushing his opponent in the back. The decision set off a pantomime, with Loveless flinging his arms in disgust. He cursed and stomped and demanded that the umpire reverse the decision. It wasn't as if the Lakers were within a whisker of victory; they were 10 goals down. But that was beside the point. Loveless was performing his curtain call. The crowd risked a few muted jeers.

The match became a procession. Ruckman Glen Hodgins directed play and the midfielders sent the ball forward. Defender Richard Ryan took a screamer to ensure that he would dominate the clubroom replays, and the celebrations began. With the game in hand, Gavin Exell jogged from the ground as Lions fans rose to applaud him. The coach had kicked 11 goals, through canny judgment and unerring accuracy. "If I have 10 shots, I know I'm going to kick nine," he said after the 72-point victory. Shane Loveless ended the match with 4.4. He trudged towards the presentations, shaking hands with opponents and chewing gum.

Near the presentations, Michael Betson cradled his baby as the odd supporter came up to congratulate him. Stanhope players tipped a tub of ice on their joyous president as Betson explained that he never really knew Loveless at Ardmona, but he knew his bag of tricks. "Today he was well-behaved," he said. Betson announced his retirement as his wife checked the baby in his arms.

Loveless announced his retirement as he lay on one elbow on the half-forward flank. "Mate, this is it," he said. He was warm and affable, and revealed that his hand had been broken early in the match. When asked for his career highlight, he said playing in six consecutive Kyabram league grand finals. "Look at this," he said, gesturing towards the milling crowd. "This is what it's all about. I left league footy at 22 years of age. This is what you play for."

Why did you leave league footy?

"Dunno," he said, shrugging his shoulders.

I asked the question in another way.

"Sorry, mate. Gotta go. I've got a plane to catch at 8.30pm. Good luck to you."

He shook my hand and trudged from the ground, a mountain of a man soaking up the stares one last time. I felt short-changed, but that was hardly a surprise. The burly forward had been a mystery for more than two decades. It was only fitting that his career should end that way.

He reached the fence and made his way to the rooms, chin held high in the spring dusk, lost to the goalsquare after all these years.

Gavin Exell kicked 124 goals for the season; Shane Loveless kicked 76. Teenage ruckman Glen Hodgins won his second successive Stanhope best-and-fairest, with Ashley Comer second and Exell third. Rohan Aldous won his fourth Nagambie best-and-fairest and his fourth Kyabram district league medal. The Lakers suffered an exodus after the grand final. Shane Loveless was unable to be tracked down for follow-up interviews. Nobody knew where he lived, not even his parents.

26

TROPICAL STORM ON
MALLEE DUST

Nyah-Nyah West United v Cohuna Kangas
the Demons and the Kangas

"I had a look on a map – 'Oh, there it is'."

Nyah-Nyah West United key defender Jason Cockatoo

Demons supporters craned their necks to catch a glimpse of the players doing stretches in the old wooden sheds at the Swan Hill showgrounds. A low hum of excitement mixed with the fear of losing after coming this far. In more than two decades since the merger, the club had never gone past the preliminary final. "You'll never get another crack like this," shouted one supporter. Even the old-timers were on the balls of their feet, willing on the young Demons, casting an eye over the key forward wrapping tape around his wrist or the defender shaking out the nerves. The weather-beaten farmers could barely believe that Nyah and Nyah West were in the same jumper, let alone in the grand final. In their day, the clubs were separated by three of the longest kilometres in Victoria. Former Nyah player Stuart Looney belied his kindly eyes with memories of the intense rivalry. "Often a bit of blood would be spilt," he said. Looney stooped and chatted with teammates from the 1963 premiership team, the last on either side of the club. The old stars continue to acknowledge the two strands of the club. Most supporters have become lazy and call it Nyah, but the old stars call it United. They believed that United were due for a flag.

The supporters watched from behind the flimsy rope that separated them from the players. Several players had backgrounds that were exotic, to say the least. Once upon a time Nyah and Nyah West had looked no further than the Murray River on one side and the Mallee paddocks on the other. In this grand final side, the coach and his offsider were from the Gold Coast and half a dozen others were from Darwin. None of them had been near a tractor in their lives.

Mark Armstrong, a policeman who played a few games in the seconds after moving up from Geelong, was the first piece in the Demons' nationwide jigsaw. A knee injury forced Armstrong to throw away his boots, so he began making himself useful by compiling a recruiting dossier. The names in the dossier were taken mainly from his home town. Then he widened his search by making regular trips to the north of the state. Tony Berry was among the players to impress him. The ruckman played in premierships on the Gold Coast before becoming part of an annual flow of players between his home club and Mildura. At South Mildura, Berry and his Queensland mates took the club to its first premiership for three decades, but the flag was barely hoisted when the recruits cleared out, unwilling to stay if the club couldn't pay. Berry stayed on to coach. His side bore no recognition to the premiership side but he impressed with his composure. Nyah knew what it was like to suffer. They wanted to know what it was like to win. Berry had experience on both sides of the ledger. The 25-year-old had no sooner led his club to the bottom of the ladder than the Demons signed him.

After signing on, Berry spent the idle months before Christmas fulfilling an ambition to play in the Top End. He joined Wanderers, where his physical style earned respect in the key positions. Against Darwin, Berry spent most of the game crashing and bashing into his opponent. At times, the contest became heated. In between skirmishes, Berry realised that his opponent could play. In the last quarter, when the sting was out of the game, the pair forgot their tiff and began talking. Berry informed his opponent that he would be in the tropics for six weeks before returning to Victoria to coach. His opponent said he'd never played in Victoria. Berry saw an opening. "Want to be my assistant?" he asked. Simon Roberts said he was keen. They would discuss the details over a beer. Darwin won the match with ease.

The pair reached a loose agreement in the tropical heat that night. Berry feared it might be the beer talking but Roberts confirmed otherwise when he asked during the week whether he could bring a couple of players with him. The news made Nyah jittery. They'd signed a coach in Mildura and now had several players ready to fly in from Darwin. The main fear was wasting money on northern recruits who would fly home at the first frost. The Demons informed Roberts that they didn't want stars; they wanted good people. They wanted players who would stick around. Leave it to me, Roberts said. Berry flew back to Victoria to begin the pre-season.

The coach received more support when Bob Suter, a former teammate from the Gold Coast, offered to join him. Suter is a lively forward with a mop of dark curls and a habit of referring to himself as "The Bob". The pair had played in premierships together. "He's my good luck charm," Berry said. They moved into a house in Swan Hill, 25 kilometres south of Nyah, and set about the pre-season. A couple of the locals looked handy and Christian Shaw, a midfielder from Geelong, was exceptional. The stand-out, however, was Ash Thompson, who'd returned home after hearing that Nyah were assembling a decent team. Thompson began training but he was wary. The Demons had such an inglorious history that any mention of success had the credibility of drop kicks on the run. He had the choice of returning to Sydney, where he was the anchor in the first Balmain premiership for almost a century, but an old promise was nagging at him. As a junior, Thompson was in a group of players that won every premiership as they proceeded through the grades. The young Demons proved their outrageous talent when three from their ranks were chosen for the Teal Cup, to play against the best teenagers in Australia. Back home, the precocious Demons took their club's senior side to the preliminary final. The next year, the team broke up. Thompson was drafted by Sydney; other young talents went away to study. "It happens in every isolated town," Thompson said. The Demons fell back towards the bottom of the ladder but not before the teenagers reminded each other of their pledge: that one day they would reunite and take the club to a premiership. After hearing of the Demons' growing player riches, Thompson decided it was time to return from Sydney and honor his word.

Former players followed Thompson's lead and returned from here and there in the north of the state. A university student agreed to drive home from Melbourne every weekend. The final pieces fell into the jigsaw when five players flew down from Darwin. Simon Roberts was tall and lean, with a floppy fringe and a drifter's ease. He had with him three young forwards, small and whippy, with silky skills and a promise to see out the winter, and a bandy-legged defender. Demons fans took a step back when they learned the pedigree of the defender. Jason Cockatoo grew up in Cairns, a member of a famous Queensland football family, before moving across to Darwin. In the Top End, he represented the Aboriginal All-Stars against Collingwood and became captain of the Northern Territory. In the south, he played in the South Australian National Football League with Port Adelaide and in the Riverina. The first step in his Victorian odyssey was discovering the whereabouts of Swan Hill, where he would live. "I had a look on a map – 'Oh, there it is'."

The Darwin recruits slotted into the Nyah side and the Demons won the pre-season grand final. The improvement continued into the home-and-away rounds, with the Demons establishing themselves among the teams to beat. Then another Darwin recruit, Shaun Hill, joined mid-season. Central Murray followers were quick to attribute the Demons' form to the recruits but Tony Berry believed these comments downplayed his side. Berry had been in teams in which five gun recruits failed to have an impact because the locals around them were unable to keep pace. He said a big factor in the Demons' rise was the change among the locals. "The talent was there," he said. "But they were always defending." The recruits had won premierships in every state in Australia. Their winning ways enabled the locals to attack. It proved a liberating experience.

The heart and soul of the local brigade was Matt Curran, who was among the teenagers to make the pact with Ash Thompson. While Thompson went to Sydney, Curran stayed with Nyah. At 25 years of age, he won his seventh best-and-fairest. The artful rover continued to burn after the northern invasion but, for the first time since his schooldays, others were burning around him. The whole side lifted and momentum began to build. It was apparent long before the finals that the Demons had the right stuff. Their biggest hurdle was Lake Boga, another brides-maid club, which defeated the Demons twice during the year. In the second semi-final, Nyah shed the last of their inhibitions with a 98-point thumping of Lake Boga.

Tony Berry sat his players on the stained floor in the wooden shed and made his speech before the grand final. The Demons players angled their necks towards him as the hubbub of the supporters tailed off. During the week, Berry asked every player to write a letter describing what the premiership would mean to him. In his grand final address, he held aloft the letter of defender Steve Wright. Players clasped their hands around their knees a little tighter as Berry began to read. "It came to the point where football was no longer enjoyable. It had become a yearly routine." Wright had described in simple, moving words the weight of defeat. Then came the lightness of victory. "To be so low for so long and to be in the side for the grand final makes my heart beat faster."

The heart of every player and supporter began to beat faster. Simon Roberts stood up and shook his limbs. He blew the fringe from his eyes and smiled as though he were about to head out for training on a balmy Thursday night. Roberts had played in pressure games in Perth and Cairns and Mount Gambier, in the bottom corner of South Australia. He played around the calendar, in Darwin over the Wet Season and somewhere down south in the Dry. In between matches, he was an artist, with a bent for abstract works. His free spirit fascinated the farmers, most of whom had been rooted to the one plot of land all their lives. Roberts was born in Kenya, of all places. The farmers looked at him, then they looked at Matt Curran, whose loyalty was a quality they knew and admired. Curran was a picture of composure, with his jumper tucked in and his shorts just right, but his mouth was set hard. His father played 180 games for the club and barely lined up in a final. Anxiety and hope showed on the faces of the Demons with years of defeat behind them. Simon Roberts remained a pic-ture of cool. A downtrodden club in a southern state had placed its belief in him. He liked that feeling. The sea of supporters parted and the players shuffled towards the door. The room went quiet. After so many years of waiting, no one knew whether to shout or cry. Simon Robert blew the blond fringe out of his eyes one last time and eased into a jog. On his back was the enigmatic No.13.

The wind blustered down from the northern plains, carrying the threat of rain over the flat grid of streets, towards the river on the edge of town. The weather failed to stop supporters pouring into the showgrounds in their thousands. The Cohuna Kangas had finished no lower than third in four years since entering the competition, but most of the crowd was here in the hope of a Nyah fairytale. Young fans wore blue and red face paint. Blue and red streamers flapped in the wintry gusts. The weather was unlike anything Jason Cockatoo had known. The whole season had been a big learning experience. Swan Hill and Nyah seemed such a long way from Darwin. Cockatoo missed his partner and two children, and the wheat-fields were no more familiar than icebergs. Even the football was from a different world. The game in Darwin is all about flow. He admires the Victorians and their willingness to sacrifice their bodies but he believes their football is stodgy. He urged his teammates to loosen up while, away from the game, he grew more uptight. Halfway through the season he flew home. The club hoped the trip would settle him down but the alarm was sounded when he flew out again after the second semi-final. Demons officials feared their star defender would miss the biggest day in the club's history. They had to work hard to persuade him to return.

A key factor in his return was the club's pledge to fly down his partner, Natasha Hewitt, for the grand final. Hewitt frowned and said she would prefer not to say much about Victoria on her first visit. Her one comment was that Darwin had better shopping than Swan Hill. The 22-year-old admitted the six months of the southern season had been tough, but not without gain. "It's brought us closer together," she said. "He's very homesick."

With Hewitt perched in the back row of the temporary seating, screwing up her nose at the blustery wind, Jason Cockatoo controlled the match from the first minute. He was dominant in the air, showing canny judgment in the tricky conditions, and dangerous with his loping runs. He was also without an opponent. The Kangas had sprung a surprise by playing Ricky Easton, their burly key forward, loose in the backline. Tony Berry could barely believe it. The coach considered Cockatoo the best attacking defender in country footy – and he had no opponent. Cockatoo continued loping downfield while Berry showed great courage in a marking contest. His team knew what he expected. The Demons pounded the packs, with the experienced players showing no sign of nerves. Ash Thompson snapped a goal at full speed to open the scoring. Tall forward Paul Walsh, recruited after destroying the Demons in their previous finals campaign, by now a distant memory, wrenched the ball from the sky and hoisted a goal from 50 metres. Thompson then gave a tantalising glimpse of his range of skills by dragging in a courageous mark and playing on in one motion. He balanced before booting long and direct to the attacking side of the ground, where Simon Roberts marked strongly on the lead. It was a passage of play straight out of a coaching manual, and all the more impressive in the conditions. Roberts made a mockery of the wind by kicking straight through the middle of the goals.

For the rest of the quarter, Thompson turned the ground into his own little kingdom. A midfielder of medium height and compact build, he showed faultless skills and he was tough. But his greatest asset is his ability to influence the match in some way when he is anywhere near the ball – a rare quality at any level. Lack of pace appeared his only drawback. There seemed no other reason why he would have missed making the grade in the AFL. Thompson admitted after the match that he was disappointed, even angry, at his failure to get a game at Sydney. He left the club after former full-back Rod Carter whispered in his ear that the selection committee would never give him a go. Thompson grew up on a farm just over the river from Nyah. He believed his background had counted against him in Sydney. "Because I came from nowhere, I think I got overlooked." The quest to earn a premiership for his cherished club from nowhere was now driving him on.

The crowd came to life at the combination of Thompson and Roberts, who was playing at full-forward. It was like Barry Price and Peter McKenna in their wildfire days at Collingwood. Children danced around with streamers as Roberts ran into another pass. He calculated the wind with precision to kick truly from 40 metres. A few minutes later, he met a pack at full pelt and took the mark. His impact left several players sprawled on the ground. For all his musings on abstract art, he was totally at home in the heat and fury of a football match. It was another canvas on which to express himself. Roberts sauntered back to his mark, blew the fringe from his eyes and booted another goal from 40 metres. The wind would have terrified most footballers but Roberts never looked like missing.

After the opening onslaught by the experienced players, the younger recruits began to work into the game. Shaun Hill, the mid-season recruit, revealed the most graceful kicking action you could wish to see, cradling the ball in the crook of his wrist and forearm before guiding it gently on to his boot, like a jeweller placing a ring on a cushion. Jason Krueger moved with fluid ease before running into an open goal. The Kangas had no answer to the Demons' talent and potency. Nyah finished the quarter five goals up.

A ripple of approval went through the crowd when Ricky Easton lined up for the next quarter at centre half-forward. Easton was the most influential player on the ground in the previous final. His team needed inspiration, but found its hopes in shreds when Simon Roberts marked just after the break. The Kangas could have built a tunnel in the first quarter and they would have struggled to move the ball into the teeth of goal; the Demons had done it in minutes. Roberts stepped in lightly and kicked his fourth goal as the rain began to dampen the dust.

In defence, Jason Cockatoo took a brave mark backing towards the goalsquare and set off towards the attacking wing, his bandy legs taking him out of reach. His one concession to the wind had been to begin his loping run from deeper in defence. Minutes later, a fellow defender urged a teammate to cut off danger like he was ordering a dog to cut off a frolicking lamb. "Way back, way back," he said. I had to smile. The words "way back" used to ring loud over familiar paddocks 30 kilometres down the road, at the farm on which my mother grew up. My grandfather was forever telling the dog to get way back. Such words are linked in my mind with the Mallee; I just didn't expect to hear them in the second quarter of a grand final. The Demons restricted the Kangas to one goal with the wind and repaired to the wooden shed. The nerves had gone and they were now seven goals in front.

My half-time was spent in a hire car interviewing visitors from interstate about their trip to Victoria. We were in the car because it was raining, an event that failed to surprise the visitors. Sue and Kevin Corrie were down from Queensland to see their son Mark play at centre half-forward, not that they knew anything about centre half-forward. "I'm a rugby league man," said Kevin, chuckling at his strange adventure. After beginning a law degree at 50 years age, it seems Kevin is a man for adventure.

His son shares his taste for new paths in life. Mark grew up playing basketball and once knocked back a scholarship at an American university because his mother was sick. In his late teens he left Cairns to see his sister in Darwin and was asked down to the local football club. Corrie had never played football but he thought it might be fun. At Darwin he met Simon Roberts, who told him about the trip to Victoria. Corrie was eager for another adventure. On the distant Murray River, he overcame his football inexperience with his zest for life. He wasn't so much a breath of fresh air as a cyclone. On the streets of Swan Hill, he called everyone "Bro". At the Swan Hill Cup, before thousands of racegoers from all over the Mallee, he whipped out his guitar and sang his lungs out. At training, he didn't shut up from the moment he tied up his bootlaces. "He's a clown," said Tony Berry. His verve helped the Demons cast off the wariness that had enveloped them during decades of failure. In the grand final, Corrie was irrepressible, barrelling around the forward line and opening up the match for his teammates. His mother seemed proud of this observation. "He lives life like he plays football," she said. "He's fun to be around."

On her one previous visit to Victoria, Sue Corrie was reminded of home. "Victoria's a beautiful state," she said. "Very English looking." Sue has pale skin and blonde hair. She was raised in Surrey before her family emigrated to Cairns, where she met her husband. Kevin is tall and broad, built like a second-row forward, with twice the grace. His background includes Torres Strait Islander, Maori, French and Filipino. Quite a cocktail, I suggested. Kevin chuckled again. The couple's spirits were high despite their demanding schedule. They'd flown from Brisbane to Melbourne before jumping in the hire car for the 350-kilometre drive to Swan Hill. In her exhaustion, Sue must have failed to look out the window. The rusted earth of the Mallee looks no more like England than Abu Dhabi does. She said it made her proud to see her son adapt to new surroundings.

Back on the temporary seating, the Corries sat next to Marilyn Suter, the mother of The Bob. Marilyn had been to Victoria once – as a child to pick grapes with her family. On her second visit, she spent most of the day shivering. Unlike the Corries, however, Marilyn was accustomed to the southern code. She was converted from rugby league after falling in love with a Tasmanian. "It was very hard to change," she said. "I didn't understand the four posts." Her husband gave her time to adjust by playing with Palm Beach for so long that he was in a premiership side with their son. The Bob later left Palm Beach to join Tony Berry in Victoria. Marilyn encouraged her son to go to broaden his horizons, but she missed watching him play. In this game, The Bob was cheeky, adding to the sense of danger in the Demons' attack. He and his mother share dark, curly hair that frames dark features. They also share determination. Marilyn makes car radiators on the Gold Coast. "I make them," she said. "I'm not a receptionist. I make them." She explained that her son was wearing No.37 because his father did.

The Demons took the foot off the pedal in the third quarter, with Simon Roberts finally succumbing to injury and the Kangas fighting back. Roberts had rarely trained since joining the Demons. Most weeks, his preparation consisted of kicking end to end with the chairman of selectors. One night he was lobbing the ball back and forth when he revealed that he was in his sixth year without a break. The chairman of selectors stopped mid-stride. "Don't you think your body's trying to tell you something?" Roberts had osteitis pubis, the wear-and-tear injury of the groin. By the finals, he was getting needle after needle so that he could take his place on to the field. Before the grand final he could barely walk. He got more needles and kicked four goals in a little over a quarter, but by the third quarter he was in agony. He made it to the bench and joined Brendan Curran, who'd been knocked out early in the match. Brendan's brother Matt helped the Demons towards four goals for the quarter.

Cohuna attacked with everything in the last quarter but the match was over. The siren rang to give Nyah victory by 33 points, a margin that flattered the Kangas. The centre of the ground erupted in a riot of leaps and hugs. Blue and red streamers began making a fast journey from the fence as Demons fans sprinted to join the celebrations. After 23 seasons, now it had happened. Nyah and Nyah West were united in a premiership.

A stab pass from the pandemonium stood a short figure with his hair swept across his forehead and his hands in his pockets. It was Bob Rose, who played for Nyah West in the 1945 premiership side, the last in the history of the club. Rose nodded his head towards the excited Demons and remembered 5000 spectators screaming at him in the grand final at the

Swan Hill showgrounds. The next year he was an 18-year-old in a Collingwood side that played before 77,000 in a final at the MCG.

Now 72, he was eager to see the spirit of Nyah West in another grand final. "I had to come up for this. I was really looking forward to it." He was praising the leadership of Tony Berry when John James, who left Carlton in the '60s to coach Robinvale, walked up.

"Gidday, Bob."

"Gidday, Jack."

The Brownlow Medallist and the multiple Copeland Trophy winner stood on the wing, chatting about old times as the Demons continued hugging and leaping in the Mallee air.

Back at Nyah, the celebrations were in the social rooms overlooking the football ground and the trotting track. As a boy, I went to the trots at Nyah during holidays at the family farm. We went on clear summer nights, with the sun burning orange on its long, slow decline. On this damp, spring night, the barbecue was burning in the open area beneath the rooms. Hungry footballers filed past, ready to fill their bellies before the long haul of celebrations. Shaun Hill was carrying his baby daughter. Fellow Darwin recruit Daniel Bromot told how he taught local children several words in the language of his people from Arnhem Land. Bromot was bright and alert. Even at 21, he knew the impact of success on a craving club. "There's so much involved. It's not just the players." Nearby, Frank and Matt Curran were enjoying a quiet drink – father and son with their dream fulfilled.

Simon Roberts absorbed the congratulations and smiled. "To have people crying on my shoulder is great," he said. In the shrill madness of the social rooms, he was unable to walk to the bar without a trail of supporters in pursuit. He was like a pop star, with admirers trying to tap his aura. Despite the overwhelming attention, Roberts had the knack of devoting attention to one supporter at a time. He cocked his head to hear their questions and answered with his eyes. Teenagers swooned. Roberts said his life as a wandering footballer had enabled him to meet good people all around the country. But his body now would need a rest. He planned to take off a couple of months before returning to Darwin after Christmas, giving him enough time to get his touch back before the finals.

I asked Ash Thompson for a word and he took me on to the decking, overlooking the trotting track. The river flowed beyond the back straight.

With a smile that threatened to hurt his cheeks, Thompson recalled the pact he made with his fellow juniors all those dark years ago. "I believed back then that, if enough of us returned, we'd play in a senior premiership with Nyah," he said. "That's what happened today."

Ash Thompson won the Nyah-Nyah West best-and-fairest from Christian Shaw and Jason Cockatoo. Thompson remained at Nyah but Shaw returned to North Shore in Geelong. Cockatoo returned to Darwin two days after the grand final and resumed at Southern Districts. He was Nyah's only Darwin recruit to play in the Top End over the Wet Season. Simon Roberts went to Perth for a rest and stayed there for the summer. Daniel Bromot did the pre-season with Westar Rules club East Fremantle. Mark Corrie spent a few months in Cairns. Jason Krueger did the pre-season with Geelong before joining Sandringham. Shaun Hill remained in the Swan Hill region but gained a clearance to Central Murray league rival Tooleybuc. Simon Roberts and Mark Corrie returned to Nyah for the new season, as did Tony Berry and Bob Suter. Back pocket Trevor Hird won the Cohuna Kangas' best-and-fairest.

FINAL SIREN

AFL statistics from Col Hutchinson at the AFL or *The Encyclopedia of AFL Footballers*

FIRST BOUNCE

1   The boys from old Fitzroy
Fitzroy Reds 13.13 (91) lost to University Blacks 14.12 (96)
April 1, 2000

The first game at Brunswick Street was on April 26, 1884:
Fitzroy 0.14 (14) d Richmond Union 0.2 (2).
The last VFL match at Brunswick Street was on August 20, 1966:
Fitzroy 5.10 (40) lt St Kilda 17.22 (124).

Players at the reunion:
John Benison: Fitzroy, 1966–71, 52 games, 2 goals.
Norm Brown: Fitzroy, 1962–73, 181 games, 77 goals.
Max Cole: Fitzroy, 1965–69, 52 games, 0 goals.
Bernie Drury: Fitzroy, 1966, 6 games, 0 goals.
John Hayes: Fitzroy, 1961–66, 94 games, 20 goals.
Bob Henderson: Fitzroy, 1953 and 55–62, 137 games, 1 goal.
Colin Hobbs: Fitzroy, 1966–71, 64 games, 6 goals.
Ray Slocum: Fitzroy, 1957–65, 121 games, 47 goals.
Bill Stephen: Fitzroy, 1947–57, 162 games, 4 goals.
Ray Wilson: Hawthorn, 1966–72, 105 games, 32 goals.

University Blacks' A-section premierships:
1928–29, 1935, 1938–39, 1946–49, 1965, 1974.

2   From wild cards to Shore things
North Shore 20.11 (131) defeated Leopold 12.17 (89)
April 8, 2000

The 11 North Shore players who represented the Geelong Football League in the grand final of the country championships in 1997:

Frank Fopiani: rover. From Corio, joined North Shore in 1993. Geelong reserves '94. Back to North Shore in 1995. Seven flags in seven years at club. Five best-and-fairests. Assistant coach from 1998.

Tom Hall: key forward. From North Shore. Geelong reserves 1996. Five premierships with Seagulls. Broke Frank Fopiani's stranglehold on best-and-fairest award in 1999.

Glenn Keast: centre, fearless, leads by example. From Mount Gambier. Geelong reserves, St Albans in Geelong league, Glenelg, assistant coach at Leopold, assistant coach at North Shore 1995–98, North Shore coach from 1998. Played in six flags in six years.

Kaine Marsh: versatile flanker, hard runner, 178 centimetres, North Shore prototype. From North Shore. Premierships 1995–98. Geelong rookie list 1999. East Perth 2000.

Billy Nicholls: half-forward. Grandson of legendary president Bill Nicholls. From North Shore. Premierships in 1996 and '97 at 15 and 16 years of age, Geelong Falcons 1998–99, drafted to Hawthorn.

Simon Riddoch: full-back since 1990. From North Shore. Played in 1990, 1993, 1995–2000. Tally of eight premierships broke John Albon's record.

Travis Robertson: key position, 188 centimetres, superb marking skills and stamina. From North Shore, premierships 1996–98. Richmond supplementary list 1999, Werribee 2000.

Darren Ryan: wing, half-back. From North Shore. Left for Geelong Amateurs in 1999, back to North Shore for 2000. Six premierships.

Darren Walsh: half-forward, kicked five goals in second quarter of 1997 grand final versus St Joseph's. From Golden Square. Arrived from Bendigo with best friend Leigh Colbert looking for a change. Stayed from 1995–98 for four premierships. Geelong supplementary list 1999, Bendigo Diggers 2000.

Danny Warren: half-back, renowned for running and kicking, kicks goals when switched up forward, including total of 15 in '98, '99 and 2000 grand finals. From North Shore. Played in all senior premierships since captaining under-18s to flag in 1992. North Shore captain in 2000.

Ron Watt: onballer, occasionally to centre half-forward to provide strength in attack, respected leader, good communicator. From Tocumwal in Geelong's recruiting zone. Two senior games at Geelong in 1984. Coached Geelong-West St Peter's in 1992. Playing coach North Shore 1993–97. Played 1998. Joined coaching panel at Geelong in 1999.

This list fails to include unsung centre half-back Tim Milsome, who – with Keast, Fopiani, Warren and Riddoch – played in every Seagulls premiership from 1995 to 2000.

3   No place like home
Castlemaine 14.7 (91) lt Kangaroo Flat 22.18 (150)
April 15, 2000

Steven Oliver: Carlton, 1992–94, 13 games, 8 goals.
Shane Robertson: Carlton, 1983–91, 80 games, 23 goals.

4   To their credit
Lavington 15.15 (105) lt Corowa-Rutherglen 20.14 (134)
April 22, 2000

Lavington's golden era
1982 second
1983 first
1985 second
1986 first
1987 second
1988 second
1990 second

Damien Houlihan: Collingwood, 1994, 11 games, 6 goals.

AFL debuts of Corowa-Rutherglen products since mid-'80s:
Jeff Bruce: Fitzroy, 1995.
Brad Campbell: St Kilda, 1997.
Michael Gayfer: Collingwood, 1986.
Aaron Henneman: Essendon, 2000.
Adam Houlihan: Geelong, 1997.
Damien Houlihan: Collingwood, 1994.
Ryan Houlihan: Carlton, 2000.
Ben Mathews: Sydney, 1997.
John Longmire: North Melbourne, 1988.
Mark O'Donoghue: North Melbourne, 1988.

Listed:
Paul Bartlett: North Melbourne.
Paul Lewis: Geelong.
Adam Matthews: Carlton.
Brett McKenzie: North Melbourne, Melbourne.

5   Fighting words
    Bungaree 6.12 (48) lt Dunnstown 15.13 (103)
    April 29, 2000

6   Rub of the green
    Dunnstown 23.18 (156) d Newlyn 6.6 (42)
    May 20, 2000

    Gerard Cahir: St Kilda, 1977–79 and 1983, 11 games, 2 goals.
    Ray Murphy: North Melbourne, 1957–58, 20 games, 3 goals.

7   Out of the fray
    Newlyn 9.5 (59) lt Hepburn 12.20 (92)
    June 10, 2000

    Jamie Grant: Footscray, 1991, 5 games, 1 goal.
    David McKay: Carlton, 1969–81, 263 games, 277 goals.

8   Devils' work
    North Footscray 14.4 (88) d Central Altona 11.4 (70)
    May 6, 2000

    Justin Charles: Footscray, 1989–93, 36 games, 24 goals; Richmond, 1995–98, 54 games, 38 goals.

9   Pride of the Yorta Yorta
    Rumbalara 12.6 (78) lt Benalla All Blacks 18.15 (123)
    May 13, 2000

10 Three's a contest
    North 18.16 (124) d Currie 12.10 (82)
    May 27, 2000

HARD YARDS

11 Heavy crowds and purple reign
    Vermont 19.17 (131) d East Ringwood 10.13 (73)
    June 3, 2000

    Vermont: 1962–2000
    Premierships: 1969, 1971, 1982–83, 1986, 1988–91, 1993–95, 1997–98
    Runners-up: 1963, 1973, 1980, 1985, 1996, 1999, 2000
    Best winning sequence: 61 games – round 2, 1988, to round 3, 1991

    Flag-bearers:
    Andrew Dwyer: 234 games and still playing, 7 senior premierships.
    Craig Gislingham: 227 games, 10 premierships (Australian record).
    Craig Coghlan: 218 games, 10 premierships (Australian record).
    Lee Bidstrup: 221 games, 2 premierships.
    Steve Tudor: 173 games, 7 premierships.
    Gary Oakman: 165 games, 7 premierships.
    Steve White: 163 games, 7 premierships.
    Andrew Moss: 148 games, 7 premierships.
    Cameron Bain: 133 games, 7 premierships.
    Mick Winter: 69 games, 3 premierships.
    John Brinkkotter: 63 games, 2 premierships.

276 | LOCAL RITES

12 Shooting Stars
Doutta Stars 16.11 (107) d Aberfeldie 14.14 (98)
June 17, 2000

Simon Minton-Connell: Carlton, 1989–91, 19 games, 50 goals; Sydney, 1992–94, 46 games, 169 goals; Hawthorn, 1995–96, 22 games, 33 goals; Western Bulldogs, 1997–98, 25 games, 53 goals.

13 Matter of faith
Ajax 9.7 (61) d Prahran 7.9 (51)
June 24, 2000

Tony Free: Richmond, 1987–96, 133 games, 46 goals.
Wayne Harmes: Carlton, 1977–88, 169 games, 86 goals.

14 Marching on
Echuca 23.17 (155) d Shepparton Swans 16.10 (106)
July 1, 2000

Simon Eishold: Melbourne, 1986–92, 77 games, 50 goals; Richmond, 1993, 5 games, 0 goals.
Ken Sheldon: Carlton, 1977–86, 132 games, 170 goals; St Kilda, 1987–89, 53 games, 24 goals.

15 Land of the Danihers
Ungarie 31.19 (205) d Girral-West Wyalong 3.8 (26)
July 8, 2000

Anthony Daniher: Sydney, 1981–86, 115 games, 62 goals; Essendon, 1987–94, 118 games, 18 goals.
Chris Daniher: Essendon, 1987–97, 124 games, 40 goals. Premiership 1993.
Neale Daniher: Essendon, 1979–90, 82 games, 32 goals. Best-and-fairest 1981.
Terry Daniher: South Melbourne, 1976–77, 19 games, 22 goals; Essendon, 1978–92, 294 games, 449 goals. Captain 1983–88. Premierships 1984–85. Best-and-fairest 1982.
Ben Fixter: Sydney, 2000– , 1 game.

Ungarie's Northern Riverina league best-and-fairest winners:

1948 Jim Daniher	1985 Garry Koop
1951 Leo Daniher	1990 Mal Williams
1954 Jim Daniher	1992 Mal Williams
1959 Jim Dainher	1997 Peter King
1974 Terry Daniher	1998 Peter King
1977 Lindsay Henley	1999 Jamie Grintell
1981 Garry Koop	2000 Chris Daniher
1982 Lindsay Henley	

16 Battle of Wills

Moyston-Willaura 5.7 (37) lt Streatham-Mininera-Westmere Rovers 31.20 (206)

July 15, 2000

17 Ups and downs

Marcellin Old Collegians 14.6 (90) d Melbourne High School Old Boys 13.8 (86)

July 22, 2000

St Kevin's Old Boys 11.11 (77) d Old Melburnians 7.11 (53)

July 23, 2000

Ian McMullin: Collingwood, 1984–87 and 1992–93, 25 games, 29 goals; Essendon, 1990–92, 24 games, 26 goals.

18 Order and the court

St Bernard's Old Collegians 13.11 (89) lt Old Melburnians 18.13 (121)

August 5, 2000

Nick Mitchell: Fitzroy, 1994–95, 9 games, 2 goals.
Shane Zantuck: North Melbourne, 1974–76, 5 games, 3 goals; South Melbourne, 1977–80, 56 games, 36 goals; Melbourne, 1981–86, 88 games, 13 goals.

19 The long-distance ruck-rover
Wickcliffe-Lake Bolac 19.8 (122) d Dunkeld 7.6 (48)
July 29, 2000

20 Portrait of Nicky Winmar
Warburton-Millgrove 23.14 (152) d Upwey-Tecoma 14.8 (92)
August 12, 2000

Nicky Winmar: St Kilda, 1987–98, 230 games, 283 goals; Western Bulldogs, 1999, 21 games, 34 goals.

Warburton-Millgrove best team since merger in 1967.
B: David Clinch, Gavin Findlay, Kevin Boyd.
HB: Roger Dunkley, Terry McAliece, Rohan Hubbard.
C: Gordon Sumner, Wayne Morris, John Winzer.
HF: Jason De Graaf, Mark Tucker, Steve Darwall.
F: Laurie Leyden, John Purdie, Rodney Summers.
R: Bob Treloar, Terry Wheeler, Jeremy Crunden.
I: Harold Hetherton, Brendan Woods, Michael Walker, Ross Watson.
Coach: Ralph Story.

Now or next year

21 Tough order at Elsternwick Park
Mazenod Old Collegians 16.11 (107) d North Old Boys 11.17 (83)
August 19, 2000

Old Xaverians 15.8 (98) d St Kevin's 14.10 (94)
August 20, 2000

22 Last rites under Waverley lights
Boronia 18.10 (118) d Blackburn 5.6 (36)
Vermont 5.8 (38) lt East Burwood 14.8 (92)
August 26, 2000

Alan Richardson: Collingwood, 1987–88, 1990–96, 114 games, 10 goals.

Division one premiers since inception of Eastern league in 1962:

1962 Ringwood	1982 Vermont
1963 East Burwood	1983 Vermont
1964 East Burwood	1984 East Ringwood
1965 East Burwood	1985 East Burwood
1966 East Ringwood	1986 Vermont
1967 East Burwood	1987 East Burwood
1968 East Burwood	1988 Vermont
1969 Vermont	1989 Vermont
1970 Mitcham	1990 Vermont
1971 Vermont	1991 Vermont
1972 East Hawthorn	1992 East Burwood
1973 East Burwood	1993 Vermont
1974 Bayswater	1994 Vermont
1975 Mitcham	1995 Vermont
1976 East Burwood	1996 Donvale
1977 Scoresby	1997 Vermont
1978 Ringwood	1998 Vermont
1979 Mitcham	1999 East Burwood
1980 Mitcham	2000 East Burwood
1981 Mitcham	

St Bernard's Old Collegians 16.5 (101) lt Old Xaverians 22.14 (146)

August 27, 2000

Old Xaverians premierships:
A: 1981, 1995–2000.
B: 1948, 1962, 1980.
C: 1938, 1978.
D: 1976

Garry Foulds: Essendon, 1974–89, 300 games, 140 goals.
Andy Gowers: Hawthorn, 1988–94, 89 games, 54 goals; Brisbane, 1995–99, 51 games, 9 goals.

23 Tyranny of distance
Pakenham 13.13 (91) d Warragul 9.12 (66)
September 3, 2000

Ashley Green: Brisbane, 1992–93, 23 games, 2 goals.
West Gippsland league premierships
1991 Drouin
1992 Drouin
1993 Garfield
1994 Garfield
1995 Rythdale-Officer-Cardinia

1996 Rythdale-Officer-Cardinia
1997 Tooradin-Dalmore
1998 Pakenham
1999 Beaconsfield
2000 Pakenham

24 Cooking The Goose
Edithvale–Aspendale 24.20 (164) d Mornington 9.11 (65)
September 17, 2000

Edithvale formed 1921, Aspendale 1924. Amalgamated in 1931. Left Federal league after 1955 without winning a premiership. Joined Mornington Peninsula league in 1956.

Edithvale-Aspendale premierships:
1965, 1978, 1987, 1989, 1999–2000
Runners-up:
1964, 1980, 1986, 1988, 1990, 1998

League best-and-fairests:
1969–70 Keith Robins
1980 Glen Moulton
1988 Brett Wright
1989 Mick Bartholomew
1992 Peter Geddes

Edithvale-Aspendale best team:
B: Bob Kupsch, Terry Davey, Dale Moulton.
HB: Ken Kupsch, Peter Geddes, Mark Alves.
C: Rod Evans, Laurie Sharp, Stan Alves.
HB: Ken Dunne, Mick Rae, Brett Wright.
F: Rob Sill, Mike Moncrieff, Aaron Martello.
R: Barry Goodingham, Gerard Healy, Greg Healy.

Inter: John Barbour, Craig Dale, Chris Hickey, Graeme Hunter, Brendan Laube, Paul Layton, Glen Moulton.

Tim Allen: St Kilda, 1991–92, 22 games, 13 goals; Hawthorn, 1993–94, 11 games, 4 goals; Geelong, 1995, 1 game, 0 goal.

Simon Goosey's Mornington hauls:

1989 – 103	1997 – 156
1991 – 86	1998 – 132
1995 – 85	1999 – 156
1996 – 126	2000 – 120

25 Beyond the big sticks
Stanhope 23.11 (149) d Nagambie 11.11 (77)
September 23, 2000

Gavin Exell: Geelong, 1987–91, 53 games, 111 goals; Fitzroy, 1992, 5 games, 2 goals.
Since 1980: Sandhurst, Carlton, Southport, Northern United, Geelong, Fitzroy, Tooleybuc, Nyah-Nyah West United, Rochester, Calivil United. Career goals: about 1200.

Shane Loveless: Footscray, 1979–81, 28 games, 72 goals.
Since 1976: 418 games, 2034 goals.

Season	team	games	goals
1976	Sale	16	24
1977	Sale	18	41
1978	Sale	16	62
1979	Footscray	10	6
1980	Footscray	10	48
1981	Footscray	8	18
1982	Glenorchy	6	22
1983	Tatura	17	84
1984	Tatura	19	106
1985	Kyabram	16	87
1986	Sale	20	110
1987	Sale	20	142
1988	Casterton	16	80

1989	South Gambier	18	78
1990	Apsley	10	51
1991	Sale	16	56
1992	Nambrok	16	32
1993	Gunbower	17	75
1994	Kerang Rovers	5	15
	Colbinabbin	10	68
1995	Ardmona	21	152
1996	Ardmona	21	140
1997	Ardmona	20	165
1998	Nagambie	21	116
1999	Nagambie	20	93
2000	Nagambie	15	76

26 Tropical storm on Mallee dust
Nyah-Nyah West United 13.15 (93) d Cohuna Kangas 9.6 (60)
September 9, 2000

John James: Carlton, 1953–63, 195 games, 31 goals.
Bob Rose: Collingwood, 1946–55, 152 games, 214 goals.

SEASON REVIEW

A-SECTION

St Bernard's OC
Old Xaverians
University Blues
St Kevin's OB
Old Trinity
Old Scotch
Marcellin OC
Melbourne High OB
Old Ivanhoe
Old Melburnians

Best-and-fairest
G Cox, Marcellin

Leading goalkicker
L Hawkins, Old Scotch, 86

Grand final
St Bernard's 16.5 (101)
Old Xaverians 22.14 (146)

BOG
A Jones, Old Xaverians

B-SECTION

Old Brighton
Mazenod OC
North Old Boys
De La Salle OC

Ormond
Old Paradians
Whitefriars OC
Old Haileybury
Collegians
Old Mentonians

Best-and-fairest
R Bonnici, De La Salle

Leading goalkicker
J Bradley, Old Brighton, 72

Grand final
Old Brighton 14.18 (102)
Mazenod OC 17.7 (109)

BOG
M Pickering, Mazenod OC

C-SECTION

Beaumaris
Therry-Penola
Ajax
Hampton Rovers
St Bede's-Mentone Tigers
Glen Eira
Prahran
Bulleen-Templestowe
Ivanhoe-Assumption
Old Geelong

Best-and-fairest
S Anderson, Hampton Rovers

Leading goalkicker
A Kalinski, Ajax, 74

Grand final
Beaumaris 9.10 (64)
Therry-Penola 12.13 (85)

BOG
M Goodwin, Therry-Penola

D1-SECTION

Old Caulfield
Old Essendon
Aquinas OC
Monash Blues
Banyule
St Leo's Emmaus
Old Camberwell
Old Carey
Oakleigh
La Trobe University

Best-and-fairest
A Cultrera, Aquinas OC

Leading goalkicker
S Amiet, Old Caulfield, 91

Grand final
Old Caulfield 26.13 (169)
Old Essendon 6.8 (44)

BOG
S Amiet, Old Caulfield

D2-SECTION

University Blacks
Yarra Valley OB
Salesian OB
Parkside
Thomastown
Peninsula OB
West Brunswick
Mentone
Kew
Fitzroy Reds

Best-and-fairest
A Campbell, Salesian OB

Leading goalkicker
S Payze, Peninsula OB, 82

Grand final
Yarra Valley OB 9.10 (64)
University Blacks 18.13 (121)

BOG
M Laffy, University Blacks

D3-SECTION

Power House
Williamstown CYMS
Richmond Central
St John's OC
Elsternwick
Hawthorn Amateurs
University High OB
Eley Park
Monash Gryphons
Albert Park

Best-and-fairest
D Williams, Williamstown CYMS

Leading goalkicker
D Williams, Williamstown CYMS, 103

Grand final
Power House 12.13 (85)
Williamstown CYMS 7.12 (54)

BOG
A Robinson, Power House

D4-SECTION

Bentleigh
South Melbourne Districts
Syndal-Tally Ho
Eltham Collegians
Bulleen Cobras
Old Westbourne

North Brunswick
Swinburne University
St Mary's
Mt Lilydale
Brunswick
Werribee Amateurs

Best-and-fairest
D Martin, Bentleigh

Leading goalkicker
C Sharp, Bentleigh, 116

Grand final
Bentleigh 14.16 (100)
South Melbourne Districts 20.7 (127)

BOG
L Hogan, South Melbourne Districts

VICTORIAN METROPOLITAN FOOTBALL ASSOCIATION

DIAMOND VALLEY

A GRADE

West Preston-Lakeside
Northcote Park
Heidelberg
North Heidelberg
Bundoora
Montmorency
Greensborough
Lower Plenty
Epping
Lalor

Best-and-fairest
P King, Bundoora

Leading goalkicker
D Yze, Northcote Park, 99

Grand final
Northcote Park 21.19 (145)
West Preston-Lakeside 10.12 (72)

BOG
S Logan, Northcote Park

B GRADE

Watsonia
Mernda
Whittlesea
Eltham
Diamond Creek
Hurstbridge
Panton Hill
Macleod
Fawkner Park
Heidelberg West
Kinglake
Reservoir
South Morang

Best-and-fairest
P Eccles, Watsonia

Leading goalkicker
G Tapner, Watsonia, 90

Grand final
Eltham 12.8 (80)
Watsonia 8.6 (54)

BOG
D Brown, Eltham

EASTERN

DIVISION 1

East Burwood
Vermont
East Ringwood
Bayswater
Scoresby
Noble Park
North Ringwood

Croydon
Mitcham
Donvale

Best-and-fairest
N Cox, Bayswater

Leading goalkicker
J Gerstman, East Ringwood, 102

Grand final
Vermont 5.8 (38)
East Burwood 14.8 (92)

BOG
D Coghlan, East Burwood

DIVISION 2

Boronia
Blackburn
Montrose
Ringwood
Mulgrave
Doncaster
The Basin
Lilydale
Upper Ferntree Gully
Warrandyte

Best-and-fairest
D Van Hoorn, Boronia

Leading goalkicker
D Franken, Montrose, 84

Grand final
Boronia 18.10 (118)
Blackburn 5.6 (36)

BOG
L Appleby, Boronia

DIVISION 3

Templestowe
Knox
South Croydon
Mooroolbark
Doncaster East
Kilsyth
Wantirna South
Mount Evelyn
Norwood

Best–and–fairest
A Sorensen, Knox

Leading goalkicker
D Mason, South Croydon, 57

Grand final
Knox 15.9 (99)
Templestowe 15.7 (97)

BOG
D Adams, Knox

DIVISION 4

Waverley Blues
Coldstream
Forest Hill
Rowville
Heathmont
Eastern Lions
Ferntree Gully
Chirnside Park
Whitehorse Pioneers
Nunawading

Best–and–fairest
A Sharp, Ferntree Gully

Leading goalkicker
E Anadoli, Forest Hill, 101

Grand final
Waverley Blues 17.11 (113)
Coldstream 7.10 (52)

BOG
G Hislop, Waverley Blues

ESSENDON DISTRICT

A GRADE

Strathmore
Keilor
Oak Park
Doutta Stars
Aberfeldie
East Keilor
Airport West
Avondale Heights
Moonee Valley
Keilor Park

Best–and–fairest
A Ibrahim, Avondale Heights

Leading goalkicker
S Minton-Connell, Doutta Stars, 108

Grand final
Keilor 12.12 (84)
Oak Park 6.5 (41)

BOG
D David, Keilor

B GRADE

West Coburg
Greenvale
Westmeadows
Tullamarine
Glenroy
Taylors Lakes
Maribyrnong Park
Pascoe Vale
Hadfield
North Coburg

Best-and-fairest
M Bangit, Maribyrnong Park

Leading goalkicker
R Capodiferro, Westmeadows, 61

Grand final
West Coburg 21.14 (140)
Westmeadows 10.10 (70)

BOG
S Vassielakopoulos, West Coburg

RIDDELL DISTRICT

Craigieburn
Wallan
Jacana
Woodend-Hesket
Riddell
Romsey
Kilmore
Lancefield
Diggers Rest
Sunbury Rovers
Melton Centrals

Macedon
Rockbank

Best-and-fairest
L Edwards, Romsey

Leading goalkicker
C McPharlane, Jacana, 51

Grand final
Jacana 14.12 (96)
Wallan 11.11 (77)

BOG
J Markham, Jacana

SOUTHERN

DIVISION 1

St Paul's
Balwyn
Parkdale
Cheltenham
Oakleigh Districts
Clayton
East Brighton
St Kilda City
Mordialloc
Caulfield

Best-and-fairest
M MacKenzie, St Paul's

Leading goalkicker
A Stroud, Balwyn, 61

Grand final
Balwyn 15.7 (97)
St Paul's 5.10 (40)

BOG
P Smith, Balwyn

DIVISION 2

Ashwood
Chelsea Heights
North Kew
Springvale Districts
Heatherton
Surrey Park
Murrumbeena
Highett
Mount Waverley
Hampton

Best-and-fairest
D Cross, Chelsea Heights

Leading goalkicker
A Higgins, Ashwood, 49

Grand final
Chelsea Heights 11.7 (73)
Ashwood 6.11 (47)

BOG
T Coote, Chelsea Heights

DIVISION 3

Tooronga-Malvern
Lyndale
South Yarra
Doveton Eagles
Canterbury
Dandenong West
Black Rock
Moorabbin West
Box Hill North

Best-and-fairest
S Miller, Tooronga-Malvern

Leading goalkicker
A Arena, Lyndale, 46

Grand final
Lyndale 14.14 (98)
Tooronga-Malvern 7.10 (52)

BOG
J Young, Lyndale

WESTERN REGION

DIVISION 1

Parkside
Port Colts
St Albans
West Footscray
Deer Park
Hoppers Crossing
Sunshine YCW
Spotswood
Altona
Braybrook
Albion
Seddon-Yarraville

Best-and-fairest
C Barker, West Footscray
Sami Sir, Parkside

Leading goalkicker
W Ramsey, Braybrook, 88

Grand final
Parkside 9.13 (67)
St Albans 7.8 (50)

BOG
A Taleb, Parkside

DIVISION 2

Yarraville
Central Altona
North Footscray
Glenorden
Kealba
Albanvale
Coburg Districts
Sunshine Heights
North Sunshine
Wyndhamvale
Western Magpies

Gladstone Park
Flemington
Brooklyn

Best-and-fairest
K Robertson, Sunshine Heights

Leading goalkicker
B Devlin, Yarraville, 100

Grand final
Yarraville 12.18 (90)
Glenorden 6.8 (44)

BOG
T Cook, Yarraville

VICTORIAN COUNTRY FOOTBALL LEAGUE

ALBERTON

Fish Creek
DWWWW
Dalyston
Inverloch–Kongwak
Korumburra
Yarram
Tarwin
Wonthaggi Rovers
Foster
Stony Creek
Toora
MDU
Bena

Best-and-fairest
M Livingstone, Fish Creek

Leading goalkicker
P Bramley, Yarram, 90

Grand Final
Fish Creek 13.6 (84)
DWWWW 10.11 (71)

BOG
N Smith, Fish Creek

BALLARAT

Darley
Sunbury
Melton
Lake Wendouree
Sebastopol
Melton South

Ballarat
Golden Point
Redan
Bacchus Marsh
East Ballarat
Daylesford

Best-and-fairest
D Stanley, Melton

Leading goalkicker
C Stuhldreier, Bacchus Marsh, 93

Grand final
Melton 8.4 (52)
Sebastopol 6.8 (44)

BOG
R Murphy, Melton

BELLARINE

Ocean Grove
Anglesea
Drysdale
Geelong Amateurs
Torquay
Modewarre
Newcomb
Queenscliff
Barwon Heads
Portarlington

Best-and-fairest
M Payne, Ocean Grove

Leading goalkicker
L Winter, Anglesea, 76

Grand Final
Ocean Grove 16.13 (109)
Anglesea 7.12 (54)

BOG
M Payne, Ocean Grove

BENALLA & DISTRICT

Longwood
Goorambat
Bonnie Doon
Devenish
Swanpool
Tatong

Best-and-fairest
S Dolling, Swanpool

Leading goalkicker
L Pollard, Bonnie Doon, 78

Grand Final
Longwood 18.12 (120)
Devenish 10.5 (65)

BOG
G Adams, Longwood

BENDIGO

Castlemaine
Kangaroo Flat
Eaglehawk
South Bendigo
Gisborne
Maryborough
Sandhurst
Golden Square
Kyneton
Lockington-Bamawm

Best-and-fairest
Reece Langan, Eaglehawk

Leading goalkicker
S Oliver, Castlemaine, 135

Grand Final
Castlemaine 12.11 (83)
Kangaroo Flat 9.17 (71)

BOG
S Milward, Kangaroo Flat

CENTRAL GOULBURN

Yea
Alexandra
Shepparton East
Violet Town
Rumbalara
Dookie United
Benalla All Blacks
Thornton-Eildon

Best-and-fairest
G Steiner, Alexandra

Leading goalkicker
D Austin, Alexandra, 72

Grand Final
Alexandra 12.9 (81)
Yea 8.14 (62)

BOG
M Johnson, Alexandra

CENTRAL HIGHLANDS

Clunes
Buninyong
Dunnstown
Learmonth
Springbank
Creswick
Gordon
Bungaree
Hepburn
Waubra
Beaufort
Ballan
Newlyn

Best-and-fairest
J Hall, Springbank

Leading goalkicker
S Basham, Learmonth, 79

Grand Final
Springbank 20.9 (129)
Clunes 9.12 (66)

BOG
A Cook, Springbank

CENTRAL MURRAY

Nyah-Nyah West United
Cohuna Kangas
Lake Boga
Tyntynder
Koondrook-Barham
Balranald
Swan Hill
Woorinen

Tooleybuc
Kerang-Rovers–Appin
Lalbert

Best-and-fairest
R Lee, Lake Boga

Leading goalkicker
N Quick, Lake Boga, 94

Grand final
Nyah–Nyah West United 13.15 (93)
Cohuna Kangas 9.6 (60)

BOG
J Cockatoo, Nyah–Nyah West
    United

COLAC DISTRICT

Lorne
Winchelsea
Alvie
Apollo Bay
South Colac
Irrewarra–Beeac
Western Eagles
Colac Imperials
Forrest
Birregurra

Best-and-fairest
S Corth, Winchelsea

Leading goalkicker
J Mawson, Winchelsea, 103

Grand Final
Alvie 13.6 (84)
Lorne 10.17 (77)

BOG
B Moloney, Alvie

EAST GIPPSLAND

Bairnsdale
Wy Yung
Lakes Entrance
Orbost
Lucknow
Snowy Rovers
Lindenow

Best-and-fairest
W Carter, Wy Yung

Leading goalkicker
D Preston, Bairnsdale, 70

Grand final
Bairnsdale 13.11 (89)
Wy Yung 9.7 (61)

BOG
D Preston, Bairnsdale

ELLINBANK & DISTRICT

Ellinbank
Bunyip
Buln Buln
Lang Lang
Koo Wee Rup
Catani
Neerim–Neerim South
Nyora
Nilma Darnum
Longwarry
Warragul Industrials
Poowong

Best-and-fairest
A Carr, Bunyip

Leading goalkicker
J Entwisle, Catani, 75

Grand Final
Bunyip 14.17 (101)
Buln Buln 5.12 (42)

BOG
D Bracken, Bunyip

GEELONG & DISTRICT

Werribee Centrals
Bannockburn
Thomson
Corio
East Geelong
Bell Post Hill
North Geelong
GWCFC
Belmont Lions
Anakie

Best-and-fairest
R O'Toole, Corio

Leading goalkicker
W Tyquin, Bannockburn, 113

Grand final
Werribee Centrals 13.10 (88)
Bannockburn 11.9 (75)

BOG
M Hallam, Werribee Centrals

GEELONG

Lara
North Shore
South Barwon
St Alban's
St Joseph's
Leopold
St Mary's
Grovedale
Geelong West-St Peters
Bell Park
Newtown & Chilwell

Best-and-fairest
G Wallace, South Barwon

Leading goalkicker
Z Suto, Lara, 87

Grand Final
North Shore 9.12 (66)
Lara 3.9 (27)

BOG
M Atkins, North Shore

GIPPSLAND LATROBE

Traralgon
Wonthaggi
Maffra
Moe
Leongatha
Sale
Morwell

Best-and-fairest
J Shields, Moe

Leading goalkicker
G Bettridge, Traralgon, 65

Grand Final
Traralgon 9.10 (64)
Moe 9.4 (58)

BOG
S Bennett, Traralgon

GOLDEN RIVERS

Murrabit
Wandella
Macorna
Nullawil
Quambatook
Ultima
Hay
Wakool
Moulamein

Best-and-fairest
G Caelli, Nullawil

Leading goalkicker
T Doran, Nullawil, 96

Grand final
Murrabit 9.11 (65)
Nullawil 18.9 (117)

BOG
D Watts, Nullawil

GOULBURN VALLEY

Shepparton
Shepparton United
Euroa
Tongala

Rochester
Tatura
Echuca
Mansfield
Benalla
Kyabram
Shepparton Swans
Seymour
Mooroopna

Best-and-fairest
S Ash, Shepparton

Leading goalkicker
A Mellington, Shepparton, 119

Grand Final
Shepparton 15.5 (95)
Shepparton United 9.14 (68)

BOG
A Bovalino, Shepparton

HAMPDEN

Camperdown
Koroit
Terang
South Warrnambool
Warrnambool
Colac
Cobden
North Warrnambool
Port Fairy

Best-and-fairest
P Jenkinson, Warrnambool

Leading goalkicker
B Hinkley, Camperdown, 68

Grand final
Camperdown 14.10 (94)
Koroit 7.9 (51)

BOG
M Bruhn, Koroit

HEATHCOTE DISTRICT

Mt Pleasant
Colbinabbin
Broadford
North Bendigo
Huntly
Elmore
White Hills
Heathcote

Best-and-fairest
F Burke, Mt Pleasant

Leading goalkicker
M Waters, Colbinabbin, 72

Grand Final
Mt Pleasant 18.10 (118)
Colbinabbin 7.12 (54)

BOG
S Dean, Mt Pleasant

HEYTESBURY -MOUNT NOORAT

Heytesbury
Noorat
Kolora
Otway Districts
Simpson
Timboon

Best-and-fairest
J Delaney, Heytesbury

Leading goalkicker
S Harriott, Otway Districts, 58

Grand Final
Noorat 9.15 (69)
Kolora 4.4 (28)

BOG
D Pevitt, Noorat

HORSHAM DISTRICT

Kalkee
Rupanyup
Harrow-Balmoral
Laharum
Stawell Swifts
Pimpinio
Noradjuha-Quantong
Taylors Lake
Ararat Eagles
Great Western
Natimuk

Best-and-fairest
S Bachelor, Kalkee

Leading goalkicker
G Nuske, Stawell Swifts, 125

Grand Final
Kalkee 9.12 (66)
Rupanyup 6.6 (42)

BOG
J Goldsmith, Kalkee

KOWREE-NARACOORTE-TATIARA

Mundulla
Kingston
Penola
Edenhope-Apsley
Kybybolite
K-L United
Naracoorte
Border Districts
Lucindale
Padthaway
Bordertown
Keith

Best-and-fairest
S Beggs, Kingston

Leading goalkicker
N Williams, Mundulla, 85

Grand Final
Mundulla 10.14 (74)
Kingston 11.6 (72)

BOG
R Hunt, Mundulla

KYABRAM & DISTRICT

Stanhope
Merrigum
Nagambie
Ardmona
Lancaster
Undera
Rushworth
Girgarre

Tallygaroopna
Murchison
Avanel

Best-and-fairest
P Trevaskis, Murchison
R Aldous, Nagambie

Leading goalkicker
G Exell, Stanhope, 124

Grand final
Stanhope 23.11 (149)
Nagambie 11.11 (77)

BOG
A Comer, Stanhope

LEXTON PLAINS

Carngham-Linton
Skipton
Rokewood-Corindhap
Navarre
Natte-Bealiba
Dunolly
Lexton
Illabarook
Avoca
Landsborough

Best-and-fairest
M Driscoll, Navarre

Leading goalkicker
S Hutchins, Dunolly, 110

Grand Final
Carngham-Linton 28.17 (185)
Skipton 5.4 (34)

BOG
T Nunn, Carngham-Linton

LODDON VALLEY

Newbridge
YCW
Bears Lagoon-Serpentine
Calivil United
Bridgewater
Mitiamo
Marong
Inglewood
Pyramid Hill

Best-and-fairest
R Pointon, Bears Lagoon-
  Serpentine

Leading goalkicker
G Gadsden, Bears Lagoon-
  Serpentine, 87

Grand Final
Newbridge 15.7 (97)
YCW 14.10 (94)

BOG
D Gordon, Newbridge

MALLEE

Beulah
Brim
Berriwillock-Culgoa
Hopetoun
Ouyen United
Jeparit-Rainbow
Woomelang-Lascelles

Sea Lake-Nandaly
Walpeup-Underbool
Manangatang

Best-and-fairest
L Wellington, Hopetoun

Leading goalkicker
J Robins, Beulah, 81

Grand Final
Beulah 11.15 (81)
Brim 10.7 (67)

BOG
M Kent, Brim

MARYBOROUGH
CASTLEMAINE

Talbot
Newstead
Harcourt
Maryborough Rovers
Trentham
Campbells Creek
Carisbrook
Maldon
Royal Park

Best-and-fairest
R Morgan, Carisbrook

Leading goalkickers
M O'Brien, Newstead, 63
J Hind, Talbot, 63

Grand Final
Talbot 10.8 (68)
Newstead 16.18 (114)

BOG
S Webster, Newstead

MID GIPPSLAND

Yinnar
Trafalgar
Newborough
Hill End
Thorpdale
Mirboo North
Yarragon
Yallourn-Yallourn North
Boolarra
Morwell East

Best-and-fairest
P Roberts, Yinnar
G Blanford, Newborough

Leading goalkicker
D Edwards, Morwell East, 75

Grand final
Newborough 17.14 (116)
Yinnar 9.9 (63)

BOG
W Vincent, Newborough

MILLEWA

Bambill
Gol Gol
Euston
Nangiloc
Werrimull
Meringur
Cardross

Best-and-fairest
D Robbins, Meringur

Leading goalkicker
B Haase, Euston, 103

Grand final
Bambill 18.19 (127)
Gol Gol 11.10 (76)

BOG
B Woulfe, Gol Gol

MININERA & DISTRICT

Wickliffe-Lake Bolac
SMW Rovers
Tatyoon
Dunkeld
Caramut
Penshurst
Woorndoo
Hawkesdale-Macarthur
Lismore-Derrinallum
Ararat United
Moyston-Willaura
Glenthompson

Best-and-fairest
D Gilmore, Hawkesdale-Macarthur

Leading goalkicker
P Campigli, Tatyoon, 88

Grand Final
Wickliffe-Lake Bolac 12.13 (85)
SMW Rovers 4.5 (29)

BOG
T Aldous, Wickliffe-Lake Bolac

MORNINGTON PENINSULA NEPEAN

PREMIER DIVISION

Edithvale-Aspendale
Mornington
Frankston YCW
Rosebud
Hastings
Rye
Pines
Hampton Park
Karingal
Cranbourne

Best-and-fairest
B Moore, Pines

Leading goalkicker
S Goosey, Mornington, 113

Grand Final
Edithvale-Aspendale 24.20 (164)
Mornington 9.11 (65)

BOG
T Shannon, Edithvale-Aspendale

PENINSULA DIVISION

Chelsea
Seaford
Devon Meadows
Berwick
Frankston
Narre Warren
Mt Eliza
Doveton
Pearcedale
Crib Point

Best-and-fairest
B Molineux, Berwick

Leading goalkicker
N Claringbold, Mt Eliza, 59

Grand Final
Chelsea 14.14 (98)
Seaford 12.11 (83)

BOG
S Kemble, Seaford

NEPEAN DIVISION

Tyabb
Bonbeach
Red Hill
Keysborough
Langwarrin
Dingley
Sorrento
Somerville
Dromana
Carrum Downs

Best-and-fairest
G Johnson, Sorrento

Leading goalkicker
G Gorozidis, Bonbeach, 156

Grand Final
Tyabb 20.9 (129)
Keysborough 10.15 (75)

BOG
M Redmond, Tyabb

MURRAY

Nathalia
Numurkah
Moama
Deniliquin
Mulwala
Congupna
Cobram
Barooga
Berrigan
Echuca United
Tocumwal
Finley

Best-and-fairest
B Hogan, Moama

Leading goalkicker
A Rudd, Nathalia, 78

Grand Final
Numurkah 17.12 (114)
Deniliquin 10.7 (67)

BOG
R McCartney, Numurkah

NORTH CENTRAL

Charlton
Wedderburn
St Arnaud
Wycheproof-Narraport
Leitchville-Gunbower
Donald
Birchip-Watchem
Boort

Best-and-fairest
M O'Meara, Charlton

Leading goalkicker
K Shevlin, Wedderburn, 103

Grand Final
Wedderburn 2.12 (24)
Wycheproof-Narraport 16.15 (111)

BOG
M Austin, Wycheproof-Narraport

NORTH GIPPSLAND

Heyfield
Churchill
Rosedale
Glengarry
TTU
Cowwarr
Gormandale
Sale City

Best-and-fairest
B Szabo, Heyfield

Leading goalkicker
D Ivey, Heyfield, 111

Grand Final
Heyfield 15.11 (101)
Glengarry 8.6 (54)

BOG
B Szabo, Heyfield

OMEO DISTRICT

Benambra
Omeo
Swifts Creek
Buchan

Swan Reach
Bruthen

Best–and–fairest
G Mooney, Swifts Creek

Leading goalkicker
G Mooney, Swifts Creek, 74

Grand Final
Benambra 10.18 (78)
Omeo 11.10 (76)

BOG
D Taech, Omeo

OVENS & KING

Beechworth
Moyhu
Rutherglen
Bright
King Valley
Greta
Chiltern
Whorouly
North Wangaratta
Glenrowan
Tarrawingee
Milawa

Best–and–fairest
S Driscoll, North Wangaratta

Leading goalkicker
D Bate, Beechworth, 79

Grand Final
Beechworth 6.9 (45)
Moyhu 4.1 (25)

BOG
D Smith, Moyhu

OVENS & MURRAY

Corowa-Rutherglen
Albury
Yarrawonga
North Albury
Wangaratta Rovers
Wodonga Raiders
Lavington
Myrtleford
Wodonga
Wangaratta

Best–and–fairest
J Brunner, Yarrawonga

Leading goalkicker
D Bradshaw, Wodonga, 75

Grand final
Corowa-Rutherglen 27.18 (180)
North Albury 11.6 (72)

BOG
D Houlihan, Corowa-Rutherglen

PICOLA & DISTRICT

Katamatite
Blighty
Tungamah
Waaia
Katandra
Strathmerton
Mathoura
Katunga

Picola United
Deniliquin Rovers
Yarroweyah
Wunghnu

Best-and-fairest
D Jenkins, Katunga

Leading goalkicker
D Ellis, Picola United, 89

Grand Final
Blighty 11.9 (75)
Katamatite 7.6 (48)

BOG
D Sexton, Blighty

RIVIERA

Boisdale-Briagolong
West Bairnsdale
Newry
Stratford
Lindenow South
Paynesville

Best-and-fairest
T Richardson, Stratford
B Dowsett, Boisdale-Briagolong

Leading goalkicker
T Light, Stratford, 100

Grand Final
Boisdale-Briagolong 19.16 (130)
Newry 5.5 (35)

BOG
C Avery, Boisdale-Briagolong

SOUTH-WEST DISTRICT

Westerns
Heathmere
Tyrendarra
Branxholme-Wallacedale
Dartmoor
Sandford
Coleraine
Cavendish

Best-and-fairest
D Hirst, Sandford

Leading goalkicker
J Duncan, Westerns, 110

Grand Final
Westerns 15.18 (108)
Heathmere 9.6 (60)

BOG
J Duncan, Westerns

SUNRAYSIA

Red Cliffs
Robinvale
Mildura
Wentworth
Irymple
Imperials
Merbein
South Mildura

Best-and-fairest
T Leng, Mildura

Leading goalkicker
R Lindsay, Red Cliffs, 124

Grand final
Red Cliffs 12.16 (88)
Wentworth 9.5 (59)

BOG
A Bounias, Red Cliffs

TALLANGATTA & DISTRICT

Yackandandah
Barnawatha
Mitta United
Tallangatta Valley
Dederang-Mt Beauty
Kiewa-Sandy Creek
Bethanga
Thurgoona

Best-and-fairest
D Mathey, Tallangatta Valley

Leading goalkicker
R Hillary, Yackandandah, 91

Grand Final
Yackandandah 17.19 (121)
Barnawatha 17.9 (111)

BOG
D McKenzie, Yackandandah

UPPER MURRAY

Cudgewa
Corryong
Federals
Tumbarumba
Border-Walwa

Best-and-fairest
L McInnes, Federals
A Frejiah, Corryong

Leading goalkickers
L Seymour, Tumbarumba, 47
G Andrews, Cudgewa, 47

Grand Final
Cudgewa 21.5 (131)
Corryong 14.9 (93)

BOG
T Purss, Cudgewa

WARRNAMBOOL &
DISTRICT

Panmure
Russell's Creek
South Rovers
Deakin University
Merrivale
Old Collegians
Allansford
Dennington
Nirranda
East Warrnambool

Best-and-fairest
P Hobbs, Panmure

Leading goalkicker
C Fleming, Deakin University, 79

Grand final
Russell's Creek 10.8 (68)
Deakin University 9.7 (61)

BOG
C Morrison, Deakin University

WEST GIPPSLAND

Pakenham
Beaconsfield
Tooradin-Dalmore
Rythdale-Officer-Cardinia
Warragul
Cora Lynn
Garfield
Drouin
Nar Nar Goon
Phillip Island
Kilcunda-Bass

Best-and-fairest
D O'Loughlin, Pakenham

Leading goalkicker
H Robins, Beaconsfield, 77

Grand final
Beaconsfield 2.0 (12)
Pakenham 7.13 (55)

BOG
M Holland, Pakenham

WESTERN BORDER

South Gambier
North Gambier
Casterton
East Gambier
Portland
Hamilton Imperials
West Gambier
Hamilton
Millicent
Heywood

Best-and-fairest
M Steel, Portland

Leading goalkicker
P Harten, South Gambier, 74

Grand Final
South Gambier 13.17 (95)
North Gambier 4.7 (31)

BOG
M Mullan, South Gambier

WIMMERA

Ararat
Stawell
St Michael's
Minyip-Murtoa
Horsham
Horsham United
Dimboola
Nhill
Warracknabeal

Best-and-fairest
M Ilsley, Stawell

Leading goalkicker
R May, Ararat, 85

Grand final
Stawell 19.11 (125)
Ararat 16.19 (115)

BOG
S Dunn, Stawell

YARRA VALLEY & MOUNTAIN DISTRICT

DIVISION 1

Warburton-Millgrove
Wandin
Monbulk
Seville
Upwey-Tecoma
Belgrave
Healesville
Olinda-Ferny Creek
Woori Yallock

Best-and-fairest
J De Graaf, Warburton-Millgrove

Leading goalkicker
A Goldsmith, Seville, 72

Grand final
Warburton-Millgrove 8.9 (57)
Wandin 7.7 (49)

BOG
J De Graaf, Warburton-Millgrove

DIVISION 2

Gembrook-Cockatoo
Yarra Glen
Yarra Junction
Emerald
Silvan
South Belgrave
Boronia Park
Powelltown

Best-and-fairest
B McGain, Silvan

Leading goalkicker
B Coller, Gembrook-Cockatoo,
103

Grand final
Gembrook-Cockatoo 18.6 (114)
Yarra Junction 17.3 (105)

BOG
J Matthews, Gembrook-Cockatoo

BEYOND VICTORIA

KING ISLAND
North
Grassy
Currie

Best-and-fairest
A Summers, North

Leading goalkicker
Q Lewis, North, 38

Grand final
North 24.14 (158)
Grassy 14.7 (91)

BOG
T McLean, North

NORTHERN RIVERINA

Ungarie
Lake Cargelligo
Barellan United
Girral-West Wyalong
Cobar
Tullibigeal

Hillston
Condobolin-Milby

Best-and-fairest
C Daniher, Ungarie

Leading goalkicker
W Kendall, Lake Cargelligo

Grand final
Ungarie 15.11 (101)
Barellan United 10.5 (65)

BOG
P Wilson, Ungarie

BIBLIOGRAPHY

Lorna Banfield, *Like the Ark: The Story of Ararat*, Longman Cheshire, Melbourne, 1986

Kevin Berry, Phil Derriman, Ray Martin, Neil Mitchell, judges, *1998 Best Australian Sports Writing and Photography*, Random House, Sydney, 1998

Geoffrey Blainey, *A Game of Our Own*, Information Australia, Melbourne, 1990

Geoffrey Blainey, *Our Side of the Country: The Story of Victoria*, Methuen Haynes, Melbourne, 1991

Peter Burke and Leo Grogan, editors, *This Game of Ours*, The Eatwarflemsd, Melbourne, 1993

Edmund Campion, *Rockchoppers: Growing Up Catholic in Australia*, Penguin, Melbourne, 1982

Cutten History Committee of the Fitzroy History Society, *Fitzroy: Melbourne's First Suburb*, Melbourne University Press, Melbourne, 1991

David Farrell, *Beyond the Boundaries*, Square Peg Publications, Adelaide, 1997

Ross Fitzgerald and Ken Spillman, editors, *The Greatest Game*, William Heinemann, Melbourne, 1988

Martin Flanagan, *1970 and Other Stories of the Australian Game*, Allen and Unwin, Sydney, 1999

Martin Flanagan, *The Call*, Allen and Unwin, Sydney, 1998

Martin Flanagan, *Western Oval, Southern Sky: A Year Inside League Football*, McPhee Gribble, Melbourne, 1994

Rodney Gillett, "Where the Big Men Fly: An Early History of Australian Football in the Riverina", *Sporting Traditions*, Vol. 4, No. 2, May 1988, pp 162–175

Rob Hess and Bob Stewart, editors, *More Than a Game: An Unauthorised History of Australian Rules Football*, Melbourne University Press, Melbourne, 1998

Stuart Hildebrand, *When the Seagull Soars*, North Shore Sports Club, Geelong, 1990

Russell Holmesby and Jim Main, *The Encyclopedia of Australian Footballers*, Information Australia, Melbourne, 1998

Garrie Hutchinson, editor, *The Great Australian Book of Football Stories*, Currey O'Neil, Melbourne, 1983

Garrie Hutchinson, Rick Lang and John Ross, *The Roar of the Lions*, Lothian Books, Melbourne, 1997

Joseph Johnson, *For the Love of the Game: The Centenary History of the Victorian Amateur Football Association 1892–1992*, Hyland House, Melbourne, 1992

Freda Jones and Tom Sullivan, *In the Path of the Roaring Forties: Memories of King Island*, Regal Publications, Launceston, 1989

Garry Linnell, *Football Ltd: The Inside Story of the AFL*, Ironbark, Sydney, 1995

Charlie McAdam with Elizabeth Tregenza, *Boundary Lines*, McPhee Gribble, Melbourne, 1995

Barry Markoff, *The Road to A-grade: A History of Ajax Football Club*, Melbourne, 1980

Ray Martin, Garry Linnell and Tracey Holmes, judges, *1997 Best Australian Sports Writing and Photography*, Random House, Sydney, 1997

Brian Matthews, *Oval Dreams: Larrikin Essays on Sport and Low Culture*, Penguin Books, Melbourne, 1991

Wayne Miller and Vikki Petraitis with Victor Jeremiah, *The Great John Coleman*, Nivar Press, Melbourne, 1997

Philip A. Mosely, Richard Cashman, John O'Hara and Hilary Weatherburn, editors, *Sporting Immigrants: Sports and Ethnicity in Australia*, Walla Walla Press, Sydney 1997

Dave Nadel, "Aborigines and Australian Football: The Rise and Fall of the Purnim Bears", *Sporting Traditions*, Vol. 9, No.7, May 1993, pp 47–63

Robert Pascoe, *The Winter Game: The Complete History of Australian Football*, Text Publishing, Melbourne, 1995

Stephen Rodgers and Ashley Browne, *Every Game Ever Played*, Viking, Melbourne, 1996

Colin Tatz, *Obstacle Race: Aborigines in Sport*, University of New South Wales Press, Sydney, 1995

Colin and Paul Tatz, *Black Diamonds: The Aboriginal and Islander Sports Hall of Fame*, Allen and Unwin, Sydney, 1996

Clinton Walker, *A Football Life*, Pan Macmillan, Sydney, 1998
Barbara Williams, convenor, *Astride the Humbug: A History of Ungarie*, Wagga
    Wagga, 1997

NEWSPAPERS

The Age, The Australian, Ararat Advertiser, Ballarat Courier, Bendigo Advertiser, Border Mail, Buloke Times, Burnie Advocate, Castlemaine Mail, Geelong Advertiser, Hamilton Spectator, Herald Sun, King Island Courier, La Trobe Valley Express, Launceston Examiner, Loddon Times, Midland Express, Shepparton News, Sunraysia Daily, Swan Hill Guardian, Wagga Wagga Daily Advertiser, Wangaratta Express, Warrnambool Standard, Weekly Times, West Wyalong Advocate, Wimmera Mail-Times, Wycheproof-Sea Lake Ensign

INDEX